GETTING INTO PRINT

GETTING INTO PRINT

The Decision-Making Process
in Scholarly Publishing

WALTER W. POWELL

The University of Chicago Press
Chicago and London

WALTER W. POWELL is associate professor
of behavioral and policy sciences in
the Sloan School of Management at
the Massachusetts Institute of Technology.
He is also associate professor of
organization and management and sociology
at Yale University.

The University of Chicago Press, Chicago 60637
The University of Chicago Press, Ltd., London

94 93 92 91 90 89 88 87 86   5432

Library of Congress Cataloging in Publication Data

Powell, Walter W.
  Getting into print.

  Bibliography: p.
  Includes index.
  1. Scholarly Publishing—United States—Decision-
making. 2. Book industries and trade—United States—
Decision-making. 3. Editing—Decision-making.
4. Authors and publishers—United States. 5. Organization theory. I. Title.
Z479.P68 1985   070:5'0973   84-23962
ISBN 0-226-67704-4

To Marianne

CONTENTS

LIST OF TABLES

PREFACE

This is a study of how editors in scholarly publishing houses decide which books to publish. Answering this question required many hours of interviews and fieldwork inside publishing houses, but the study also took me outside the formal boundaries of the firms and into contact with authors, reviewers, advisers, brokers, and patrons. In tracing how choices were reached on particular manuscripts, I came to see the ways in which publishing departs from many of the assumptions commonly found in the literature on organizations. Markets and hierarchies, the twin concepts on which so much contemporary theory and research on organizations are based, presuppose that organizations are independent entities, separate from society, driven by economic and administrative logics. Contact with suppliers, consumers, or other organizations is guided by contract and principles of economic exchange. Yet in book publishing, and, I suspect, in many other organized economic endeavors, it is hard to tell where society ends and economic organization begins. Decisions are embedded in an environmental context that can transform the choice process in a number of surprising ways. The rational elements in formal decision processes often turn out to be more symbolic than real, while chance, or serendipitous contact, appears to be strongly tied to one's location in the social structure. Editorial decisions are a form of mating—a matching of editors looking for manuscripts to make

up their lists with authors searching for a publisher to dissemi-
nate their ideas and to enhance their career prospects. Both
parties to this mating process are frequently guided by a sense
of appropriateness, and long-term relationships are sealed by
an implicit norm of reciprocity. Years of contact with editors
and the social worlds they inhabit have made these observations commonplace to me, and it is only in the context of
reading otherwise superb work in organization theory that I
am reminded of the disjunction between the world I have
observed and the world our theories purport to describe.
While the primary purpose of this book is to explicate the
decision-making process in scholarly publishing, I hope that
the observations and explanations I offer will raise questions
about current theories and stimulate the development of
models of organizations that do a better job of capturing the
richness of organizational choice processes and their intimate
linkage to a broader social context.

This book has had a long gestation period. It began in 1975
as a pilot study of two organizations. That research grew into
a large-scale study of the book industry, undertaken by Lewis
Coser, Charles Kadushin, and me. In an earlier form, the
book was my doctoral dissertation, but the manuscript that
the University of Chicago Press accepted five years ago bears
little resemblance to this final version. The first half of the
earlier manuscript became the basis for three chapters in
Books: The Culture and Commerce of Publishing, the larger
industry study to which this volume, an expansion of the
second half of my dissertation, is a companion. My work on
Books required setting aside the revisions for this book, and a
new job, teaching, other writing, and another research project—this one on public television—also intruded. But the
study of Apple Press and Plum Press did not sit idly gathering
dust. I kept in contact with my respondents, even following
them as they moved to other houses. My understanding of the
industry was enhanced by my participation in various publishing conferences and annual meetings. Most important,
the passage of time allowed me to gain distance from the case

studies and to see beyond them to more general social processes.

Along the way I have incurred a great many debts. Like most people, I get by with a little help from my friends, and I have been blessed with many supportive colleagues at both Stony Brook and Yale. The members of my dissertation committee at Stony Brook—Lewis Coser, Charles Perrow, and Mark Granovetter—were both exemplary teachers and good friends. I learned from and shared many good times with the members of our research team—Lewis Coser, Charles Kadushin, Michelle Caplette, Laurie Michael Roth, and Frank Sirianni. Richard Peterson and Barry Schwartz provided insightful comments on the dissertation, which greatly improved it, and I benefited immensely from the careful reading of the revised manuscript by Becky Friedkin and Connie Gersick. For me, the best thing about Yale has been my friendship and collaboration with Paul DiMaggio. Not only is Paul all that one could ask for in a friend; he is a marvelous and speedy editor as well. I also had the good fortune that Chick Perrow "followed" me to New Haven. He has provided the kind of advice and criticism, on this book and on much else in my life, that comes only when the best of friends also happens to be an excellent scholar. Finally, for the past eight years, Dan Deutsch has been a dear friend and probing critic of everything I have written.

My research was supported by NIMH grant MH-26746, and release time for writing was made possible in part by a grant from the Yale Program on Non-Profit Organizations. The Yale School of Organization and Management has provided excellent support facilities. Very special thanks are due to Linda Vessicchio, Dolly Bonisch, and Linda Knudsen for their expert typing of the manuscript.

Finally, my greatest debt is to the many people whom I cannot thank publicly: the employees and executives of Apple Press and Plum Press and the many other members of the book community who gave so generously of their time. Without them, this book would never have been possible. Their openness and accessibility were extraordinary, and I am extremely grateful for their help.

I would like to thank the publishers of the following articles of mine for permission to draw on these papers for use in this book: "Publishers' Decision Making: What Criteria Do They Use in Deciding Which Books to Publish?" *Social Research* 45:227–52 (used in chapter 5), and "Political and Organizational Influences on Public Television Programming," pp. 413–38 in E. Wartella and D. C. Whitney, eds., *Mass Communication Review Yearbook*, vol. 4 (Beverly Hills: Sage, 1983) (used in chapter 6).

INTRODUCTION

Publishers are the key intermediary between writer and reader. This book describes two successful scholarly publishing houses that perform this linkage, thereby providing the institutional and organizational framework for the production and dissemination of academic research. The book thus offers a map and an interpretation of a sector of the book industry that is central to the intellectual advancement of our society.

Books compete with newspapers, radio, and television for the shaping of public discourse. In part because of their comparative cheapness and convenience, books enjoy some advantages that newer forms of communication lack. Books are more respected than the more ephemeral media, and they still carry a measure of dignity. Books have more permanence; the reusage rate for books is vastly higher than for the other mass media. The tactile pleasures and physical attractiveness of books are unmatched by other means of transmitting the written word. Books are also an individual medium: the reader proceeds at his or her own speed. While the growth of the modern electronic mass media has stripped publishing houses of some of their formerly uncontested influence in the cultural arena, publishing nevertheless remains a vital force in the world of ideas.

Publishers, like classical entrepreneurs, link creators of products with interested consumers. Publishers decide which kinds of books will be offered to the public and how vigorously they will be marketed. In doing this, they shape the creation and dispersion of ideas, scientific knowledge, and popular culture. But, despite the publishers' central role, we have only recently begun to learn why some book manuscripts get published and others do not.[1] This is not to say that little has been written about the book trade. There are many histories of individual companies,[2] treatments of key periods in the industry's history,[3] memoirs and biographies of editors and publishers,[4] informative journalistic accounts,[5] and treatises on the nature of the book business.[6] There are many fine studies of the development of reading publics and of the social context in which literature is produced.[7] There are, however, few systematic analyses of the decision-making process in book publishing.[8] Compared to the attention paid to other media, such as newspapers or television, the book industry has gone unnoticed by those who could provide rigorous analysis.

Book publishing is a commercial enterprise, and product design, sales strategy, pricing, and order fulfillment are just as important in it as in any other business. Yet, as we shall see, book publishing is a fascinating and complex industry, with traditions that often frustrate the standard business practices associated with other, more bureaucratized industries. As Charles Horton Cooley (1929:188) observed many years ago:

> Commercial institutions . . . have in general obvious functions, but an adequate characterization of a successful institution of trade would have to include all those subtle traits of organization and spirit which explain how and why this institution is viable while others, if they are viable, are so in a different way. I have had to do, for instance, with several publishing concerns, and am of the opinion that their distinctive behaviors would make an instructive study.

As an industry, book publishing is beset with a number of competing demands and internal contradictions. It is both a labor-intensive craft and a business that realizes economies of scale from high-volume production. Highly dependent on the success of a large number of new "products" issued annually, some firms are nevertheless sustained by the steady earnings of their backlists. In recent years the industry has experienced both an exceptionally high birthrate of new firms and a pronounced tendency toward mergers. The labor force is generally overeducated yet is frequently ill prepared for careers in publishing. There is widespread use of subcontractors for nearly every function save the initial decision to publish. The most persistent and unresolved problem has been distribution—how to get books into the hands of interested consumers (see Shatzkin 1982; Powell 1983). College and university libraries, themselves major consumers of scholarly books, offer books as public goods, obviating the need for scholars to purchase them.

A thorough study of the sociology of scholarly publishing must address a wide variety of concerns. The decision to publish a book involves such factors as the credentials of authors ("He's from Stanford," "Her previous book won the C. Wright Mills Award," or "He's an unknown"); the social networks in which authors and editors are enmeshed ("This editor, who is a good friend of mine, is coming for a visit. Would you like to join us for dinner and tell him about the book you are working on?"); the process through which decisions are made (which is sometimes a slow, cumbersome affair, bogged by delays; sometimes a lengthy period of solicitation of an author by an editor; sometimes fast—a snap decision resulting from a chance encounter on an airplane); the occupational characteristics of editors ("I'm not a professional, I'm more like a skilled craftsman" or "An editor is like a cabdriver: he knows the feel of the road, where the ruts and bounces are"); and the mechanisms through which employees are socialized ("After you are here for a while, you acquire a kind of cognitive map—you learn what goes over and what doesn't").

The relationship between scholarly publishing and social science research is an intricate one. One task of this book is to analyze the way in which the success of two scholarly publishing houses is inextricably tied to the organization of the

American academy. The forces of supply and demand and the pressures of environmental selection do influence the growth and development of scholarly publishing, but these pressures are strongly attenuated by the network ties and the cultural and historical elements that form the nexus of social relations between editors and academics. Of course, any recurrent economic transaction becomes overlaid with social content (see Macaulay 1963; Williamson 1975:106–8; Granovetter 1983a:31–38 and 1983b:33–35); however, in book publishing preexisting social relations often form the basis of economic exchange.

For the community of American scholars, books are very important commodities. They are written, read, debated, and reviewed. Reputations are tied to the success or failure of one's latest book. Promotion, tenure, and even one's first job are tied to the quality of one's writing. Publishing is the primary measure of academic achievement. A few scholars and unattached intellectuals command so significant an audience that their writings are also a source of considerable income. So, for the academic community, books serve a highly utilitarian purpose, and it is scholarly publishing houses that are the gatekeepers to this important medium of communication.[9]

The primary focus of this book is the local political economy—the set of relations both within the two houses that I studied and between them and a variety of external advisers and service-providers. The immediate ties to the task environment form a critical part of this local political economy. A publishing house lies at the center of a large and complicated web whose strands reach out in a variety of directions: to authors and the social worlds they inhabit; to libraries; to the reading public; to employment agencies and to unions; to banks or parent corporations, which extend credit or lend money; to the federal government, which sets policies dealing with copyright legislation, the tax treatment of books held in inventory, postal rates, and import regulations; and to the scientific communities in foreign lands.[10]

The case studies on which this book is based describe the boundary-spanning roles played by editors and explain the influence exerted by such key outsiders as senior academic advisers and series editors. I present a detailed ethnographic account of how the structure of social relations, both inside and outside the firm, influences the crucial decisions about what should be published. In general, I am concerned with three main questions. (1) How do editors decide which few manuscripts to sponsor, out of the hundreds that flood their desks? The view of the decision-making process presented here suggests that choices are seldom strategic, nor are they guided by stable preferences. Choices more commonly represent the fulfillment of duties and obligations. Preferences and meaning develop in the course of making decisions, through a combination of socialization and experience. (2) What is the nature of the editorial task? In short, how do editors ply their trade? Here I analyze the different strategies employed by editors to acquire manuscripts and show how the search process fits into a network of social relations among editors and authors. I illustrate the way in which the structure and operation of the two publishing houses I studied create standard operating assumptions that guide editorial activities. (3) What are the specific ways in which scholarly houses are embedded in a larger social context? To answer this, I describe the relationships between the two scholarly houses and their respective parent corporations, discuss the role of the two houses within the scholarly sector of the book industry, and illustrate how most of the activities that publishing houses must engage in—the acquisition and evaluation of manuscripts, the promotion and sale of books—require making contact with outsiders. The formal organization of the two houses—and of the publishing industry in general—is not well suited to meeting these demands; recurrent informal connections are one way of filling in the gaps in the formal structure.

In chapter 1, I provide an overview of the publishing industry. Several trends—in particular, increased concentration and commercialization—have of late been attracting a considerable degree of attention. It is my view that culture is more resilient and resourceful than we generally take it to be. Periodic crises in the publishing industry have come and gone, and the feared collapses have not occurred. The history of the industry can be characterized as a long series of conflict-laden episodes, none of which has proved terminal, however threatening each seemed at the time. In taking this long view, I do not intend to understate the risky, unsupportive financial environment in which some sectors of the book industry currently operate. Yet, however much we may deplore the blockbuster complex in trade publishing or the production of "managed" textbooks, it is not only the economic structure of publishing that has changed in recent years. As Elisabeth Sifton (1982) suggests, it is not rapacious, profit-minded corporations that threaten quality work so much as the sad but simple fact that, for the first time since the early eighteenth century, readership is declining.[11] A complete assessment of the health of scholarly publishing must ask whether scholars read outside the narrow confines of their disciplinary sub-fields. Do they buy books within their fields, or do they rely on libraries to purchase them? How valid are the charges made by some scientific publishers that books are no longer bought but instead are photocopied?

The most significant feature of book publishing as an industry is its internal diversity and segregation into a number of distinct, separate worlds, marked by important cultural and organizational differences. Across industry sectors we find significant variation in recruitment patterns, career security, interfirm mobility, and promotion prospects.[12] Each sector of the book industry operates within a distinctive institutional environment, with dissimilar amounts of risk and uncertainty. The various types of publishing houses are staffed by people from different social backgrounds, and the status and influence of the occupants of similar positions contrast significantly across industry sectors. Such sectoral differences influence the quality of an employee's life: the nature of interdepartmental conflicts, patterns of friendship, and leisure-time activities all vary according to the branch of publishing in which a person works.[13]

In chapter 2 I introduce the two companies that I studied. One of them, Apple Press, is a small scholarly house that publishes fewer than a hundred books a year, almost exclusively in the social sciences. The other, Plum Press, is a large monograph house that publishes over four hundred books a year, of which fewer than a hundred are in the social and behavioral sciences. Apple has approximately thirty employees; Plum, more than four hundred. Both companies are on a sound financial footing. In the years just preceding my fieldwork the smaller one cleared a double-digit profit margin, while the larger one had a somewhat smaller profit margin on annual sales in excess of forty million dollars. At both Apple and Plum the organization of work shapes the editorial process in important ways. As I argued in an earlier book, "What directly affects an editor's daily routine is not corporate ownership or being one division of a large multidivisional publishing house . . . ; on a day-to-day basis, editorial behavior is most strongly influenced by the editorial policies of the house and the relationship among departments and personnel *within* the publishing house or division" (Coser, Kadushin, and Powell 1982:185). We shall see that, although both Apple and Plum direct their books toward an audience of academics and professional practitioners, there are sharp differences between them with respect to organizational structure and editorial policy and practice.

In chapter 2 I also look at an intriguing dimension of publishing: the time cycle. Publishers engage in a delicate balancing act involving previously published books that continue to generate revenue, the search for new acquisitions, and books that are presently being released. The various departments of a publishing house operate within very different time frames, and the disparity between their perspectives is, in addition to being an indicator of an employee's discretionary power, a frequent source of conflict and disagreement. Cyert and March (1963) observed that finance departments estimate resource requirements on the low side, whereas comparable estimates by sales departments are high. This is not at all surprising, given that it is the task of finance to conserve resources and of sales to stimulate growth; yet it serves to emphasize that organizations have multiple goals and perspectives and that these often conflict.

Organization theorists are familiar with numerous studies that point to the tensions that arise between administrators and professionals, between the demands of the organization as a whole and the personal concerns of career-minded individuals. Nowhere is this tension more evident than among book editors. For no one person oversees or controls the whole publishing process, and at no one time do all or even most of the personnel work on the same set of manuscripts; yet it is the editor who decides which book others in the house will have to produce and sell, and this clearly is the most important decision to be made in a publishing house.

Editors, as we shall see in chapter 3, are situated in structurally ambivalent positions: loyalty to their authors and their craft often outweighs their allegiance to the firm that employs them. All but one of the editors at Apple and Plum had worked for three or more different companies. The high turnover commonly reported in publishing partially reflects the extent to which craft loyalties outweigh corporate ones. Theodore Caplow (1954) and Rosabeth Kanter (1968) have noted that many organizations attempt to instill commitment in their members by inducing newcomers to renounce previous associations. Editors, however, are frequently hired precisely because of their extensive contacts. When editors change houses, some of their authors move with them. Indeed, the number of authors that follow an editor from one publishing house to another is a good measure of that editor's prestige and influence. In chapter 3 I look at the craft of editing and examine the daily tasks performed by editors, paying particular attention to the different search methods used by editors, the problems involved in rejecting authors, the services that editors provide for authors, and the extent to which editor's jobs spill over into their private lives. A great part of an editor's skill lies in his or her ability to judge which topics will attract a sufficiently broad audience. At both Apple and Plum the editors were continually looking for books with the backlist in mind, for an ideal book is one that will sell steadily for many years.

The editors I observed rebelled at any overt attempts by their bosses to tell them how to do their work. They claimed that editing demands special sensibilities and that they knew their subject matter better than anyone else. Their descriptions were very much akin to Mary Quant's characterization of fashion designers: "Good designers . . . know that to have any influence they must keep in step with public needs, public opinion . . . and with an intangible 'something in the air'" (Quant 1965:74).

In chapter 4 I discuss a variety of situations that illustrate the degree of discretion that editors are allowed. Most editors have a considerable amount of freedom in conducting their daily affairs. Indeed, they all made a point of telling me this and offered data in support of this view. For example, one editor had had only one book proposal turned down in four years, and another estimated that 95 percent of his projects were approved without question. What are the reasons for this apparent autonomy, and how real is it? The second part of chapter 4 provides an answer and offers an alternative account of editorial discretion. Despite considerable evidence of editorial freedom and autonomy, it often seemed to matter very little which particular editor happened to make a decision. I argue that editorial choice is strongly shaped by the force of moral and organizational obligations. As Howard Becker (1974:770) shows, "People who cooperate to produce a work of art do not decide things afresh. Instead, they rely on earlier agreements that have become customary." These agreements become conventions and suggest a shared understanding that allows for easy and efficient coordination of activity. The routinization of the decision process at Apple and Plum allows for the appearance of autonomy while simultaneously enforcing limits beyond which decisions rarely stray. I describe the methods publishers use both to socialize editors into organizational roles and to shape the premises of editorial decision-making. Once editors accept their employer's premises, they can then be permitted considerable latitude. Of course, conventions are seldom rigid and unyielding; much may be left unsettled and subject to interpretation and negotiation. I conclude the chapter with a discussion of how the tastes of individual editors blend with the overall "character" of their respective houses.

In chapter 5 I examine the criteria that influence an editor's decision to accept or reject a manuscript. A crucial reality of editorial work is that the demand for editorial time far exceeds its supply. At both publishing houses, systems of preemptive priorities allow some clients to jump ahead of earlier arrivals in the queues awaiting editorial attention. The conventions vary with the context of production. There are significant differences for authors with regard to waiting and access, and this variation in queuing at the two houses helps amplify some of the differences between them. As we shall see, authors located in different positions in the respective queues meet with different rates of acceptance and rejection.

Queuing rules operate as filtering systems; however, even in the most preferential queues, only a minority of the authors receive contracts for their manuscripts. A variety of other factors—the house's history and tradition, finances, and scheduling considerations—influence the decision-making process. An author's academic status is reputed to determine his or her chance of being published, yet, as we shall see, the actual influence of an author's academic position is modified by his or her position in social networks.

Many of the chapters provide examples of how authors are cared for by editors, how authors may suffer from delays they experience during the review process, and how they may be mishandled during the production process. Publishing houses and their employees treat as routine what authors regard as their crowning achievements. There is obviously considerable opportunity for disparities of opinion to emerge. Meyer Schapiro (1964), in describing the system through which an artist agrees to exhibit and sell exclusively with a particular dealer, notes that the contractual relation is beset with many strains and difficulties. There are clearly many parallels between the author-publisher relationship and that of artist and dealer. It is worth quoting Schapiro at length:

> The dealer may be dissatisfied with the artist, either because he has produced too little altogether or falls below the expected level of quality. The artist may not approve the looks or location of the gallery, the method of publicity, the clientele, the dealer's personality and calculations; he may feel less favored by the dealer than other artists in the same gallery who are more successful in attracting purchasers; he may suffer because the works of the others cast a shadow on his own, because they are better or worse, or in a style with which he feels no sympathy. There are then many tensions within this freely chosen relationship of artist and dealer. In general, an artist desires a dealer who admires his work wholeheartedly and will continue to show it even though there are few sales; who gives no sign of disapproval when the artist changes his style and passes through a period of searching or experimentation, without fully realized results; whose publicity is dignified, original, or personal in a way that appeals to the imagination and taste of the artist; and who respects the personality of the artist. There have been dealers for whom the art business was a genuine personal expression, a means of participating in the deeply interesting, often exciting world of original artists with whom they have formed lasting friendships. [Schapiro 1964:368]

The comments of authors illustrate the separation process that occurs as an author gains distance from his or her work with the passage of time. As one author whom I interviewed stated, "When it comes to my scholarly work, I consider it tinkering with my soul. I went through a period where I would have liked to shoot my editors and copyeditors. But, in retrospect, I now think the job they did was quite good . . . I'd readily publish with them again."

In the sixth and final chapter I place the analysis of the choice processes at Plum and Apple in the context of recent debates within organization theory. Most formal theories of organization-environment relations ignore both the role of organization qua organization (see Zucker 1983) and the manner in which organizations represent clusters of patterned relations embedded in more inclusive social arrangements (see Granovetter 1983a). Prevailing conceptions of organizations view firms as being at the mercy either of the internal necessities of production or of external market forces over which they have little control. I argue that the comparative case studies I present here suggest the need for a rethinking of the relationship between organizations and their environments. I draw upon my research on another industry, public television, and contrast the fragmented environment of public TV with the tightly coupled world of scholarly publishing. I show that environments are enormously invasive and that firms are capable of altering and managing them. I close by examining how the decision process at Apple and Plum in particular, and in scholarly publishing in general, influences the academic development of the social sciences.

When Lewis Coser, Charles Kadushin, and I began our study of the book-publishing industry, we were motivated above all by our common love for books, our interest in the institutions responsible for producing and disseminating ideas, and our conviction that much of the fate of our culture and our educational system hinges on the health of the publishing industry. I have painted scholarly publishing with all its warts precisely because I care about books so deeply. Even if, on the basis of our research, my colleagues and I can give only two cheers for the publishing industry as it is presently constituted, we can give three wholehearted cheers for the future of ideas, writing, and the book in America.

Research Chronology

In order to judge the reliability of many of the observations in this book, the reader needs to know something about my research methods and the arrangements I made with the two publishing firms. Case studies have many virtues and many liabilities. They avoid some of the simplistic causal assumptions found in some quantitative work. Thick description is necessary if we are to capture the range of events and practices that go on within organizations. But a publishing house does not sit still while we study it. Indeed, any organization that did not change while being studied would be a peculiar one. And a case study can give too much credence to the interpretation favored by its author. Selective emphasis of material and decisions about what to include and exclude are, however, problems shared by both qualitative and quantitative research. I have attempted to avoid overemphasizing my own views by systematically describing the two publishing houses and the events that I observed within them. The reader can thus use the ethnography to develop his or her own explanation. In some cases, I suggest competing analyses for interpretation of the field data and argue why I think a particular interpretation is the correct one. Of course, it is almost always possible to find a plausible explanation for a set of observations; the reader will have to judge how systematic and consistent the views offered in this book are.

When I began my research in May, 1975, my central concern was to locate publishing houses that would give me more or less free rein to study them. I drew up a list of prominent scholarly or monograph houses in the New York City metropolitan area, developed a prospectus that outlined the aims of my work, and began contacting the firms. The first two companies declined; although they expressed interest in the research, they maintained that their staffs were overworked and could not spare the time I would require of them.

Apple Press

I used a well-known academic as an intermediary to introduce me to the editor-in-chief of the third house I approached. For purposes of confidentiality, this very successful and well-regarded scholarly publishing house will be referred to as Apple Press. The editor-in-chief consented to my studying the house. I was introduced to the company's employees as a graduate student in sociology who was interested in understanding how the publishing business operated. Being re-

garded as a novice was extremely useful in establishing rapport with people. I was not viewed as a threat by anyone; in
fact, I was treated very much like someone who had just
started to work for the company. I began visiting Apple Press
in late May of 1975 and spent at least one day a week there
during the months of June, July, September, October, and
November. These visits were generally arranged in advance. I
would telephone either the editor-in-chief, a department
head, or one of the editors and arrange to spend the day with
the person I had contacted.

During this initial period, I listened to people describe
their work and explain the details of the specific projects with
which they were involved. A typical day would find me sitting
in someone's office, reading mansucripts that had been submitted, going through editors' correspondence with authors,
and looking at sales records. During this time the person
would carry on with his or her business more or less as usual,
with the exception that about fifteen minutes out of every
hour would be spent in answering my questions.

By December, 1975, my visits became less frequent, and
they were not arranged in advance. The nature of my interaction with Apple Press changed considerably. Several factors
influenced this. First, I had formulated hypotheses I wished to
test, and I had specific requests for information that I wished
to collect. My questions were no longer general inquiries but
detailed, specific probes, aimed either at explicating processes that were unclear to me or at filling in gaps in my
knowledge. Second, in the fall of 1975 I assumed a position as
field director of a major study of "publishers as gatekeepers
of ideas," funded by a grant from the National Institute of
Mental Health to Lewis Coser and Charles Kadushin. In that
capacity I was responsible for overseeing the interviewing of
over a hundred people in editorial positions in a variety of
houses throughout the United States. With the added resources provided by the grant, in terms of both personnel and
finances, I was quickly becoming more knowledgeable about
all aspects of the book business.

I was no longer regarded as a novice at Apple Press; in fact, my opinions and advice were sometimes solicited. I was recognized and greeted by maintenance staff and employees of the parent company located in the same building. Whether they thought I was a meddlesome author or an employee I do not know. With the added responsibilities of the grant, I had less time for fieldwork. Instead of spending the day from 9:00 A.M. to 5:00 P.M., observing the goings-on, I would see people for lunch or for short, focused interviews. This continued until July, 1976, when I finally concluded my work at Apple Press. In retrospect, I realize that the patience of these people and their willingness to spend countless hours with me were truly remarkable. I hope the final product of my work will in some small way compensate for their generosity.

Plum Press

My next attempt to gain access to a publishing house was made within the context of our larger study of the publishing industry. I was rebuffed by an independent house that I sought to use as a comparison to Apple Press, since Apple was a division of a large corporation. Then one of the senior investigators of our research team received the approval of the chief executive officer of a very large publishing corporation to study all of the company's operations. I was assigned to the task of studying a monograph house that was one of its major subsidiaries. I lost the chance to draw a comparison between independent and corporately owned firms, but I gained the opportunity to study a very large, commercially successful, and academically reputable monograph house.

Again for the sake of confidentiality, I will refer to this house, pseudonymously, as Plum Press. My field relations and experiences at Plum were substantially different from those at Apple. In a real sense, my presence was imposed on the company. The nature of my first meeting with the editor-in-chief and the psychology editor was indicative of this: they took me to lunch at a posh restaurant. (On my first day at

Apple Press the editor-in-chief and I had had sandwiches at a nearby fast-food stand.) In short, I was treated as a professional social scientist involved in organization research, not as a young graduate student. This created some problems in building rapport, but, in general, these difficulties were overcome. For example, my first introduction to production and manufacturing personnel occurred at a transmittal meeting, where the social science editor presented me as having "the imprimatur of Mr. ——— [the president of the parent company] and God." One young union organizer was taken aback by this and asked what, if any, association I had with a recent management consulting team that had been at the house. He asked if I had spoken with any of the participants in the union drive. I mentioned that I had talked to the union's leaders at the union office and that I knew of the organizing drive that was presently under way at Plum Press. I later met with several union organizers off the job site and gained their confidence and trust.

Establishing rapport with the social and behavorial science editors at Plum Press was not difficult, since we had a number of interests in common. Regrettably, I never established good relations with the company's editor-in-chief, who found my presence intrusive and bothersome.

My field experiences at Plum Press were both more focused and more concentrated than at Apple. By this time I had accumulated a great deal of general knowledge about the publishing industry, so that my concern now, in addition to collecting specific data, was to learn what, if any, characteristics were unique to Plum Press. My observations were not stretched out over a period of months. Instead, I visited the company two to three times a week from mid-September, 1976, through mid-December of that year, for a total of about thirty observations.

Other Sources of Information

In addition to my fieldwork at Apple and Plum, I visited a large university press, where I interviewed several editors and the director. I also attended a variety of industry meetings and workshops, such as the annual meetings of the American Booksellers Association, the Society for Scholarly Publishing, and the Association of American University Presses, and I closely followed events in various trade publications, among them *Publishers Weekly*, *Scholarly Publishing*, the *Author's Guild Bulletin*, and the *BP Report on the Business of Book Publishing*. I also read numerous reports issued by the Association of American Publishers, the Association of American University Presses, Knowledge Industry Publications, and the Book Industry Study Group. Finally, my associates and I formally interviewed approximately one hundred thirty people in editorial positions and informally interviewed roughly four hundred other publishing personnel. I also supervised participant-observation studies of eight other publishing houses.

A word of explanation about the sources of information cited in this study is necessary. In the course of our research, my colleagues and I promised confidentiality to all the people with whom we talked. Since people were rarely aware of the ultimate use that I would make of the information they gave me, it is important that their confidence not be violated. Occasionally, I have altered minor details of incidents in order to protect respondents' identities. All data collected at Apple Press and Plum Press (as well as additional material collected in the course of the general research project on publishing) are reported anonymously. When individuals or corporations are identified by name in the text, it is because this information was obtained from publicly available sources.

1

THE ORGANIZATION OF AMERICAN BOOK PUBLISHING

Publishing has acquired something of a mythic heritage as a genteel profession that attracts people because it is a lively and urbane occupation concerned with ideas, contemporary affairs, and literature. The traditional prerequisites for being a successful publisher are a certain flair—a certain taste and sense of discrimination. How close this myth is to reality would be difficult to ascertain, but, suffice it to say, it has had considerable staying power. As recently as 1976 the Association of American Publishers sponsored a seminar called "The Money Side of Publishing," and one of the speakers, Erwin Glikes, criticized the seminar for perpetuating the pervasive myth that the industry has two sides, the "sunny side of editors, writers, and other gentle folk sitting at sidewalk cafes, sipping aperitifs, talking about Art," and the shady side, where the sun does not shine, where "sharp-eyed accountants and heavy-jowled financial types pause every now and then to shake their fists at the children of the sun across the street, who sit there, oblivious to the bottom line, whiling away their hours and the profits in blissful ignorance."[1] Much of the current outcry over commercialism in publishing is a reflection of the belief held by some parties that book publishers should be concerned with more than just making money. These tensions between the demands of commerce and the obligations of culture have persisted throughout the history of the book trade.

1

Such debates go back over a century and a half because book publishing is one of the oldest industries in the United States. There are few other American businesses in which it is possible to trace a direct family lineage from the original founders to the executives of contemporary firms. Nor are there many industries where so substantial a number of the leading companies have maintained their dominant position since the turn of the century. Moreover, some of the practices and policies associated with the book trade's cottage-industry era persist in modern-day publishing. Nevertheless, there have been a number of profound changes, particularly during the past three decades. In the 1950s, William Jovanovich regarded his occupation as "a halfway house between art and business."[2] By the late 1970s, Michael Korda, editor-in-chief at Simon and Schuster, quipped to an interviewer, "We sell books, other people sell shoes. What's the difference? Publishing isn't the highest art."[3]

In this chapter I briefly review the principal changes that have shaped the social and economic organization of the book industry in recent years and assess the consequences of these changes. In particular, I review the emergence of various market segments within the industry, the rapid growth of the past few decades, and the bifurcation of the industry into large vertically integrated publishing and entertainment firms and smaller specialist houses that cater to well-defined audiences. I conclude with a comparative analysis of the three branches of the industry—general "trade" books, college textbooks, and scholarly monographs—that are most significant for the production and dissemination of social science knowledge. Although editors in almost all branches of the book industry share a common task—the location of manuscripts with sales potential—the means for accomplishing this task vary, depending on the sector of publishing in which the editor works.

Differentiation: A Highly Segmented Industry

A great many different types of books—textbooks, encyclopedias, reference books, Bibles, mass-market paperbacks, serious fiction, and research monographs, to mention only a few—are produced by the publishing industry. Each type of publishing commonly requires special skills and knowledge. As we shall see, the problems that people must solve in their work roles differ significantly across the different branches of the industry. Given the varying requirements for successfully publishing a particular type of book, it is not surprising that publishing houses tend to specialize in one type of book or that, in the larger firms, such as McGraw-Hill or Harcourt Brace Jovanovich, there are separate divisions or departments, each concentrating on a particular type of book.

In terms of its social organization, the book-publishing industry is a universe of loosely connected firms, linked sometimes by ownership but more often by nothing more than the common enterprise of producing books. This universe of firms is subdivided into a number of smaller, distinct, and tightly knit social systems. This process of differentiation, or the creation of various subsectors within the industry, dates back to the nineteenth century. John Tebbel (1974:119) reports that, "by 1860, book production had assumed the general proportions it has today—that is, textbooks were the largest part, 30 to 40 percent of the whole." Book publishers have long known that publishing "trade books"—books of wide general appeal—"has ordinarily been too shaky a business to stand firmly by itself" (Miller 1949:19).

By the early part of the century, many of the larger publishers of general literature had expanded the scope of their operations to include the more reliable and predictable areas of publication, such as medicine and law and, especially, school and college textbooks. Macmillan was the first house to establish a college textbook division, which it did in 1906 (see Madison 1966). By 1913, George P. Brett, president of Macmillan, observed that few large publishers were confining their publications to books in general literature (Brett 1913:455). The strategy of diversifying into new areas was a means of reducing the risks typically associated with trade publishing.

Not only publishing houses but a wide variety of American industries began to diversify during the early years of this

century. As the historian Alfred Chandler (1977:473) has
shown, the strategy of diversification evolved from the concept of the "full line," the adding of new product lines which
permitted companies to make more effective use of their
expertise and to exploit the by-products of their existing
product lines. Initially, many of these moves were ad hoc
responses of middle managers to fairly obvious opportunities.
By the 1920s, however, in much of American industry, diversification became an explicit strategy of growth. By diversifying, businesses hoped to achieve several aims: to decrease
risks by spreading resources across several domains of activity; to achieve economies of scale in those activities that were
common to all lines of the business; and to smooth over rough
periods and allow for the maintenance and development of
product lines during periods of adversity.

Book publishing lagged behind these general business developments, pursuing its own independent path. Some publishers diversified into new lines of publishing, but the industry did not grow. In fact, in the period 1911–45 it had a
negative compounded annual growth rate of − 0.8 percent
(Noble 1982:100). After a remarkable year in 1910, when
13,470 books were published, an increase in the number of
new books and new editions released annually did not occur
again until almost five decades had passed. Although these
years were not propitious for growth, they were years of
significant literary and intellectual accomplishment. Books of
genuine merit commonly made the best-seller lists. This was
also the heyday of valuable and productive editor-author
relations, typified by the legendary Maxwell Perkins of Scribner's and his close association with, among others, Thomas
Wolfe and Ernest Hemingway (see Wheelock 1950).

Although the book industry began to develop distinct submarkets early in the twentieth century, it was not until mid-
century that it began to grow. And grow it did, turning out
14,876 titles in 1959, more than 30,000 by 1966, and reaching
a peak of 48,793 in 1981.[4] The number of publishing companies jumped from 804 in 1954 to 1,650 in 1977.[5] I turn now
to a discussion of this growth and the changes that have

accompanied it, but we should not lose sight of the fact that the industry's recent growth has also accelerated the move toward differentiation. Thus any effort to chart overall industry trends is risky, because book publishing today is not so much a single industry as an assemblage of subsectors, and few trends or changes are uniform in their consequences across industry sectors.

Expansion and Modernization

The speedy growth of book publishing since 1960 is the result of the confluence of a number of factors. In the midst of the baby boom and post-Sputnik funding, higher education burgeoned. As the globe shrank and literacy rates increased, there was a worldwide information explosion. The popular entertainment industry, with its insatiable appetite for new products, also grew at a rapid clip. Publishing-industry analyst John Dessauer recalls that the sixties were

> times when books seemed to sell despite the inadequacies of their publishers, when even inferior materials were readily absorbed by a well-funded, gluttonous market. So many factors worked together to benefit the various segments of the industry that almost everyone enjoyed a slice of the pie. Research projects supported by government and foundation grants encouraged acquisition of professional books; generous federal and state budgets, bringing unaccustomed affluence to colleges, universities, and their faculties, augmented sales of scholarly materials; newly founded colleges were stocking libraries; parents eager to strengthen their children's educational resources avidly bought encyclopedias for the home; general and specialized book clubs were flourishing. [Dessauer 1974:8]

The expansion of the book industry attracted many outside interests. Companies such as Time, CBS, ITT, Xerox, and others in the information or entertainment fields were eager to join in the book trade's growth or to finance it. Publishing houses themselves raised new sources of capital by public stock issues or by merger, the latter route becoming very common. This outside capital further fueled the industry's swift rise. The book industry became rife with mergers and acquisitions, and during two peak periods, 1965–69 and 1974–80, the merger rate in publishing was four to five times higher than in most American industries. Outside ownership also brought modern management practices that fundamentally altered the craftlike nature of book publishing. These changes, as I discuss in more detail below, have been a mixed blessing.

The debate over the consequences of the book industry's growing absorption by the entertainment industry, through the acquisition of publishing houses by film companies and television networks, has been loud and long. Some have termed these developments a "sinister process," while others have welcomed them.[6] Statistics on the publishing industry are sparse, and one can easily marshal data to support a wide variety of competing arguments. Heather Kirkwood, the attorney who coordinated the Federal Trade Commission's investigation of media concentration, has remarked:

> I have been frequently startled by the amount and intensity of disagreement which revolves around the media. Yet I have found that little of this controversy involves disagreement on facts. Instead, people disagree on how the facts should be categorized, judged, analyzed, or valued. Hardcover trade book publishing provides a good illustration of this type of controversy . . . ; frequently one side will point to a particular set of figures as proof positive that the industry is, indeed, concentrated. The next day, a different group will point to the exact same figures as proof positive that the industry is unconcentrated.[7]

A plausible case can be made that industry concentration has been enhanced by the formation of large vertically integrated publishing/entertainment companies. Huge multimedia giants, such as MCA, Gulf and Western, Times Mirror, and Time, Inc., own various combinations of magazines, television stations, film companies, cable television, and other entertainment activities. The ten largest mass-market paperback lines, all owned by large corporate entities, accounted for 83.3 percent of mass-market paperback sales in 1980.[8] The eleven leading hardcover trade publishers were responsible for 71 percent of the sales of hardcover titles in 1980.[9] Six of these houses are owned by larger corporations; the others are themselves large diversified publishing companies. These figures suggest that certain subsectors of the industry are controlled by a small number of firms, many of them in cross-ownership of other mass media. But other statistics paint a very different picture. Measures of overall industry concentration show scant change. The four largest firms accounted for 18 percent of the industry's sales in 1947, and in 1977 the four-firm concentration index was 17 percent. The U.S. Bureau of the Census considers the publishing industry to be "one of the least concentrated sectors among all U.S. manufacturing activities."[10] A recent Congressional Research Service report notes that the number of publishing establishments increased by 45.2 percent over the 1972–77 period and concludes that the industry is highly competitive and open to new entrants (Gilroy 1980).

I find that neither set of statistics—those that stress the industry's competitive health as against those that indicate a trend toward concentration and a narrowing of editorial choices—fully captures the complex reality of contemporary book publishing. The interviews and field observations that my colleagues and I obtained in our general study of book publishing provide a different perspective. I argue that changes in ownership have had a subtle but nonetheless significant impact on the manner in which many publishers conduct their business. I will also suggest—and this may initially strike the reader as counterintuitive—that the heightened quest for large audiences, common in many corporately owned houses, has provided new opportunities for specialist firms. The basic economic structure of the book industry is fragmented, and only in a few submarkets do any significant financial gains accrue from large size.

Changes in the Labor Process

Arthur Stinchcombe's (1959) classic paper on bureaucratic and craft modes of production beautifully delineates the difference between work systems that are bureaucratic and hierarchical and those that are autonomous and personal. In bureaucratic mass-production systems, both the product and the work process are planned in advance by persons who are not members of the work crew. The engineering of work processes and the evaluation of work by economic and technical standards takes place in specialized staff departments. Such systems are hierarchical in nature, and communication generally is in a vertical direction. In contrast, Stinchcombe observed that the construction industry consists of a loose coalition of small organizational units, each having considerable autonomy. In construction, the task calls for many intermittent and highly skilled operations that follow a sequence. The skills are such that control by direct surveillance or by rules will not render the desired outcomes; considerable reliance must be placed on workers making their own judgments. Management confines itself largely to inspecting outcomes. In a craft system of production, such as construction, the work process is governed by workers in accordance with the empirical lore of their occupation. Planning and execution are decentralized at the work level, where entrepreneurs, foremen, and craftsmen carry the burden of technical and economic decision-making. Such systems are not bureaucratically organized except for their administrative components, which generally are considerably smaller in size than their counterparts in bureaucratic organizations. Stinchcombe finds a strong association of craft systems with a minimization of fixed overhead costs. This is necessary because of variations in work volume and product mix.

Occupations that involve the production of cultural goods exhibit many of the characteristics associated with craft systems of production. Because of their uncertainty about the necessary ingredients for a successful book or phonograph record, executives are forced to trust the professional judgments of their employees, relying on their track records as indicators of their abilities (Peterson and Berger 1971). Paul Doebler, a publishing-industry analyst, has described these arrangements in the following way:

Unlike many other industries, where costs can be managed more tightly from higher echelons, book publishing costs depend heavily on the actions of those working at the lower and middle levels of the organization. It is impossible to centralize all the myriad decisions to be made on the thousands of books published each year, and these cost-determining decisions are spread throughout the company in publishing. So, in a very real sense, people at most levels of publishing have direct impact on how well the organization uses its resources to attain its goals, whether to earn a profit or to produce fine books or both. [Doebler 1976:33]

For years, the view that publishing is a craft was the orthodox one. The following comments, made by two highly regarded senior editors, both with distinguished careers in trade publishing, aptly summarize this perspective. One of them had this to say:

Publishing is a very chaotic industry . . . ; it begins with the fact that you exert very little control over the person who creates the product. Nor does anyone actually know what the public wants or what it will buy. I think it would be impossible to try and create a list of books, each of which would have high-volume sales. I don't think it can be done, not intentionally anyway. Over and over, publishers are surprised by their lists. Some books sell better than expected, others do much worse. What I try to do is to publish books I think are important, or informative, or needed by someone out there. I think about the "market," but, in my mind, what is crucial ultimately is how I feel about the book.

The other said:

I firmly believe that publishing cannot be made rational or efficient because it is like a factory that turns out sixty, eighty, a hundred or more custom-produced objects . . . each of which has to be sold to a different market, talked about in a different way. Each book is a separate product, with an essentially autonomous fate.

Not only has the nature of the labor process in publishing long resembled a craft occupation, but the industry as a whole has been able to maintain low operating costs by arranging for services on an as-needed basis. Overhead costs are minimized by contracting with authors on a royalty basis, and editors' salaries may sometimes be tied to the sales of the books they sign. Even the largest houses routinely call upon free-lancers, either individuals or agencies, for such services as copyediting, design and artwork, indexing, promotion, and publicity for individual books; smaller houses rely on free-lancers to an even greater extent. The overwhelming majority of publishing houses contract with independent firms for the printing, binding, and manufacturing of books. Additionally, many publishing houses market a substantial number of their books indirectly, through independent distributors or wholesalers, who sell to libraries and bookstores. This is true even for large houses who have their own sales staffs. Most of the small and some of the medium-sized houses have no in-house sales force; instead, they contract with either commission salespersons or larger publishing houses, or they form a consortium with other small publishers to handle the sales, distribution, and warehousing of their books.

Yet, in the past decade or so, many of these features have disappeared from the publishing scene, usurped by new arrangements and practices. The conversion of a craft occupation into a corporate enterprise has been initiated in part by new owners and managers, who have sought to rationalize book publishing and bring its idiosyncratic and often determinedly old-fashioned habits into line with modern management techniques. Much more attention is now paid to orchestrating a book's release and reception. Both trade and textbook publishers have embraced the idea that books should be carefully packaged. Houses now have large and sophisticated marketing and publicity departments, whose advice is frequently sought, and in some instances is required, before any publishing decisions are made. The result is that more attention is paid to actually selling a book; this is in marked and rather welcome contrast to the previous notion that a book sold itself by favorable word-of-mouth. The down side, of course, is that not all books are deemed worthy of such favorable treatment.[11] At some publishing houses, it does not seem worthwhile to crank up the marketing machinery for a book of quality and merit but of only modest commercial potential. (Such books, I should note, are not going unpublished. As I discuss in more detail later, they are increasingly likely to be published by small specialized firms, or under a special imprint by a larger house, or by a nonprofit university press.)[12]

Other changes in the work process are the natural by-product of the close alliance of publishing with television and film.[13] The huge sums paid for the subsidiary rights to hard-cover books have kept many trade houses afloat;[14] at the same time, these developments signal a displacement of editorial prerogatives. Editors in trade and textbook houses can no longer simply sign a book and then tell their house to sell it. Instead, other departments must be consulted before decisions are reached. The task of negotiating a trade-book contract has become quite complex, involving complicated subsidiary-rights agreements. Negotiations require hard bargaining, legal expertise, and shrewd manipulation. For assistance, authors have turned to agents and lawyers to help them stay abreast or ahead of the publishing community. The links between authors and agents are but one part of a more general reduction in contact between authors and major publishing houses.

Perhaps the most fundamental shift has been in the role of the editor, especially in large trade and textbook houses. Publishing-industry historian John Tebbel observes (1981:732) that the widely used term "acquisitions editor" is an indicator that today's editors seldom edit. He notes that, in the 1940s, "acquisition editors were confined to textbook publishing, and the so-called line editors of the 1970s had not been invented." Editors used to be generalists who did everything. Now the time of an acquisitions editor is considered too valuable to be spent on working with an author. In the past, editors read manuscripts, worked with authors, assisted them, and edited their manuscripts to whatever extent was required. Today's editors spend much more time talking, arranging deals, and consulting with lawyers, corporate managers, and marketing and subsidiary-rights directors. This not only signals a power shift within publishing houses—one in which editors are on the decline and others are in ascendance; it has also led to a restructuring of the relationship between authors and editors.

One editor described the changes in his work at a large trade house by noting, "I'm spending a lot more time planning the lives of my books. Much less time is spent with authors and much more time with other departments—marketing and subsidiary rights, especially." Another trade editor, commenting on the hurly-burly pace of his job and the need to move quickly, remarks that, "with multiple submissions, editor and author never get together to judge the chemistry between them, and we find ourselves up against fifteen other houses, having to make fast decisions." Moreover, both authors and editors seem to move from one house to another more frequently than they used to. A *New York Times* story on publishing's declining sense of community summed up the state of affairs by noting that loyalty is now spelled "M–O–N–E–Y."[15] Of course, few complaints are being voiced by the authors who are reaping the benefits of the new era of large contracts or by the employees, who have found that the highest salary levels are paid by houses owned by large corporations or conglomerates.[16]

Transformation or Transition?

How fundamental or permanent are the changes I have just described? One indicator of whether new forms of ownership and work organization will endure is the strength of their financial performance. Clearly, when measured by increases either in sales receipts or in the number of new titles and editions, the book industry's gains have been remarkable. But have the new methods and practices resulted in higher profits? The data needed to fully answer this and related questions are not available;[17] however, the calculations of J. Kendrick Noble, analyst of media stocks and vice-president of Paine Webber Mitchell Hutchins, Inc., offer us some insights. It is important to note that, prior to the industry's recent transformation, hardcover trade publishing was a marginally profitable activity, while textbook publishing was fairly stable and prosperous. Have the new practices altered these traditional standards of performance? Moreover, are the greatest financial gains realized by the largest firms within specific industry sectors? And, finally, is it the more concentrated sectors of publishing that earn the more robust profits?

Tables 1 and 2, below, provide tentative answers to these questions. They report 1980 profit margins for different sectors of the book industry, as well as a trendline, based on normalized estimates of operating margins for the period 1971–80. Noble (1982:113–16) cautions that these data, which are derived from voluntary reports by member firms of the Association of American Publishers, have several limitations. The number of companies reporting varies annually, and it is reasonable to assume that the larger publishers are more likely to report. It is best to regard the data as reflecting the performance of members of the AAP and not as necessarily representative of the entire industry.

Table 1
Estimated Operating Margins of Publishing Firms, by Sector

Sector	Operating Margin 1980 (%)	Rank	Trendline, 1971–80 (%)	Rank
College textbooks	20.4	1	16.3	3
Trade books (total)	8.2	10	0.9	9
Adult hardbound trade (subcategory of above)	5.6	11	4.2	7
Mass-market paperbacks	1.4	14	− 5.6	11
Professional books (total)	12.4	7	10.6	5
Technical and scientific books (subcategory of above)	9.4	9	18.6	1

NOTE: Operating margins are pretax.
SOURCE: Excerpted from Noble 1982: 113. The full table includes data for fourteen industry sectors.

Table 2
Estimated Operating Margins for Different-sized Publishers, 1980

Sector	Smallest Third (%)	Middle-sized Third (%)	Largest Third (%)
Trade books (total)	8.8	8.8	8.7
Trendline, 1971–80	1.6	9.8	8.5
Professional books (total)	12.8	11.3	13.0
Trendline, 1971–80	9.6	10.2	12.0
College textbooks	9.4	14.2	25.4
Trendline, 1971–80	1.9	17.1	25.4

SOURCE: Adapted from Noble 1982:114.

In 1980 and for the period 1971–80, college textbook publishers performed very well. They were the industry leaders in
1980 and were among the top performers in the previous
decade. Textbook publishing's economic status clearly did
not suffer from any changes in work arrangements or increases in concentration; in fact, this sector's financial performance was quite likely improved as a result of these developments. Trade publishing presents a different story.
Financially, it remains a fairly marginal activity. Of course, it
is possible to argue that, had there been no changes in operating practices, trade publishers might have fared even worse
than they did; but that is hardly a strong justification for
significant changes in the organization of work. It is also
worth speculating that, while trade publishing is not particularly lucrative in and of itself, firms that own trade publishing
houses in tandem with film companies or television studios
realize some economies of scope. That is to say, they benefit
from common ownership of several media, and they gain
added understanding of their markets as well as greater access
to potential "products" from such arrangements. The data do
not permit us to assess whether this is true, but this would be
one reason for remaining in this line of activity. Note that
mass-market paperback publishing, one of the most concentrated sectors of publishing, is also one of the least rewarding
financially. Finally, professional books, the unglamorous and

seldom-recognized sector that we will shortly be examining, performed extremely well in the decade 1971–80.

The data in table 1 do not provide strong support for the notion that changes in the organization of work have dramatically improved performance. Textbooks continue to be rewarding, while trade books are not. Nor do the data offer a clear picture of the advantages of market concentration. The college textbook market is fairly concentrated, with a small number of firms controlling the lion's share of industry receipts. On the other hand, mass-market paperback publishing is even more concentrated, and the performance of these dominant firms is hardly auspicious.

When we turn our attention to differences in the size of houses within specific industry sectors, we find somewhat more stable results. The larger companies in each sector tend to show the highest profit margins. The advantages of bigness seem particularly strong in the college textbook market, somewhat less powerful in trade publishing, and even more modest in professional books. Nevertheless, the message of table 2 is fairly clear: greater financial gain is associated with larger size. We should, however, be somewhat cautious about the actual importance of size. The proposition that large size generates high profits raises tricky problems of causality. Both size and profitability may be the result of growth, of expertise, or of historical trends. The strongest association between size and high profit margins is found in college textbook publishing, a sector of the industry which has long been regarded as highly predictable and profitable. Textbook publishing is one of the few areas of the industry where there are any significant economies of scale. Large textbook publishers, unlike large houses in other sectors of the industry, appear to be able to maintain high profits without facing significant challenges from new entrants, whom we would normally expect to be attracted to this rewarding line of activity.

If the available data on financial performance do not provide an unequivocal rationale for the recent alteration in the traditional practices of book publishers, are there other reasons why we might expect the developments of the past decade to be more or less irrevocable? For example, to what extent are there sunk costs, either psychological or economic, attached to existing modes of operation? The general portrait of the rise of modern business enterprise sketched by such scholars as Max Weber, Alfred Chandler, and Oliver Williamson suggests an evolutionary progression. Weber averred that rationalization was the dominant trend in modern industrial societies. Bureaucracy, as an organizational form, has rendered calculable and predictable what was once governed by intuition, personal appeal, or passion. Once established, bureaucracy is very resilient in responding to challenge. Chandler (1977) and Williamson (1980) see the growth of modern corporate organization as the triumph of a superior form of administration, one that is able to outperform competing modes. Hence, once an economic activity moves from a decentralized, craft form of organization to a more centralized corporate form, it is unlikely to return to its earlier craft status. Though they differ in some important respects, the implication to be drawn from Weber, Chandler, and Williamson is that a return to a craftlike form of organization would be an unexpected regression. These broad portraits of social change are meant to capture general trends and are not necessarily applicable to specific industries, particularly one as idiosyncratic as publishing, but they do suggest that, in the absence of strong contrary factors, we should expect the recent changes in publishing to constitute a fundamental transformation in both the means and the relations of production. Thus we now turn to the key question: Are there any factors that would render the recent changes in book publishing more transitory than transformative?

Mergers by themselves do not necessarily make companies any less efficient or their activities any less valuable. But as the concerns of book publishers shift in a way that leads them to spend more time on business issues and less time on cultural matters, it is natural to worry that the social consequences of these developments may not be altogether beneficent. The production of books is a special enterprise. What may be logical from the point of view of efficient management may not be beneficial when examined with respect to such different criteria as enhancing cultural diversity, promoting civil liberties, or advancing scientific knowledge.

There is little evidence, however, that books of merit are going unpublished. Even the Authors Guild, the most vehement critic of recent changes in book publishing, observes that "it is not that fewer books are being published than formerly, or even, at least not provably, that books of exceptional merit are going unpublished."[18] The Authors Guild points instead to a kind of degradation of the publishing process. But books of quality continue to be published, occasionally with considerable success, both critical and financial. *The Name of the Rose*, a demanding first novel by Umberto Eco, a professor of semiotics at the University of Bologna, spent many weeks in 1983 and 1984 atop both the hardcover and paperback best-seller lists. Successes such as this are, however, uncommon; more typically, books that are challenging and rewarding are published with limited fanfare. The works of a great number of talented novelists, historians, social scientists, and foreign writers are currently in print. One may have to look carefully for these books and pay dearly, because their prices are generally very high even when they are published in a quality-paperback format. And, outside of a few large cities, such books may require special ordering. Yet they are available.

One reason for this relatively promising state of affairs is the growing specialization of the book industry, brought about, in part, by the proliferation of small publishing concerns. The rate of merger and acquisition in publishing is high in comparison to other industries, but it is only a fraction of the rate of formation of new publishing companies. As a result, the industry's overall concentration rate does not increase. Noble (1982) shows that the average new book is selling fewer copies and that the average firm has fewer employees than before; hence the book industry's productivity is being achieved in terms of more titles per employee. In short, the industry is becoming more specialized.

These new houses are not replacements for the medium-sized firms that have been gobbled up in the recent mergers. The publications of small firms do not receive the attention in national review media that books published by larger houses do. Small firms also lack the distribution capability of larger publishers.[19] What is significant about the small publishers is that they are demonstrating that a specialist strategy—that is, catering only to particular segments of the reading public—is quite viable in book publishing. A small but highly specialized publisher can make as much profit with small print runs of expensive titles as the very large publisher of titles can with big print runs and low prices.

Glenn Carroll (forthcoming) has pointed out that many industries are characterized by the simultaneous success of apparently opposing strategies. In such industries as brewing, newspapers, music recording, and book publishing, generalist firms and specialist firms not only coexist but are fundamentally interrelated. The success of the generalists creates the conditions for the success of the specialists. Carroll (1984) describes this phenomenon as "resource-partitioning," a process which results in an environment that is split into general and specialized markets. In the newspaper industry, for example, general-audience newspapers strive to reach the widest possible audience; in so doing, they are vulnerable to the competition of specialized newspapers, who appeal, for example, to ethnic or suburban readers or to those interested in business news (Carroll, forthcoming). More generally, "by attempting to secure large market shares through universalistic appeals to all potential customers, generalists avoid making extended particularistic appeals to special groups of customers" (Carroll 1984:131–32). The net result is that, by pursuing large audiences, generalists neglect many specialized pockets of consumers.

Resource-partitioning seems to be an apt characterization of the current state of the book trade. As large trade and also college textbook publishers increased their expectations about the number of copies that a book must sell in order to be considered successful, they became less willing to take on eminently worthwhile books that had modest sales potential. This change in the marketing strategies of many large publishers has created new opportunities for small trade houses, scholarly houses, and university presses, all of whom are moving into the territory the large trade houses have vacated in their quest for blockbusters. Other small publishers have found specialized niches and have concentrated on how-to books or books of regional interest. There are also small publishers driven by social, religious, or political causes. Still other small houses, such as David Godine, are concentrating on books noted for their exceptional design. And there are small firms that are surviving by reissuing titles that the large companies have allowed to go out of print.

Perhaps the key difference is that, unlike general-interest publishers, small specialty houses operate with the knowledge that the readers of their books are, to a large extent, the same kind of people as those who write them or else are professionally like them. This makes information-gathering much simpler. It is easier to stay in close contact with authors who are more likely to know one another. Decisions can be made faster. The marketing advantages of specialization are even more pronounced. Direct-mail advertising can be highly targeted and cost-effective. Special markets have more predictable sales. The same benefits of specialization also extend to finding skilled copyeditors, compositors, and other production personnel. The growth of special-interest publishers is only one factor, albeit a significant one, in the dramatic increase in the total sales of books, from approximately half a billion dollars' worth in 1952 to more than eight billion in 1983.

Part of the success of the small, more specialized houses is due to the declining quality of author-publisher relations in the larger houses, along with the exceptionally high rejection rate for manuscripts that is characteristic of almost any publishing house of significant size. Small firms and large firms not only aim at different audiences; they also differ with respect to their internal structure and operating policies. While the books published by the small, specialized houses generally receive less national exposure and attention, the titles are kept in print longer than the typical book published by a large house. Employees are likely to feel a stronger sense of identification with a small press, even though their pay is usually less than they would receive at a large firm. The administration of a small house tends to be fairly simple, in contrast to the intricate organizational structures, involving complex decision rules and costly monitoring practices, that are standard at many large houses.[20]

Of course, not all small houses are specialists, and not all of the large publishers are generalists. Although organizational size and strategy are correlated, the association is not terribly strong because other factors affect this relationship. Despite the many problems faced by small houses in their struggle for survival, particularly with regard to access to bookstores in general and to chain bookstores in particular, some do succeed. A crucial issue is how they react to success. Do they continue their specialty operations or attempt to standardize their products and enlarge their resource base? Or do they become acquisition targets for larger houses, who can provide much-needed financing for the smaller firm? Some may even go out of existence if the person who founded them dies.

Moreover, I have treated large publishing houses as if they are uniform in their policies when, in fact, they are not. The relationship between one division or subsidiary of a large firm to the corporate office is rarely the same across companies. Ownership strategies and practices vary considerably. Some parent companies follow a hands-off policy with their divisions and subsidiaries, while others become involved in the minute details of daily business. Many large houses and conglomerates encourage internal competition among their various divisions and subsidiaries.[21] And, as the specialist strategy has demonstrated its viability, large firms themselves are embracing it, whether through diversification into specialized lines of publishing, the establishment of personal-imprint lines within trade publishing houses, and the spinning-off of small subsidiaries, or directly, via the acquisition of successful small publishing houses.

This diversity of practices reflects the basic fragmentation of the book business. In order to retain authors as well as valuable personnel, large houses have moved to set up small "boutique" or personal-imprint lines within their larger operations. In this manner, editors enjoy some freedom from corporate constraints and responsibilities and are freer to stay in close contact with their authors. The diversification into new areas of publishing is a recognition that some of the less glamorous areas of book publishing are the most remunerative. But, most broadly, these developments illustrate that even large publishers have found it difficult to transform some of the basic structural features of the book business. It is a type of work in which there are some important diseconomies of scale (Porter 1980:197–98). There is a constant need for new products. These products have a creative content that cannot be supplied by the publishing house itself but must be competed for in the marketplace. While the competition for authors is sometimes determined on financial grounds, it also frequently rests on personal service and matters of image and reputation. Outside of the textbook and mass-market paperback fields, there are neither barriers to entering the publishing business nor economies of scale to be reaped from high-volume production. And there are "peculiar" barriers to exit, such as a strong emotional desire to be associated with books, that keep people and firms in the business for reasons other than financial reward. In sum, these enduring features of the book trade have led to a fairly diverse, highly segmented industry, populated by corporate giants, semiautonomous firms backed by corporate owners, and small "Mom and Pop" houses, all competing in many different areas of book publishing.

Major Sectors of the Industry

Although I maintain that it is the branch of publishing—not ownership or size—that has the greatest influence on the way people carry out their jobs, it is by no means easy to come up with a widely shared set of definitions that nicely discriminate

among the various sectors of the industry. The fact that
people distinguish between types of books, not only locating
them individually but also categorically, is nothing new. Jane
Austen, in *Northanger Abbey*, made the point for her own
generation in this ironic passage:

> "I am no novel reader—I seldom look into novels—Do not
> imagine that I often read novels—It is really very well for a
> novel." Such is the common cant. "And what are you reading,
> Miss———?" "Oh! It is only a novel!" replies the young lady,
> while she lays down her book with affected indifference, or
> momentary shame. "It is only *Cecilia*, or *Camilla*, or *Belinda*"
> . . . Now, had the same young lady been engaged with a
> volume of the *Spectator*, instead of such a work, how proudly
> would she have produced the book, and told its name . . .
> [Quoted in Lane 1980:13]

The definitional problem is further confounded by the fact
that few publishing houses catalogue their books in the same
way. The primary consideration may well be the overall con-
stitution of a house's list, and this will therefore influence how
individual books are to be typed. For example, a publisher
whose list is largely trade-oriented may designate as academic
a book that a scholarly house would regard as "general." Nor
would it be correct to claim that publishers never handle
books that lie outside their normal range; for a variety of
reasons, many publishers do books that seem out of character
for their particular house. But these exceptions only serve to
emphasize the extent to which publishers' lists do have an
identity, which can be described in terms of the types of books
they have previously published.

A number of different methods are currently used for
categorizing books. There is the Dewey system, which clas-
sifies books according to twenty-three subject categories.
This method is not particularly helpful for our purposes here,
because it does not allow us to distinguish among publishing
houses. (It also appears to have its share of problems with
subject matter; to take an example from my local library,
Union Democracy, a classic study of the politics of the typog-
rapher's union, is classified as a book about printing.) Nor are

the thirteen categories established by the Association of American Publishers (AAP) all that useful from a sociological standpoint. (We will, however, have to rely on the AAP statistics, because other figures are virtually nonexistent.) The problem with the AAP categories is that they fail to employ a consistent set of criteria for discriminating among houses. Some categories are based on type of publisher (textbook); others signify the manner in which books are distributed (mass-market paperbacks, mail order, book clubs); still others rely on a book's content (religious); and one describes ownership (university press).

Another manner of classifying books is by their channel of distribution. There are five major means of distribution: general retail stores, college stores, libraries and institutions, schools, and export.[22] While the great majority of texts are sold in college stores, and most trade books are handled by retail outlets, neither professional books nor university-press titles have a primary distribution outlet. For example, in 1981 professional publishers used a variety of channels, with direct sales to consumers, sales to libraries and institutions, and export sales the three primary means of distribution. University presses relied on sales to libraries and institutions, to college stores, and to general retailers, in that order of importance (Dessauer 1983:101–4).

I choose instead a simple typology that distinguishes among three sectors of the book industry—publishers of trade books, including adult hardcover and trade paperbacks, as well as mass-market paperbacks; publishers of college textbooks; and scholarly publishing, including specialized commercial monograph publishers, nonprofit university presses, and for-profit generalists who publish primarily for an academic audience. The usefulness of this scheme is that the interviews and fieldwork that my colleagues and I conducted revealed significant differences in the organization of work across these three sectors; hence it is a sociologically interesting way of dividing up the industry.

The three sectors differ in the following important ways: the audiences they seek to reach and the methods they employ to reach them; in the standards and criteria they use for accepting manuscripts; in the differential chances for unpublished authors to be discovered; in the size of their print runs and in their time schedules; and in their definitions of what is successful, as well as in their strategies for attaining success. Scholarly editors seek the approval of the oligarchs of academic networks or "invisible colleges."[23] Trade editors try to create the illusion of success by generating media publicity, talk-show spots for authors, and high-priced subsidiary-rights auctions. Textbook editors rely on research that purports to tell them what professors who teach introductory college courses are looking for. While Harvard University Press would be pleased with a book that sold 5,000 copies in a three-year period and garnered a Bancroft Prize as the best book in the field of history, Prentice-Hall or Simon and Schuster might be very disappointed by a book that sold "only" 20,000 copies during its first six months of shelf life. It is a business in which one publisher's peacock is another's turkey.

Perhaps most important, the three sectors show very significant differences in profitability. One review of the performance of the industry in 1981 concludes, "As usual, text and professional books were among the profit leaders" (Dessauer 1983:100). Table 3 shows estimated book-industry sales according to the AAP classification. If we combine the categories that I have marked 1, we approximate what I call the trade sector. College texts are marked 2, and the categories labeled 3 roughly correspond to my definition of the scholarly sector. These are general approximations, but they will prove useful in the context of a discussion of profitability and market shares. Professional books and college texts have both been consistently strong performers over the past decade (see, for example, Most 1977 and Quirk 1977). The 1981 pretax operating margins of around 13 percent for professional books and an even stronger 22 percent for college texts typify the year-in, year-out solidity of these two sectors. In contrast, adult hardcover trade, trade paperbacks, and mass-market paperbacks all had lower than 10 percent operating margins in 1981, which, though weak, represented a marginal improvement over 1980 (Dessauer 1983:100). If we use the data in table 3 for 1982 book sales, we find that trade books accounted for 22.8 percent of total industry sales, professional books for 15.7 percent, and college texts for 14.6 percent. The three sectors combined account for more than half of all book sales. I turn now to a brief overview of the major features that distinguish these three branches of book publishing.

The nature of college textbook publishing has undergone tremendous change since the 1950s and 1960s. Back then, all manner of books—research monographs, basic texts, paperback anthologies, and books designed for advance upper-level courses—were published by textbook companies. In the interim, textbook publishing has witnessed a growing concentration of ownership and a reduced willingness to take risks.[24] Since the 1970s, the large textbook houses have concentrated on producing books for the largest undergraduate courses. They no longer produce for the smaller upper-level and graduate courses, and they publish no research monographs at all. These large textbook publishers may employ more than a hundred college travelers, who visit the campuses, urging adoption of the latest texts. Orders are placed with college bookstores, who obtain the books from the publisher at a discount of 20–25 percent.

In contrast to the large houses, the small college publishers, frequently located in publishing's hinterland, outside the New York metropolitan area, survive by locating the specialized niches that the large firms disdain. They concentrate on producing one "quality" introductory text, on doing books for smaller advanced courses, or on publishing texts with a particular point of view, such as a Marxist political sociology text. Medium-sized text houses face the greatest threat to their survival, because they are too large to rely on specialized texts, yet they lack the sales force and other economies of scale necessary to take on the dominant giants, such as Prentice-Hall or McGraw-Hill.

The days when a college text editor would "eyeball" the

Table 3
Estimated Book Publishing Industry Sales
(In Millions of Dollars)

	1972 $	1977 $	1977 Pct Chg From 72	1982 $	1982 Pct Chg From 77	1982 Pct Chg From 72	1983 $ (Preliminary Est.)	1983 Pct Chg From 82
Trade (Total)	444.8	887.2	99.5	1344.4	52.8	204.7	1595.2	17.7
(1) Adult Hardbound	251.5	501.3	99.3	671.6	34.0	167.0	807.6	20.3
(1) Adult Paperbound*	82.4	223.7	171.5	452.0	102.1	448.6	531.6	17.6
Children's Hardbound	106.5	136.1	27.8	180.3	32.5	69.3	190.3	5.5
Children's Paperbound	4.4	26.1	493.2	51.5	97.3	1071.3	65.7	27.6
Religious (Total)	117.5	250.6	113.3	390.0	55.6	231.9	454.9	16.6
Bibles, Testaments, Hymnals & Prayerbooks	61.6	116.3	88.8	163.7	40.8	165.8	182.0	11.2
Other Religious	55.9	134.3	140.2	226.2	68.4	304.7	272.9	20.6
(3) Professional (Total)	381.0	698.2	83.2	1230.5	76.2	223.0	1373.0	11.6
Technical & Scientific	131.8	249.3	89.2	431.4	73.0	227.3	491.0	13.8
Business & Other Professional	192.2	286.3	49.0	530.6	85.3	176.1	561.2	5.8
Medical	57.0	162.6	185.3	268.5	65.1	371.0	320.8	19.5
Book Clubs	240.5	406.7	69.1	590.0	45.1	145.3	654.4	10.9
Mail Order Publications	198.9	396.4	99.3	604.6	52.5	204.0	554.5	−8.3

(1) Mass Market Paperbacks							
Racksize	250.0	487.7	95.1	665.5†	36.5	166.2	706.1	6.1
(3) University Presses	41.4	56.1	35.5	122.9†	119.1	196.9	129.9	5.7
Elementary & Secondary							
Text	297.6	755.9	51.9	1051.5	39.1	111.3	1149.7	9.3
(2) College Text	375.3	649.7	73.1	1142.4	75.8	204.4	1228.6	7.5
Standardized Tests	26.5	44.6	68.3	69.7	56.3	163.2	79.7	14.3
Subscription Reference	278.9	294.4	5.6	396.6	34.7	42.2	443.0	11.7
AV & Other Media (Total)	116.2	151.3	30.2	148.0	-2.2	27.4	143.0	-3.4
Elhi	101.2	131.4	29.8	130.1	-1.0	28.6	124.3	-4.5
College	9.2	11.6	26.1	7.9	-31.9	-14.1	7.6	-3.8
Other	5.8	8.3	43.1	10.0	20.5	72.2	11.1	11.1
Other Sales	49.2	63.4	28.9	77.1	21.6	56.8	80.0	3.8
TOTAL	3017.8	5142.2	70.4	7844.3	52.5	159.9	8592.0	9.5

SOURCE: *Publishers Weekly*, June 22, 1984, p. 34.
*Includes Non-racksize sales by Mass Market Publishers of $113.5 million in 1982 and $139.9 million in 1983.
†Previously reported 1982 figures revised to conform to information available at a later date.

market to see what was needed, find a professor to write a book on the subject, wait for it to be written, and then hope the book would sell have largely passed from the scene. One reason for this is that the process took too long. Sometimes as many as three or four years would be spent in writing the text. Nowadays college publishers are anxious to produce books that are lively and topical. They are also asserting much greater control over both the writing and the content. Textbooks no longer just get written; they are now carefully designed packages, heavily illustrated and accompanied by manuals, test banks, and other paraphernalia. In other words, college texts are now produced with the very active participation of the publishing house, much as elementary and high-school texts have always been prepared. Utilizing market-research data, editors develop a plan for a text and then carefully oversee the writing, testing, design, and manufacture to make sure that the plan is followed. The editor-author relationship is essentially a buyer-seller relationship in which the editor contracts for certain specified services from the author. There are tight deadlines and strict controls. The aim is to produce a small number of products that have been carefully researched and tested in advance of publication.

College text publishing is strongly sex-typed: nearly 75 percent of the college text editors whom we interviewed were men who had begun their careers in sales or marketing (see Coser, Kadushin, and Powell 1982: chap. 4). Thus, editorial decisions—which ultimately determine what college students will read—are influenced by historical patterns of career mobility, the market demands of a highly concentrated sector of the book industry, and a set of internal social relations in which an emphasis on sales predominates. Introductory texts are expensive to produce; a quarter of a million dollars or more is often spent before the first copy is adopted for classroom use. This large expenditure puts heavy pressure on editors to ensure that their decisions will pay off. As a result, the majority of college editors handle less than a dozen books each year—much less than the yearly workload of scholarly editors. Much of their time is spent in meetings—much more than is the norm for editors in scholarly or trade houses. Every step of the production process is closely coordinated by editors and key members of other departments.

Competition among text houses is fierce. Unlike scholarly or trade publishers, text houses are in direct competition with one another for customers—the professors who decide which text to adopt. One indication of the competitive nature of text publishing is the reluctance of text editors to assist their counterparts at other houses; they are the least likely of all editors to refer manuscripts to editors at competing houses. The decision process in text publishing is highly formalized; text houses are among the most bureaucratic of publishing firms. In Perrow's (1967) terms, the task of the text publisher is routine. There is little variation in the production process even though the subject matter of the books may differ greatly. With such high stakes involved, most houses opt for a fairly conservative strategy, and there is a good deal of imitation of competitors' products.

Text editors feel that their skills are interchangeable from discipline to discipline (one text editor claimed that he could "easily be as efficient in electrical engineering or physics as in psychology"), but scholarly editors take a different perspective on their work. Although few scholarly editors profess to be experts in their respective fields, they do believe that a certain amount of knowledge of a subject—whether acquired through education or experience—is necessary. "You *have* to understand the differences among subfields within a discipline," an editor at Plum Press asserted. More generally, our interviews revealed a difference in intellectual disposition between scholarly and text editors. The latter believe that they possess a general skill, while the former have more passion for a particular set of interests. Scholarly editors read much more widely and well; they were more likely to read such periodicals as *Science*, for example, and more than a third of the scholarly editors we interviewed regularly read three or more "highbrow, intellectual" magazines.[25] In contrast, college editors were light readers; they seldom read publications such as the *New York Review of Books*, the

American Scholar, the *Atlantic*, or the *New Yorker*. Most scholarly editors attended top undergraduate colleges and universities, and more than a third had one or more advanced degrees. Of all the editors we interviewed, it was the scholarly editors who were the most likely to have done some writing themselves, while the text editors were the least likely to have done so.

Many scholarly editors underwent some anticipatory socialization before entering a career in publishing. Almost half intended to pursue a career in book publishing. In contrast, text editors typically entered publishing by accident. Scholarly editors honed their network-building skills early: many used personal contacts to land their first job. As a group, scholarly editors are, by publishing standards, the most diverse; for example, the largest percentages of females and Jews are found in the ranks of scholarly editors. This diversity also holds up in terms of career mobility. Scholarly editors started in a much wider range of positions than did editors in either textbook (where sales is the entry point) or trade publishing (where editorial secretary or assistant is the first step on the ladder).

Academics and other professionals constitute the primary audience of scholarly publishers. Within this terrain, however, there is room for a considerable variety of publishing houses. There are a small number of for-profit scholarly houses, as well as the elite, nonprofit university presses, who try to reach what is, by scholarly standards, a fairly wide audience. These houses publish books aimed at a broad spectrum of academics from several disciplines rather than a narrow subfield of specialists. Ideally, their books either deal with important public issues or make a serious contribution to scholarship and thus continue to sell for many years. In addition, there are also a great many professional monograph houses who publish for very specialized audiences. Whether the audience is broad and interdisciplinary or narrow and specific, the comments of the editor-in-chief at a large monograph house aptly summarize the intended model: "The best scholarly books are those that professors have to buy for their personal libraries—the ones they have to read in order to keep up with their field."

The economics of scholarly publishing is the major factor that distinguishes it from trade publishing. While there are trade publishers, such as W. W. Norton or Pantheon, whose lists bear some resemblance to those of scholarly presses, the manner in which their books are costed out and distributed is fundamentally different. Trade books are sold at a trade discount (40–45 percent) in general bookstores. Their print runs are typically much larger than those of a scholarly book. Scholarly publishers survive by conservatively estimating a book's sales potential and then budgeting the book in such a way that a small profit can be made on a limited number of sales. The amount of money involved in terms of advances, production costs, and advertising budgets is relatively small. It is not unusual for a small scholarly book to cost less than $15,000 to produce.

Professional monograph houses represent the most specialized branch of the scholarly publishing field. The essence of monograph publishing is the delivery of timely research to small groups of consumers in need of the information. The editor-in-chief of a large monograph house described his firm's activities in the following way: "The way we look at it is that we don't publish books; we produce research tools—the latest in scientific advances. Scientists need our books the same way they need a new piece of hardware. We are at the cutting edge of science."

As scientific fields have become more specialized, and as new areas of professional activity have opened up, the number of monograph houses has grown dramatically. Among the many monograph houses or companies with monograph divisions are Wiley Interscience, Greenwood Press, Lexington Books, Jossey-Bass, Praeger Special Studies, Routledge and Kegan Paul, Ballinger, Academic Press, JAI Press, McGraw-Hill, Plenum Publishing, Transaction Books, Sage, and Westview Press.

The very specialized content and audience are the key factors, and they are unique to monograph publishing. Because the audiences for them are small, monographs are extremely high-priced. Authors receive low royalty rates, and advances are rare. The assumption is that an author's main interest is in rapid dissemination of his or her ideas to relevant colleagues. It is not unusual for a monograph to be published in less than six months. Little editing is done, and artwork and design are minimal. It is a steady and profitable, if unspectacular, business in which cash-flow problems are minimized by low overhead costs and by the short publishing schedules, which result in money returning much sooner than in other types of publishing.

The ninety-odd university presses can be arrayed along a continuum from general scholarly publisher to specialized monograph publisher. The larger and more prosperous ones, such as Oxford, Cambridge, and the university presses at Chicago, Harvard, California, and Yale, are very similar to commercial scholarly publishers and, in fact, frequently compete with them for authors. The smaller university presses have lists that are more like those of the commercial monograph publishers. One important exception is the fact that many university presses publish books in the humanities and even fiction, both of which are regarded as unprofitable by commercial scholarly houses.[26]

University presses, however, operate under different economic circumstances and, as a result, decision-making in university presses is less oriented toward the profit motive. As a part of nonprofit educational institutions, these presses are tax-exempt. Their overhead costs are lower because they are typically located in university towns rather than metropolitan centers, and their parent universities may assume various expenses for them. Many presses have endowments or other forms of subsidy. As a general rule, it would be fair to say that most university presses would be satisfied to break even. But university presses face other, more stringent constraints than do commercial houses. Manuscripts undergo much more critical scrutiny at university presses. Any manuscript that is seriously considered for publication must be favorably reviewed by two experts in the field and must later pass muster with a governing board composed of members of the senior faculty. As a result, the decision process is often lengthy, and university presses may lose authors to commercial scholarly or trade publishers. As one university press editor-in-chief remarked ruefully, "We publish an author's dissertation and then they take their next book to commercial publishers in Manhattan."

If, in trade publishing, the importance of editors is being challenged internally by subsidiary-rights personnel and externally by agents, and if, in text publishing, an editor's duties are segmented and often subservient to the marketing and sales departments, in scholarly publishing the role of editor remains the most powerful position. Scholarly editors often oversee the publication of twenty-five or more books each year. That may sound like a lot, but we will soon see that the academic community greatly assists these editors in carrying out their duties.

While scholarly publishers generally operate in a context of low risk, the high-stakes world of hardcover trade books and mass-market paperbacks is characterized by considerable risk and great uncertainty. On the other hand, the readers of scholarly books are a demanding lot, and a publisher's prestige can suffer if books of little substance are issued. In particular, the elite university presses and top scholarly houses are quite concerned with maintaining prestigious reputations. (For large monograph publishers, who issue hundreds of very specialized research treatises, reputation is not so overriding a concern.) Trade publishers compete for a broad mass audience and often publish outright junk with little negative consequence. Authors, agents, librarians, and others in the book-buying trade may be put off by a list of dubious quality, but the general book-buying public is not considered to be sensitive to a trade publisher's reputation. Each trade book is regarded as an individual commodity in its own right.

Trade editors lack both the market-research data that college editors utilize and the tightly connected academic circles that scholarly editors depend on. Text and scholarly editors readily turn to outside experts for advice; in contrast, trade editors rely on other members of their house for guidance. The world of academic and professional authors is well organized; there are even regular gatherings, such as conferences and annual meetings, where text editors and scholarly editors come in contact with authors and with one another. A consensus on what is new and valuable is developed through these institutionalized contacts. For trade editors, the outside world is much more anonymous; they lack easy access to authors, and they also tend to be somewhat isolated from editors in other houses.[27]

Trade books, whether published in hard covers or in rack-sized mass-market paperback format, are regarded as "perishable" commodities.[28] A scholarly book is sold over a fairly long time period and may wait a year or more for recognition, but a trade title has but a few months in which to make an impact or else be forgotten. If they are published with little fanfare, trade books will die a quiet death upon publication. Mass-market paperbacks expire in a most unceremonious fashion: their covers are ripped off and returned to the publisher for reimbursement by the bookstore. Hardcovers that do not "move" are consigned to be "remaindered"—that is, sold at sharply reduced prices in discount bookstores. But when success strikes, trade publishing comes alive with a kind of intoxication. Subsidiary rights are auctioned off to the highest bidder, with book clubs, movie studios, and others all clamoring for a piece of the action. Authors jet around the country on whirlwind tours, promoting their books on television and radio talk shows. Books are reviewed in newspaper and magazine columns, and large sums may be spent on publicity and advertising.

Trade publishing is a high-stakes world, with little room for the cautious. The president of a major trade house sadly notes that "only one out of every seven or eight titles pays for itself."[29] Because of the risks involved, most trade houses rely on established writers, well-known public figures, and those temporarily in the limelight as sources for new books. Trade editors typically receive a good portion of their books from agents, who have already carefully sifted through the ranks of potential authors. Few of the major trade publishers will take a chance on a manuscript from someone whose name is not known. Previously published authors or celebrities are much more likely to receive attention from reviewers and book-buyers.

Although it may not be as lucrative as text or scholarly publishing, trade publishing plays an enormously important role in shaping our popular culture. The debate over whether the high-powered world of entertainment has eclipsed the less exciting but more consequential world of serious literature cannot be resolved here; we can, however, note that the two currently coexist, with the lists of various trade publishers tilting more strongly toward entertainment or toward litera-ture, depending on the predilections of their editors and owners.

* * *

The revenues of book publishers pale in comparison with those of other mass media. The policies of the book industry are discussed infrequently in the halls of Congress. We sel-dom read about book publishers in the business press, nor should we expect to, since, as a whole, the industry employs only about 66,000 people. But we should not allow its com-paratively small size to obscure the book industry's impor-tance. Moreover, in contrast to other media industries, where decisions are dictated by the imperatives of mass production, the book industry does a better job of serving the diverse interests of small groups of consumers with special tastes. We move now from a discussion of the general landscape of the industry to specific portraits of two scholarly publishers. In doing so, we move from an assessment of the direction the industry is taking to the question of how a very small number of individuals make choices of considerable consequence for the academic community.

2

THE SETTING

Apple Press occupied a portion of one floor of a multistory building located in one of Manhattan's main business districts. The other floors of the building were inhabited by the various divisions, and also several of the subsidiaries, of the parent corporation. There were many other publishing houses in the neighborhood and also an abundance of restaurants, shops, and department stores. Editors could choose among a wide variety of restaurants, their selection often guided by the status of their lunch date.

The offices at Apple were cramped, with books and manuscripts stacked everywhere. Employees frequently inquired if and when they could get more space. The editors, department heads, and production editors all had small personal offices. The two top executives—the president and the vice-president, who was also the editor-in-chief—had somewhat larger, but by no means spacious, offices, which doubled as reception areas for guests and visitors. The remaining staff had desks in a small open area. The personal occupancy of the offices and desks was marked by posters, plants, and family pictures.

Besides offices, the building contained a newsstand, a company cafeteria for employees, and a posh corporate dining room for executives, which was rarely used by the editors of Apple Press. Each floor had a bulletin board for posting job openings within the corporation, company news, and special-interest stories, such as the one that announced the winners of the college-scholarship competition among the children of company employees. There was a monthly company newsletter, which sought to boost the company's internal image. This reflected a recent effort by the parent company to repair the damage that had stemmed from serious labor-relations problems a few years earlier. While some Apple Press employees welcomed the corporation's increased concern, others viewed it with suspicion. Contact between Apple and members of the parent company was both formal and infrequent.

The working conditions at Apple were "hygienic," or, as one employee described it, "nothing to get excited about . . . I mean, we don't have a great view or fancy chairs or anything, but it's all right." The offices were close and compact. All employees were on a first-name basis. Contact among the employees was both frequent and informal. If the head of production had a question for an editor, he would walk into the editor's office to get an answer. When a member of the manufacturing department wanted the editor-in-chief's approval of a book's jacket design, it was easy to obtain. There was a great deal of socializing both on and off the job. Employee birthday parties were common, and if the press gave a party for an author when a professional convention was in town, the entire staff was invited. Apple Press had something of the image of a happy team, working together in pursuit of a common goal. This was clearly the picture that Apple's executives drew for me. As we shall see, it was not entirely accurate. I should note, however, that, despite constant questioning on my part, few employees voiced wholesale dissatisfaction. Most of their complaints were more on the order of frustrated suggestions as to how things could be done more efficiently.

At Plum Press, the atmosphere and setting were markedly different from this. Plum occupied most of the floors of a multistory building that was located in a part of Manhattan where there were few other publishing houses and a limited number of restaurants and shops. The editorial offices were on one floor; production and manufacturing, accounting, sales and promotion, customer services, and the journals department were on other floors. Two floors were occupied by subsidiaries of Plum Press. Most of the contact between personnel on different floors was formally arranged. Employees comported themselves in a quiet and reserved manner. On-the-job socializing was limited to pleasant exchanges. Editors and executives were often referred to as Mister or Doctor by rank-and-file employees. The formality of social relations was of course due in part to the large size of Plum Press, which precluded face-to-face working relationships for most people.

The offices at Plum were not well furnished. The building was old and undergoing renovation. On very cold days the heating system warmed the building to the point that fans or air conditioners had to be turned on for relief. Top executives, editors, and managerial personnel had private offices that could best be described as adequate. Other employees worked at desks that were crowded together and separated only by short glass partitions. There were few signs of personal occupancy of offices or desks. Reception areas were sparsely furnished. Bulletin boards on the editorial floor listed the weekly travel schedules of the editors; on the other floors there was only information about fire regulations and company rules. There was little, if any, company "news" or publicity.

A Short History of the Two Firms

Apple Press was founded after the Second World War with an initial investment of less than two thousand dollars. In its early years, reprints of classical European works in the social sciences were its staple publications. One employee who worked with the company during the 1950s reports that Apple in those days was "chronically undercapitalized; we operated on a shoestring." Another remarked, "We were always stalling off creditors." The company had only five full-time employees during the mid-1950s, so it relied heavily on the services of free-lancers and a number of academics who served as advisers and uncommissioned scouts. The company's founder was a "master at exploiting personal ties," according to one former editor. He got authors to forgo royalties until their books had recouped their production costs. He found scholars who were willing to translate foreign classics for very small fees. During most of the 1950s Apple Press published fewer than thirty titles a year.

In the late 1950s and early 1960s the publishing industry was rife with mergers and public stock issues. College enrollments were expanding rapidly, and publishers wanted a piece of the burgeoning educational market. Apple Press was constantly short of money, a chronic problem for many fast-growing but small companies. To remedy this, the president of Apple agreed to an acquisition offer from a larger publishing company. At the time of the merger, the firm had annual sales of somewhat less than a million dollars.

Initially, Apple Press was "lost" within the larger parent corporation. The founder of Apple moved on to "bigger and better things with the parent company." During the 1960s there were frequent corporate reorganizations, and Apple Press eventually wound up as a division within another publishing division of the parent corporation. The parent firm itself then became, through the merger process, a large diversified, multinational educational corporation. Apple Press was encouraged by the parent company to become more textbook-oriented and to publish in a wider range of fields. The press experienced some initial but short-lived success with college textbooks. The transition to more texts and fewer scholarly books was reflected in the smaller number of titles published by the press in the late 1960s.

An editor who was with the company in the 1960s and is now editorial director of another house had this to say:

I believe that ——— [the parent corporation] thought they had purchased a potential textbook house. But clearly Apple Press lacked that capability. We were encouraged to go after college adoptions, and we didn't even have a sales force! We relied on theirs [the parent corporation's], but they were busy selling their own books. The press wasn't successful in changing its list. There were rapid changes in leadership. The house's economic performance was poor. There was no direction to their program. Their relations with authors deteriorated, and they lost many of the good ones. The publication program suffered [and, with it,] their reputation, performance, and profits. It was not until the current management redefined itself that they came near to making the kind of impact they made in the 1950s.

The parent company grew dissatisfied with Apple Press and installed a new administration in the early 1970s. The new president and the editor-in-chief were promoted from within the parent company. In the editor-in-chief's words, "We were hired to do a full-scale first-aid operation." Major changes soon took place. The new editor-in-chief described them as follows:

> Only six of our present employees worked for the press under the previous administration. We've tried to disassociate ourselves from that period. I guess it started going downhill about eight or ten years ago. [This conversation took place in late 1975.] The press published a freshman English textbook with spectacular success—it sold something like 40,000 copies. That won everyone over—texts became the order of the day. They quit selling scholarly books that sold only 2,800 copies. They didn't work with their superb backlist authors. They did not develop good relations with authors. They started publishing readers and texts—both of which can require big investments. Then, if they don't click, you lose big! Plus, they were not contributing to their backlist or promoting it. Their sales sagged. They lost their contacts and the authors who used to publish with them . . . Shortly after we took over, we had to destroy thousands of copies of textbooks the press had done in the sixties. It was a difficult decision, but there was no way these texts were ever going to sell, and warehousing costs aren't cheap!

The new president of Apple Press took a somewhat more sanguine view of the past:

> You must realize that it was a minority opinion, both within the parent corporation and among authors, that Apple Press

was seriously deteriorating. You might say that it was also the more perceptive opinion, but there were plenty of people who would have been delighted to have their books published by Apple. You should remember that the press published some of the leading social scientists in the world during the sixties. Many of these books did a lot for the house's reputation and also sold extremely well. But clearly a lot of errors were made. It was essential for me to reestablish a certain sense of trust in the press, both within the parent corporation and among authors.

One of the current employees who had worked with the press in the 1960s recalled that "the delays were just incredible. It often took two years to put a book between covers. There were no schedules. No one talked to each other. Authors were furious at us. Now we are a professional publishing house."

The two new top executives hired their own staff, reestablished contacts with authors who had left the press, instituted more efficient production schedules, and exploited the press's fine backlist, which had gone relatively ignored. Both of them told me it was impossible for them to come into Apple Press with any preset philosophy about what types of books they wanted to publish because, for the first year at least, they were saddled with publishing books that had been signed by their predecessors. In fact, manuscripts of books that had been contracted for in the late 1960s sometimes arrived at the press as late as 1976 and 1977.

By 1974, in the opinion of Apple's executives as well as in the minds of the top people in the parent corporation, the press had made a successful turnaround. This was a very good year financially for the press. Most of the books published had been signed during the reign of the current administration. Publications in the humanities had been cut back, and very few texts were published. Once again the house was publishing "respectable works of scholarship in the social sciences." In contrast, the parent corporation of Apple Press fell on hard times in the mid-1970s, partially as a consequence of their aggressive and rapid growth during the prosperous sixties. As firings and layoffs became part of "a general strategy of corporate belt-tightening," the corporation received a considerable amount of bad publicity as a result of charges of "unfair labor practices." Apple Press had only an indirect involvement in this tumult. Moreover, the success of Apple Press was a small beacon of light in the generally gloomy corporate picture; as a result, it was permitted to operate increasingly under its own direction.

In the years since my fieldwork at Apple, the press has gradually moved from publishing basic social science research into more applied areas. It has expanded its list into economics, law, management, and policy analysis and has trimmed the number of monographs in anthropology, history, political science, and sociology. There is greater concern that a new title in, say, the sociology of deviance also appeals to potential readers in the fields of criminal justice, law, and police administration. The number of titles published has remained fairly constant, ranging between sixty and eighty annually. The most pronounced change has been the editorial turnover. Only one acquisitions editor remains from the period when I did fieldwork. The president has moved on to an important position at a larger publishing house, and the editor-in-chief also has changed jobs. The reputation of Apple Press in the scholarly community remains strong, despite the changes in the nature of its list and its staff.

Plum Press was founded by an émigré during the Second World War. Few commercial publishers at that time were specializing in professional monographs in the hard sciences. The founder was the company's president for over two decades. His second-in-command—the vice-president and editorial director—assumed the presidency in the '60s, upon the founder's death.[1] There has been stability at the top executive levels throughout the press's existence. Plum Press remained relatively small during the 1950s; not until 1960 did it begin to publish more than a hundred books a year. A London branch was established in the mid-1950s, and it has developed a separate editorial program. A reprint program and a small monograph house were also set up as Plum Press subsidiaries.

The company went through a period of accelerated growth in the 1960s, publishing more than two hundred books in 1963 and topping three hundred by 1968. It also started a number of journals, opened a west-coast office, and established branches in Europe and Canada. A specialized textbook program was begun, but its record has been spotty. Textbook sales have never exceeded 10 percent of the company's total sales. The text department has had a number of different directors, in sharp contrast to the relative absence of executive turnover in other departments.

The press began publishing in the fields of chemistry, physics, and the earth sciences, later branching into the biological sciences, mathematics, medicine, and engineering. A publishing program in the behavioral sciences, defined by the press as psychology and as the speech and hearing sciences, was begun in the mid-1960s, but the emphasis has always been on the "hard" sciences. It was firmly believed that other disciplines, such as the social sciences and the humanities, were not sufficiently empirical and could not support the publication of expensive monographs.

The press went through a series of significant changes in the late 1960s. First, it went public in order to raise capital for expansion. Second, the founder of Plum Press died. The editorial director assumed the presidency, and other executives moved up a level in the hierarchy. Most of the top executives whom I met in the course of my fieldwork moved into middle-management positions at Plum during the late sixties. The new president's family became the company's major shareholder. Third, a few years after the founder's death, a merger agreement was reached between a large publishing corporation and the new president's family, in which the family's majority holdings were exchanged for stock in the larger publishing company. Plum Press and its subsidiaries became part of a conglomerate that had, like Apple Press's parent corporation, embarked on a campaign of mergers and acquisitions throughout the sixties. One key difference is that Plum Press's parent corporation continued its active expansion into the 1970s.

By the early 1970s, Plum Press was issuing more than four hundred books a year. This growth was partly attributable to a decision to initiate a publishing program in the social sciences. At the outset, a separate imprint for the social sciences was established, because there were fears that the social sciences were not "scientifically respectable." The press did not want to damage its reputation in the "hard" sciences through association with the "softer" sciences. The social science editor recalls that, "after a few years, in which I demonstrated that an estimable list could be developed in the fields of anthropology, archeology, demography, linguistics, and sociology, the separate imprint was dropped."

A major falling-out occurred between Plum Press's president and the parent corporation's top executives in the mid-1970s. As a result of the exchange of stock at the time of the merger, the president of Plum Press and his family had become large shareholders in the parent corporation. Whether the president of Plum Press was regarded by the parent firm as a potential threat or as too independent is not clear, but relations were not good. The president of Plum Press soon left the press, sold his stock in the parent firm, and formed a small publishing company of his own. His second-in-command assumed the position of editorial director.

The parent corporation was then restructured into a multidivisional firm. Plum Press, which had not been very visible within either the parent corporation or the industry, now became the major component of one of the divisions; in fact, it was one of the largest subsidiaries of its parent corporation. Plum's parent, like the parent of Apple Press, is a large diversified multinational educational and communications conglomerate, and Plum Press itself is an international publishing company, with branch offices in numerous foreign countries and, in some disciplines, very sizable foreign sales. In addition, much of its printing, mainly in the fields of mathematics, chemistry, and physics, is done by specialized printers in foreign countries.

Since the period when I did my fieldwork, Plum Press has continued to grow and to expand its publishing programs.

There has also been some editorial turnover, but the personnel changes have not, it appears, led to any changes in editorial policy or corporate strategy; however, Plum's position within the hierarchy of its parent firm has changed somewhat of late. The parent firm has continued to expand into the areas of educational and entertainment services while selling off or reducing many of its traditional publishing operations. Plum Press is now the major publishing arm of the corporation. While the parent firm's involvement in trade and textbook publishing has been reduced, its commitment to Plum Press has strengthened. A good example of this support has been the elevation of several Plum Press executives to high-level staff or advisory positions within the parent company.

Domain

James Thompson has argued (1967) that every organization must establish a "domain": the claims that it stakes out for itself in terms of goods or services produced, client population, geographical location, and services rendered. Organizational domain is a primary concern of the top administrative levels of responsibility and control in an organization. For-profit organizations have considerable freedom in choosing their domain. It is important to understand, however, that the selection of a domain is also the selection of an environment in which to operate. The domain determines the points at which an organization is dependent on its environment. A domain can be viable only if an organizations's claims to it are recognized by the essential forces in the environment that provide the organization with its necessary resources. Thus the environment poses both constraints and opportunities for organizations that seek to exchange their goods and services for resources. (We shall see that this process of exchange in publishing houses is characterized by strong norms of reciprocity.) The choice of domain is both fundamental and strategic. Thompson (1967) and also Hannan and Freeman (1977) have maintained that no two domains are identical and that two organizations cannot occupy the same domain. A good portion of the success that both Apple Press and Plum Press have achieved can be credited to their ability to stake out domains in a way that was recognized and accepted by key external actors. In short, they have achieved what Thompson (1967) refers to as "domain consensus"—a set of expectations, both for the members of the respective houses and for outsiders with whom they must interact, about what the houses will and will not do.

Plum Press is, according to the vice-president for sales, a "well-established scientific publishing company that does four to five hundred books a year in over three-hundred subfields." He went on to say, "We also do over a hundred journals. With the exception of business, law, the humanities, and history, we cover almost every scientific discipline." Plum Press titles are almost always done in hardcover and are sold to individuals through direct mailings and at conventions. Library sales are also a substantial part of total sales. "It would be odd if you saw one of our books in a regular bookstore. You'll find them in a few college bookstores but never in your local shopping-mall bookstore," remarked another member of the sales department.

"Normal science" was clearly the dominant model at Plum Press. One editor described the press as "a very conservative house":

> We'd never do anything earth-shaking. We tend to stay away from controversy or anything topical. The emphasis is on signing books that deal with significant empirical research. That way, scientists who are working in the area will have to buy our books. We want our books to be an essential part of the research process. We like books with numbers in them because we think people will be attracted to them, not just for the book's arguments or thesis, but because they contain useful data sets.

The economics of the publishing program were deceptively simple. A senior editor summed it up well:

> It is a low-investment, low-return operation. All sales are projected for a five-year period; that means that, at a mini-

mum, the book will not go out of print for five years. We rarely give advances. A book is expected to sell at least 600 to 800 copies, and that covers the cost of investment; if it sells another 600, then we have covered the cost of our overhead. Above that, it's gravy. So you can see that, if a book sells 1,500 or 1,800 copies in its first year, that's fantastic.

The director of sales elaborated on Plum Press's marketing strategy, noting that

> It's fairly unusual for one of our books to sell more than 4,000 copies. Oh, sure, some of the books signed by [the social sciences editor] have sold more. But his books are different. We have trouble promoting books to a larger audience. We don't do enough to enjoy any economies of scale, and ads for one or two books in the major media are too expensive. We just aren't equipped to promote them. We have several books that have received a great deal of attention and are selling well. We're trying to promote them accordingly . . . but, by the time all is said and done, they probably will turn out to be less profitable than a steady monograph, where we printed 1,800 copies, advertised them through the mail and in professional journals, and sold most of them over a several-year period. That's the name of our game.

The great majority of Plum Press's publications were monographs and treatises dealing with a particular subfield or topic and published as part of a series. The strategy of concentrating on well-defined topics was one means of attracting attention to, and facilitating the advertising of, their new books. Given the large number of scientific monographs on the market, a series of books has definite advantages over individual books. If a publisher has a particularly strong series in, say, anthropology, it is likely to attract new authors who wish to be associated with the series. Series are particularly economical to market and promote. It is anticipated that libraries and institutions will want to have a complete series and so will purchase new additions to it as a matter of routine. If the series prospers, it will grow in reputation and attract both authors and purchasers.[2]

Plum Press has been particularly adept at recruiting well-known academics to serve as series editors. These editors receive a small royalty, usually of 2 or 3 percent, on books published as a part of their series. Then, for books that they locate that do not appear in their own series, they may receive a finder's fee of several hundred dollars. Series editors are efficient and inexpensive talent scouts. They are the functional equivalent of quick and accessible market research. Monetary gain is not what motivates someone to take on the task of editing a series. For all the time and effort involved, the pay is quite low. More likely, the power and influence to shape the development of a field of research is a key incentive for many academics. Yet we should not underplay the fact that the position is also an obligation that is owed to the profession that has accorded one a position of prominence. Moreover, being a series editor gives one access to new work that may not become available to others for several years; it also affords one the opportunity to offer one's students and colleagues a publication outlet.[3]

Multiauthored serial publications are equally attractive to monograph publishers like Plum Press. Among the various types of multiauthored volumes regularly published by Plum are Proceedings, Recent Advances, Current Topics, and Annual Reviews. The audiences for these publications are quite small, but they are well defined and easily reached.[4] Prices for these volumes are extremely high. Print runs can be accurately predicted because the market is ascertainable—a limited but definite number of scientists, libraries, and institutions will purchase each volume in these series. Despite all these advantages, there are certain problems connected with serial publications. The new growth area one decides to exploit may fail to develop rapidly, or other publishers may overcrowd the market in this area. Editors also have to be concerned with ensuring a continuous flow of books of consistently high quality; several poorly done volumes can give an entire series a bad name and do irreparable damage.

Plum Press is not highly visible either within the book industry or to the reading public at large. In part this is because its books are rarely reviewed outside the professional journals. The company's executives tend to regard their house as unique and so do not compare themselves to other publishing houses. While few of the general developments within the publishing industry are of concern to Plum Press, events in the scientific world, or developments that affect the academic community, such as government spending for basic research, are of considerable importance and are closely watched by company executives.

The strength of the list at Apple Press was in the social sciences, particularly in international affairs, criminology, sociology, and political science. During my fieldwork, Apple Press was rapidly expanding into new areas, such as history, law, and psychology. The house was strongly committed to its backlist, and in fact most of its annual sales came from books that were more than a year old. The editor-in-chief echoed this commitment in his description of an "ideal" Apple Press book:

> The perfect Apple Press book is well reviewed in the major journals, cited for many years . . . it's a book of lasting value . . . it does not have to sell spectacularly, but [it should sell] steadily over the years. As a result, we stay away from fads, and we don't try to keep up with intellectual fashions. If good stuff is being done by important people, then we will either hear about it or they'll come to us. We may not always live up to this image, but that's our goal.

Like Plum Press, Apple Press was not very active in book-industry affairs. The president commented, "I'm certainly not very flamboyant personally, and the house reflects this somewhat. We don't belong to the AAP [Association of American Publishers], and none of us is part of any cocktail set. We don't have much pizzazz, I guess you could say." Apple Press editors and executives did stay informed about what was happening in other scholarly publishing houses, and contact with editors and personnel at competing houses was frequent. The primary focus of attention, however, was the academic social science community. Extreme importance was given to maintaining good relations with house authors and to fostering a positive image of the house. As an example of the concern about image, the top executives felt that it was "very tacky to remainder books. Authors wouldn't care for that." The press routinely called on its authors for advice, and the more prestigious senior authors were heavily relied on. As the president of the company remarked,

> It has been my viewpoint for a long time that there are people out there in academia and the foundations who will act as scouts for us and that, if you treat them right, you will build up a loyal relationship. There are probably forty to fifty people we rely on. [I act surprised at this large figure.] You just can't survive on only six or seven scouts. We won't publish everything they refer to us, and sometimes they tell us we made a mistake when we turn down one of their referrals. But they know it will get a fair shake—that the project will receive serious attention.

Apple Press's strategy of using a large number of "scouts" on an informal basis was a sound one from both a business and a sociological point of view. As Emerson (1962), Blau (1964), and Pfeffer and Salancik (1978) have demonstrated, if a much-needed resource can be obtained from a variety of sources, the power of any single source is reduced. Moreover, the referral of manuscripts by scouts is a flexible and manageable way for editors to cope with the great mass of projects that cross their desks. The scouts used by Apple Press were commonly senior academics who acted as patrons and brought younger academics to the attention of the house.[5] The role that such patrons play in scholarly publishing is in certain respects equivalent to the role of literary agents in trade publishing. Like agents, they help to screen potential manuscripts. These informal ties are bound by a norm of reciprocity but have the appearance of serendipity. Unlike agents, the scouts do not receive financial remuneration or any fixed reward. They may receive a polite note from an editor, a free book or two, or a dinner invitation. Bourdieu (1977) has pointed out that it is of the essence that reciprocal relationships not be openly acknowledged as formal exchanges. Calling attention to the exchange nature of reciprocity offends participants. In contrast to formal exchanges, in which there is a quid pro quo, reciprocal ties are highly implicit, returns are uncertain and long-range, and compensation may occur at a much later date. It is precisely these characteristics that make reciprocal relations more trustworthy than formal exchanges. And, as Kenneth Arrow (1974:23) has noted, trust is "extremely efficient; it saves a lot of trouble to have a fair degree of reliance on other people's word." In sharp contrast was the disdain with which literary agents were generally regarded by most scholarly editors. Apple Press understood altruistic ties very well and used them frequently. It had a large circle of scouts whom it could count on for referrals and for advice. As we shall see later, these scouts were amply rewarded, in a noneconomic sense, for their assistance.[6]

Apple Press published a wide range of social science titles in both hardbound and paperback editions. The bulk of its list consisted of scholarly professional books whose average print runs ranged between 2,500 and 6,000 copies. These books were the press's "bread and butter." The president underscored this publishing philosophy when he stated:

> As you know, we estimate things conservatively; our print runs are small. You call it the "cover your ass" principle. Well, it is. But I try to encourage my editors to translate unit sales into income and return on investment. Many publishers talk only about unit sales, especially in trade publishing but in our business too. But often big sales don't mean big profits. You have to consider all the angles, the costs and discounts involved . . . Looking at it from this perspective, you can see how a small book can make a good contribution. The important point is that the book doesn't have to be a big seller for us to do it and consider it a success.

The press also published a small number of reference books and an occasional specialized multivolume encyclopedia. Each season they did a few upper-level, advanced textbooks as well as several books targeted for a general trade audience. The print runs for the few trade books were considerably larger, as many as 15,000 copies for a biography of a major politician or a book on the history of an important institution. There were even instances when a successful hardcover book was released in a mass-market paperback format with an initial printing of 25,000 copies. The press was also developing an agency account, whereby a bookseller commits himself to stocking some minimum number of copies of Apple Press titles in a given subject area and in return receives an intermediate discount (generally 33.33 percent as opposed to the more common "short" discount of 20 percent for professional books). The press's parent corporation handled the sales of the texts and trade books; the press itself was responsible for direct mail and library sales. When Apple Press (or, very rarely, Plum) published a book with potential broad appeal, the parent company's trade sales force was responsible for placing the book in the bookstores. As can be expected, such arrangements did not always work well. A trade sales force is usually not well prepared to handle academic or professional books. The sales force's performance is usually evaluated on the basis of how successful they are in selling the parent company's list, so there is little incentive to work hard at promoting Apple Press books. Bookstores are seldom enthusiastic about ordering one or two copies of an academic title. Nevertheless, through a variety of means, some Apple Press books received limited distribution and were available in more discriminating bookstores, particularly in university towns.

Apple Press sold its books in a wide variety of ways. The editor-in-chief estimated that the sales breakdown in 1976 of the various channels of distribution was as follows:

Library and institutional sales	25 percent
College adoptions	25
Direct mail	20
General bookstores	20
International sales	10

Many academics are accustomed to ordering scholarly books directly from a publisher. Scholarly houses also advertise widely in journals like the *New York Review* or the *American Scholar*, and if readers cannot obtain an advertised book in their local bookstore, they can write the publisher directly. A house like Apple Press may sell several thousand copies of a book individually, filling one order at a time.[7] Both Apple and Plum did a considerable amount of their promotion and sales through direct mailings to academics and other professionals. Plum Press maintained up-to-date mailing lists of academics and professionals, while Apple Press more commonly leased appropriate mailing lists from professional societies, scholarly journals, or list brokers. The mailing lists allow houses to pinpoint the professionals who are likely to be interested in their recent publications. Even if the recipients of a catalog or mailing do not purchase a book, they may recommend purchases to their university libraries. Direct mailings permit flexibility in the design and format of advertising copy, and it is easy to chart and analyze their effectiveness. Publishers can build a data base from mail-order responses that will help them determine print runs and audience size for comparable books in the future.

The more specialized a book's topic, the more the publisher will rely on direct mailings rather than other sales methods. When it comes to specialized monographs that are not addressed to a whole academic discipline, say, economics, but to a narrower field within a discipline, such as industrial organization, total sales will be comparatively modest, but knowledge of who will buy the book is quite high. The publisher, or the academic editor of a specialized series, knows with some accuracy who will be inclined to acquire a particular book. This is why Plum Press monographs, though usually priced very high, have a relatively certain market and so can be profitable even with very modest print runs.[8]

Another important outlet for Apple and Plum was library sales. Editors at both houses mentioned that if they chose the right books, they could count on anywhere from one to two thousand sales to libraries. For some books, this alone would put them into the black. Here again, a publishing house's reputation is important. With declining library budgets, li-

braries have become more selective and will rely on publishers with a reputation for, and tradition of, publishing good
scholarship.[9]

During my fieldwork at Apple Press in 1975 and 1976 and
in subsequent interviews in 1977 and 1978, I observed that
Apple editors were signing more books with trade or agency
potential. The current sales mix would probably include a
larger percentage of trade books. Even with the somewhat
increased emphasis on "bigger" books at Apple Press, the
publishing philosophy did not change. Almost all of its books
were written by academics or professionals. Advances were
seldom extravagant. The average advance in 1975 was approximately $1,300, which masks a range that includes many
authors who received no advance at all and a handful who
were given several thousand dollars.[10] The press took a conservative approach to academic books that might possibly
appeal to a wider audience. They usually waited until the
publication date drew near; then any of a number of factors,
such as a rave prepublication review in *Publishers Weekly*,
enthusiastic comments from reviewers, heightened interest in
the book's subject, or an excited response from the parent
company's sales force, would increase confidence in a book,
and the size of the printing would accordingly be increased.
The important point, however, is that Apple Press was very
careful in these matters. Its prices for trade books were comparatively high, and the books were budgeted to earn back
their initial investment on a limited number of sales.

The Structure of the Two Houses

Apple Press is a small house and is organized quite simply.
There are two chief executives: the president, who is also an
officer of the parent corporation, and a vice-president, who is
the editor-in-chief and also an executive of the parent firm.
There are four departments: editorial, production, manufacturing, and marketing. All other functions are performed
either by the parent company or by free-lancers. The formal
chain of command is simple: each employee reports to his or

her department head, who then reports to the editor-in-chief, who is responsible to the president. In daily practice, since it is a small company, there is constant interaction among almost all staff members.

The editor-in-chief functioned as the company's chief troubleshooter. His days were characterized by constant interruptions, telephone calls, visitors, and employees dashing in and out of his office for advice. He worked on many projects simultaneously, juggling problems and projects back and forth, jumping from issue to issue, depending on the needs of the day. His office door was almost always open. Because of the many intrusions on his time, his attention span was short, and many tasks were glossed over. If he had something very important to attend to, such as a monthly report for the president or an important manuscript he wished to read or edit closely, he took it home with him. Like most managers, he thrived on oral communication (see Mintzberg 1973).

The editor-in-chief usually had several major appointments a day. Often they were of a ceremonial nature, such as taking an important author or a visiting foreign publisher to lunch or meeting with an important member of the parent corporation. During such occasions there were rarely pressing items that demanded discussion; the meetings served as an opportunity to exchange pleasantries and information and to do some public relations work for the press. Most of the editor-in-chief's daily work contacts were unplanned.

When key employees were absent or there was an important position that was temporarily vacant, the editor-in-chief would often fill in. He functioned as the sociology editor for a nine-month period and, for a shorter period, helped out with marketing and promotion. The latter task was shared with the president until the help of a free-lance person was secured. Eventually, a full-time department head was hired. The editor-in-chief still found time to acquire manuscripts, and he was personally responsible for dealing with some of the press's most prestigious authors. The time span of matters under his attention varied from the short run of daily and mundane affairs to long-range projections, often several years into the future. At one moment he would be concerned with prodding employees, approving the jacket copy for a new book, or sending out an advance copy of a book in the hope of obtaining an important person's favorable reaction. At the next moment he would be working out future scheduling problems, analyzing the backlist, or planning a new reference series that might reach fruition in five years.

In contrast to the editor-in-chief's harried pace, the president of the press maintained a low profile. A large portion of his time was spent in interaction with the parent corporation. He wanted "the corporate shadow to end in his office and not affect the rest of the press." His primary duties were fiscal management, planning, and the preparation of detailed monthly summaries for the parent company that reported Apple Press's progress in title acquisitions and sales. The weekly meeting of the four department heads was run by the president. He wanted lines of communication within his company to be direct and open; however, he was acutely aware that satisfied employees were a small factor in the parent company's evaluation of how well he was performing; it was interested strictly in the bottom line, in seeing that Apple did as well or better than had been predicted at the year's outset. Occasionally the president signed a few titles—in his words, "for the sake of my own sanity."

Both of the top executives worked long hours and were very devoted to the press. Both maintained that "companies are reflections of the people who run them." They prided themselves on their style of collegial leadership. They wanted their employees to identify with the company and to be committed to their work, yet they also believed in hiring bright young people, knowing full well that they would not remain with the company for very long. The parent company's personnel office had a different approach, preferring to hire prospective employees who professed a long-term commitment. They were therefore reluctant to hire college-educated people for low-level positions. The attitude of Apple Press was, "Why shouldn't you hire educated persons if they want a job? Hell, nobody that's any good should want to stay in a lousy job very long anyway."

For most of my fieldwork period, the editorial department consisted of two senior editors and an assistant. Their principal responsibility was manuscript acquisition. Editorial turnover is commonplace in book publishing and is a key source of author dissatisfaction (see Coser, Kadushin, and Powell 1982: chapters 4 and 9).[11] Within commercial scholarly houses and university presses, career patterns are even more varied than in trade or textbook publishing, where career ladders are fairly standard and recognizable. The editors whom I interviewed, not only at Apple Press and Plum Press but at other scholarly houses as well, began their publishing careers in a variety of different positions. A fair percentage were once editorial assistants or secretaries, a few began as salespeople or in promotion departments, and a surprising number were hired as editors from the beginning and did not have to work their way up. Almost all of the latter were people with academic backgrounds; frequently they were advanced graduate students who, for one reason or another, never completed their dissertations. Knowledge of a particular discipline, however, does not seem to be a particularly valued asset in scholarly publishing. Only a few editors actually did advanced studies in the field in which they became editors. The psychology editor at Plum Press had an advanced degree in biology. He explained that he was better off working in a field in which he was not an expert because he could be more "objective."

A key feature of editorial work is its forward-looking character. An editor's primary interest lies in finding manuscripts that will constitute future lists. Few of their concerns lie in the present, except for worrying over the whereabouts of an author's long-overdue manuscript or the status of a reviewer's promised critique. Editors are structurally conditioned not to pay much attention to books that are currently being released (for a more detailed discussion, see Coser, Kadushin, and Powell 1982:244–59). For most editors, this is a taken-for-granted aspect of their work, and few reflect on the unusual temporal nature of their activities. One exception, however, was a woman I interviewed at a competing house. She was an author and had previously worked as a magazine editor. When she became a senior editor at a scholarly house, she brought with her a very different personal time frame. Her reactions to the reviews of her first crop of books are most suggestive.

> This is a very anxious period for me. I discovered that I respond to the reviews of the books that I published—that I care about—very badly. Not as much as if they were my own books, but almost. The big difference is that, as an editor, you are already busy doing other things. As an author you are not as busy, so reviews can really get to you. What keeps you from worrying too much around here is that you learn that it is all in a day's work. By the time you face the prospect of success and failure of a particular project, you're already very much involved in another. You're too busy doing other things. And then, of course, if you see someone with long experience who laughs about the failures that he's had, then you learn to take it all in stride. They're part of the whole scene. But it horrified me at first.

The production department at Apple Press was responsible for overseeing the editing of manuscripts for style, consistency, spelling, and punctuation. It consisted of a department head, three to five production editors, and a department secretary. As a rule, the production editor did not work on more than eight books at the same time. The manuscripts were farmed out to free-lancers for the actual copyediting, which was then checked by the production editors. In a year's time, a production editor would see between twelve and fifteen manuscripts "put between covers." The time frame of these editors was very limited, since they were always focusing on manuscripts that would by published in the upcoming months.

The manufacturing department at Apple was similarly organized, with a department chief, three manufacturing editors, two clerks, and a secretary. This department spent the bulk of the press's money. Manufacturing was responsible for creating books as physical entities, which involved making cost estimates, scheduling, planning an overall uniform design, selecting suppliers, purchasing paper and cover materials, and supervising the typesetting, printing, and binding. All of the artwork and design were done by free-lancers. The head of the department also kept track of the inventory of the backlist.

The press's smallest, and most overworked, department was marketing, staffed by the marketing director, two copywriters, and a secretary. They were responsible for advertising, publicity, and promotion for all of the press's titles except the textbooks and trade books, which the parent company handled. Other marketing functions, such as the sale of translation rights and book-club rights, were also performed by the parent company. During my stay at the press, the marketing director was never satisfied with the efforts of the parent company, and she increasingly took on the tasks herself. This built to a point where she was working seventy hours a week, and she eventually resigned. It was six months before a full-time replacement was hired.

This department was the press's weakest link. In contrast to Plum Press, Apple Press did not have an easily identifiable style of promoting its books. Each year a new format was adopted. Various experiments were tried with journal ads, but no consistent promotional strategy was evident. Marketing experts in scholarly houses are split in their evaluation of the utility of journal ads. Most believe that, at the very least, they have "institutional" value, in that they promote the publishing house's reputation and show that the house supports its authors. In addition, readers of scholarly journals may also be potential authors, so that advertising current books may help to insure a future supply of publishable manuscripts. Whether the ads also sell books is a matter of some dispute.

Both Apple Press and Plum Press knew that successful promotion of a scholarly book depends on utilizing the author's network and the "invisible college"—a fact that many authors do not fully appreciate.[12] Publishers provide authors with a questionnaire, asking them, in effect, to describe the key nodes of their academic network and the key access points to the "invisible college" to which they belong; they are also asked to list the names of professional journals in which it would be appropriate to advertise. The author naturally knows much more about these matters than the publisher does. More frequently than not, however, the author naively thinks that book promotion is solely the publisher's responsibility. The publisher may know the principles of promotion, but the author knows who the audience is.

While Plum Press used its proven mailing lists for book promotion, Apple Press exerted more effort at obtaining good prepublication blurbs from noted persons in an author's academic discipline or in an important policy-related position. Blurbs are used by all types of publishers, but they are especially useful for the scholarly market, since the network of potential readers and opinion leaders is so clearly delineated. Apple Press was most successful in getting favorable quotes to grace the covers and ads for new releases. They were less successful in bringing new books to the attention of the "intelligentsia press"—such journals of opinion as the *New York Review of Books*, the *New Republic*, and *Commentary*. When its books were reviewed in these "elite" magazines, Apple Press seldom knew about it in advance and would have to scurry about trying to place copies in bookstores. To this observer, the most surprising market strategy was an omission: Apple Press had no catalogue of its backlist titles, nor did it distribute seasonal catalogues, describing its new titles. Nor were there separate catalogues for the various social science disciplines. In effect, the press's impressive backlist sold itself. To some extent, it can be viewed as a testament to the quality of the press's publications that, with the exception of ads in professional journals and some promotional work on a title-by-title basis, little was done to sell them. The press was a very profitable operation, so additional marketing efforts were perhaps viewed as unnecessary.

Plum Press had twelve times more employees than Apple Press and published approximately six times more books. Doing fieldwork in a large organization presents many more difficulties. One is not afforded the luxury of sitting in one particular office where, in the course of the day, the majority of the company's employees would come and go. Large corporations appear more reserved and formal because face-to-face interaction is limited and the pace of activity seems much slower. Top executives are surrounded by assistants and secretaries, who shield them from intrusions. As a result of their relative isolation, the actions of individuals seem to have less consequence. One editor at Plum Press noted, "It's very easy to become detached from the actual process of publishing books. All the work is done by people on other floors; you have to go out of your way to see what's going on. And that means extra work, which you seldom have time for."

Hence Plum Press seemed like a large machine with replaceable parts. No employee or executive appeared to be indispensable. This was in sharp contrast to Apple Press, where the absence of a few key employees or executives threw the firm into turmoil. Georg Simmel (1950) was one of the first social scientists to eloquently analyze "the bearing which the mere number of associated individuals has upon the forms of social life." In small groups, the views and needs of individuals are a more immediate consideration. In large groups, individuals are submerged in the mass and count for less. Studies that have assessed the effects of individual administrators in large organizations have found that they account for, at best, 10 percent of the variance in organizational performance (Lieberson and O'Connor 1972; Salancik and Pfeffer 1977). Moreover, Pfeffer (1977) has shown that personalities and personal characteristics are more apparent, and that factors of personal style have a greater effect on career progress, in smaller organizations. The differences in size and strategy at Apple and Plum created different organizational climates, which greatly influenced the nature of intraorganizational relations and conflicts. The latter are discussed in more detail in the next section.

Besides its much larger size, Plum Press differed from Apple Press in the manner in which it was organized. Unlike Apple, it was not broken down into specific departments, each with a department head of equal importance; instead, it was run by ten executives, two of whom were on the premises on only a part-time basis. The company's president was also an executive of the parent corporation and president of the London branch of Plum Press. His time was thus divided among three commitments. There were three senior vice-presidents. One was the editorial director, another was the chief financial officer, and the third was head of the sales department. This third man was also an executive of the parent corporation and spent time there as well. The sales department was run on a day-to-day basis by one of the six company vice-presidents. Two of the other vice-presidents were senior editors, who, along with the editorial director, constituted the editorial committee, which met weekly. Another vice-president was the company treasurer, and the head of the textbook division was also a vice-president. The only woman in the executive group was in charge of the journals. The company's various floors were overseen by floor managers.

One of Plum's senior vice-presidents described departmental responsibilities in the following way:

> It's the duty of the editorial department to acquire, sign, and contract for manuscripts, to oversee the reviews and refereeing process, to recheck final manuscripts and ready them for production. The function of production is to take a finished manuscript and produce it. We do very little artwork and our designs are standardized. Some free-lancers are used for copyediting. The sales department handles the promotion, marketing, distribution, direct-mail advertising, and library sales.

The company's concentration and strength lay in two areas: editorial and sales. In the New York office there were twenty-five people involved in editorial acquisitions. This group included twelve Plum Press editors, each in charge of monograph publications in a particular set of disciplines; six editors in the textbook department; and four in one of the company's small subsidiaries. Each editor reported to one of the two editorial vice-presidents, who in turn reported to the editor-in-chief. Plum Press also had a field office on the west coast, where three additional editors were located.

The sales department was extremely large, with over seventy-five employees in its various branches. It was one of the company's best assets. Every book that was published was featured at least once in a direct mailing and a journal ad, and, if a book belonged to a series, it was likely to be promoted many times a year. The sales department kept hundreds of mailing lists on computer file, which greatly facilitated promotion. The importance of international sales has already been mentioned; one consequence of the overseas sales was that few translation rights were sold. Book-club sales were not common; the largest order on record was for 2,000 copies.[13]

Interdepartmental Relations and Conflicts

As I have argued elsewhere (Coser, Kadushin, and Powell 1982:198–99), conflict is endemic to the publishing process. It is not at all surprising that different departments within an organization develop different outlooks on the organization's activities. Certain departments have tasks that require them to focus inward while others face outward. Differing perceptions of similar situations easily occur. As Dearborn and Simon (1958) noted, executives perceive situations in terms of the specific activities and goals of their own departments rather than from a company-wide viewpoint.

Furthermore, employees will attempt to use an organization to achieve their own ends and maximize their own careers. People also identify with their jobs and derive status from their positions. Within an organization, status is commonly associated with discretion in the use of time and freedom from routine. Publishing houses generally are two-tiered systems, with executives and editors enjoying the lofty positions and the rest of the employees consigned to the routine, more mundane, chores. Ever since the work of March and Simon (1958) and Cyert and March (1963), organization researchers have viewed organizations as political arenas, characterized by subgroup struggles and attempts at maximizing subunit interests. Organizations are commonly rife with internal disagreements over the distribution of power and discretion. One of the paradoxes of organizational life is that while the division of labor into specialized departments encourages the development of expertise and the coordination of activities within a department, such an arrangement can also create coordination problems and conflicts among departments. Different departments, particularly in large organizations, can become so isolated from one another that they develop their own goals and perspectives. An editorial department wants all books promoted heavily, while the marketing department wants to get the maximum use of its small advertising budget by promoting only the few titles that have potentially broad appeal. In publishing we find that authors are often caught in the crossfire of battles between different departments.[14] Such disputes are not uncommon in cultural industries.

Intraorganizational conflicts in publishing are further complicated by the particular character of publishing's labor force and the unusual temporal phasing of the publishing process. Publishing has long had a strong, somewhat romanticized, attraction for many young people, fresh out of college, who have dabbled in writing or worked for campus publications. Publishing also is an appealing occupation for frustrated teachers, librarians, journalists, and writers who are thinking of changing to a second career. It is an occupation that is tempting to people who believe they have creative talents. This attraction results in a perennial supply of new recruits for most publishing houses. Unfortunately, most of these people aspire to editorial positions. Starting positions, however, are usually at lower levels, often in noneditorial departments. At both Apple and Plum a significant proportion of the rank-and-file employees were highly educated. Yet they were saddled with low-paying and not very glamorous positions, with few prospects for advancement. This situation is not unique to publishing; Hagstrom (1976:94) notes that young persons employed at substandard wages are important in almost all types of cultural endeavors. Epstein (1977:435) finds that one of the marks of a "romance" industry is that it can get away with paying small salaries at its lower echelons because so many are lined up outside, waiting to get in.[15]

The temporal phasing of work has significant consequences for intraorganizational conflicts. The pace at which work proceeds depends on one's position. While editors are concerned with the lists that will be published two and three years down the road, the rest of the house is struggling to produce next season's list. Publishing is arranged in interlocking lines of work, so that the output of editors—that is, manuscripts—constitutes the input of the production, manufacturing, and marketing personnel. In effect, the rest of the company is preoccupied with books that have left the purview of editors. There are even formal occasions—called "launch meetings" at Apple Press, "transmittal meetings" at Plum Press—where editors turn manuscripts over to the other departments. As the editor's concerns must turn to other matters, the launch or transmittal meeting is the first step in an editor's gradual relinquishing of control over a manuscript. From this point on, the manuscript becomes increasingly remote from an editor's interest. Yet it is the editor who is generally the author's sole contact with the publishing house.

It is at this point that conflicts and disagreements most often develop. Authors feel they are at the mercy of members of the publishing house whom they have never met. The employees of the house will have a much closer relationship with the free-lancers to whom they regularly farm out work and with whom working relations are established. Authors are frequently wary of the way their books will be copyedited, designed, and promoted, but at this stage they have very little voice in these matters and can only react to more or less finished work. Authors can, of course, complain; but to whom and with what effect? Their editors are now in pursuit of other authors. Moreover, at least at Apple and Plum, authors who become extremely bothersome can be threatened with cancellation of their contract.

At both Apple and Plum, books were normally produced in a period of seven to nine months. A large number of "raw materials" were always being transformed at the same time. Every employee had a sizable workload and a schedule to meet. To work in the face of a deadline is to work under pressure, and this affects the way employees evaluate their work. Given this pressure, we should not be surprised that the service-providers occasionally expressed irritation at clients—in this case authors, who were a source at once of livelihood and burdensome demands.

Other factors also create conflict. At Apple Press, the top executives encouraged the active participation of all members of the company. They frequently said, "Everyone around here contributes." One of the biggest problems of the previous administration at Apple was an erratic and slow production schedule. The new administration wanted books published promptly and on schedule, a sensible philosophy, since, the quicker you publish a book, the sooner the money that you've invested begins returning.[16] In order to produce books efficiently, the press allowed the noneditorial departments a sense of responsibility and autonomy. These departments were also staffed by young well-educated persons. Once they were encouraged to play an active role, it is not surprising that they sometimes attempted to alter an author's work to bring it more into line with their image of the type of books their press should be publishing.

The head of the production department at Apple remarked, "I like to challenge the author. When a manuscript needs a lot of work, I let it be known. A lot of manuscripts we get are very uneven." Authors frequently did not welcome these changes. In some instances serious disputes arose, and the acquiring editor or the editor-in-chief had to intervene. This was usually done on the author's behalf, and the editor would inform the employee, "If we hadn't liked this manuscript in the first place, we wouldn't have signed it. So cool it!" This fostered disagreements and led employees to question whether their contributions were really valued. Some of the turnover in the production and manufacturing departments was attributable to disagreements of this type.

The situation differed at Plum Press, for a number of reasons. First, although the rank-and-file at Plum were also young and well educated, they did not receive any signals that could be read as encouragement to devote themselves to a manuscript. The suggestions for improvement that were made by employees were seldom received with enthusiasm. Hard work on a manuscript was not rewarded. Second, over four hundred books were produced yearly. This meant that the manuscript that an author regarded as a unique accomplishment was, to Plum employees, a routine product in need of prompt processing. Third, working conditions were not good; lunch breaks were only forty-five minutes long, and supervision was tight. One response of employees was to initiate a union-organizing drive. In the opinion of several key organizers, this drive improved morale, but it also met with difficulty precisely because turnover was so high. One organizer remarked in the autumn that over 30 percent of the employees who had signed union cards during the previous summer had since left the firm. Fourth, the type of books being produced also had an effect on employee involvement. At Plum Press the products were highly technical treatises that were usually of little immediate interest to those working on them. At Apple Press, more of the books appealed to the employees who worked on them; the staff enjoyed reading some of the titles and occasionally took copies home. This increased attachment, however, could result in greater disappointment when an employee's efforts to "improve" the books were rebuffed. I once asked a production editor if employees ever took Plum Press books home as personal copies. He responded, "Who would want to? Besides, no one can ever read them. They are really very difficult books." Disputes at Plum were, as a rule, less often between departments than was the case at Apple. Instead, conflict more typically pitted the rank-and-file against top management. Editors who were members of top management were identified as hostile to the rank-and-file, while other editors were seen as bystanders to the conflict.

In sum, we see that a number of features of book publishing—a talented, young, and underpaid labor force; problems in keeping to tight schedules; and a craft legacy that frowns on one department's offering too much advice or commentary on the activities of another—all contribute to organizational conflicts. The very common organizational problem of attributing credit and responsibility for successes and failures often boils down in publishing to disputes between the editorial and sales departments, and the perennial question of which books should receive the most promotion is an ongoing debate that involves, the editors, the sales and promotion departments, and the top executives.

Summary

How do we account for the differences between Apple Press and Plum Press? Apple is more informally organized, the work process is less standardized, and a lively atmosphere pervades the house. In contrast, Plum is more bureaucratic and routine, and, for most employees, it is rather dull. At Apple there are disagreements among the staff and between departments over the handling of particular books. At Plum there is little comparable debate over publishing matters; conflict there is more like the traditional production politics that characterize labor-management relations in other industries. Questions about the amount of time that employees had for lunch or for breaks and conflicts over the prohibition of fraternizing on the job or the quality of work conditions were continually arising at Plum but seldom at Apple.

Both houses were owned by a parent publishing corporation. In neither case did the policies of the parent firm influence decisions made by the subsidiary. Both parent companies were pleased with the financial performance of their respective subsidiaries and generally left them alone. One obvious difference is the disparity in size between Apple and Plum. Work is much more likely to be formally organized in large organizations than in smaller ones. However, Plum differs from other large scholarly publishers in that the work process is not finely distributed among numerous departments. There were only a few departments at Plum, and they were quite large. The two houses were roughly comparable in age, but Apple had installed a new management team, while Plum had had considerable continuity of leadership.

Perhaps the most significant difference between the two firms is in the relationship between the type of books they publish and the degree of uncertainty they feel about selling their books to the scholarly market. I argue that while both houses had considerable ability to influence and manipulate their operating environments, the technology adopted at Plum Press was so effective that it permitted the routinization of the work process. By "technology" I refer to the strategies and techniques utilized to get work done. At Plum Press there was very little uncertainty about its publication strategy. There was a clear notion of what a scientific monograph was. Ideally, it was a book for which there was a limited but known demand—a book that could be sold easily. There was little variance from the practice of publishing this kind of book. Indeed, when the social science editor occasionally had a "surprise" on his hands—a book that was reviewed in the popular media and had the potential for sales outside a particular discipline—the sales director was not thrilled, because such a book would disrupt well-established routines.

Apple Press showed mastery in exploiting external contacts with senior-scholar brokers and journal editors. While Apple did publish some scholarly monographs, similar to those published by Plum, it also published a mixture of textbooks, some trade books, and professional books aimed at a wider audience. Plum was highly effective in selling its monographs by direct mail, targeting them to carefully chosen lists of people with similar professional interests. Apple used a variety of promotional and distribution mechanisms: direct mail, ads in the *New York Times Book Review*, and general bookstore sales. In short, while Apple's list was more interesting than Plum's, it was the diversity of its list that created uncertainty and led to internal policy debates. The comparison of the organization of work at Apple and Plum suggests a general logic that informs the production of cultural goods: as a firm's work process becomes more rationalized, its output becomes more homogeneous and its capacity for innovation diminishes.

I should note that, personally, I would much prefer to work at Apple Press. There is more opportunity for having a voice in decisions, and the list is more varied and interesting. At Plum there is little voice but ample opportunity for exit. The publications are highly specialized and routinely handled. However, as an author, and depending on the type of book in question, I might take a different view of the two houses. Apple Press did fairly well in terms of author-publisher relations. Most authors were happy with the services they received, but there were "horror stories": cases where an enterprising staff member decided that the author's manuscript needed improving and the author was not happy with the wholesale revisions. Author-publisher relations at Plum Press, on the other hand, were extremely good, partly due to Plum's adroit use of its series editors, who served as vital links between the house and the scholarly community. Given the limited advertising done by Plum Press, I was particularly struck by the fact that over 70 percent of its authors responded to a questionnaire I sent them by stating that they were extremely satisfied with the advertising, promotion, and distribution their books received. Slightly less than half of the Apple Press authors expressed similar satisfaction.

The initial acceptance of a book and, many months later, its publication occasion great expectations in an author. The book is a product of years of research and writing. The author naturally hopes that his or her efforts will be repaid, if not in money, in attention and prestige. It is precisely such expectations that explain why the majority of authors are displeased with their publishers (see Coser, Kadushin, and Powell 1982: chap. 9). That Plum Press is an exception to this unhappy rule is due to its unusual approach to its authors. Plum Press editors were direct and open: they told their authors what kind of services they would receive; explained that every book is featured in a direct-mail ad and in an ad in a major journal; solicited the author's advice about the appropriate audience for the book and asked for useful mailing lists; and followed up on the author's suggestions.[17] They were honest about the very limited sales prospects, were open to ideas, and were responsive to the author's concerns. Plum compensated for the lack of widespread exposure for its books by bringing new titles to the attention of the author's invisible college. By contrast, Apple's efforts to reach a broad audience occasionally resulted in a failure to bring the book to the attention of an author's professional colleagues, thus creating author dissatisfaction.

3

THE NATURE OF
EDITORIAL WORK

Editors are the essential players in the publishing process.[1] They are responsible for acquiring the manuscripts that the rest of the publishing house will turn into books. They start the wheels turning. In essence, it is their job that is unique. The director of a leading university press reinforced this view when he said:

> Let me tell you something, and don't you repeat it to anyone else around here. Editors are irreplaceable! I think very highly of the staff I have assembled. They are very good; but if any one of them left, I could find someone else to do their job. That's not true with my editors. If one of them left, it would be a disaster. Editors are very special people.

The majority of the people employed by a publishing house are administrative and clerical workers whose skills are easily transferable to any of a number of commercial or public organizations. Those with more specialized talents could find work in other media organizations or advertising agencies. Then there are executive positions, such as president or director, that pay much better and carry more power than editorial jobs. Such positions, however, require that considerable time be spent on administrative matters and managerial duties. They afford little time for locating new authors and working with them. In fact, executive positions, such as editorial director, require that the executive be the manager of an editorial staff. Chester Kerr, former director of Yale University Press, described a meeting with another press director in the following manner:

> "The list," said Arthur Rosenthal, "the list is everything. So if you don't have any smart editors, you don't have any list." He had just become director of Harvard University Press, after a brilliant performance as founder and head man of Basic Books, and I was having lunch with him in Cambridge to see how things were going. He had walked into a bad financial picture, not to mention a somewhat disoriented organization, and I had supposed the marketing and business sides would receive his first attentions. But here he was firing and hiring editors, just as though new feats of list-building could be performed overnight. [Kerr, 1974:211]

An editor at a scholarly or monograph house performs a set of varied tasks.[2] Perhaps the key to scholarly editing is staying informed about developments that are taking place in various academic fields. Knowing who the leading scholars are, who the up-and-coming people are, and what fields are growth areas is an editor's primary responsibility. The extent of an editor's knowledge is a key measure of his or her skills, and many editors jealously guard their talents. A senior editor at Apple Press was very clear about this, as his comments to me attest:

> The president will send me suggestions from time to time . . . ideas from the newspaper or somewhere. But they are just suggestions. If I deem them useful, I'll follow up on them . . . We don't have any editorial meetings. Why should we? I don't see how someone can tell me what's best to sign. It's *my* area; I *know* it. Who else around here knows anything about cognitive psychology or what new developments are taking place in administrative science? The normal course is for me to develop things on my own. When I give the editor-in-chief the rough draft of the "proposal to publish" form, it is usually the first thing he knows about the project.

Another important task for editors is to establish good relations with authors, because this enables an editor to use

them as sources of information about what is going on in their
specialty, as reviewers of manuscripts, or as sources of news
about college enrollment trends. Editors must also stay informed about new lines of research in the various disciplines
they cover. It is their job to evaluate these developments and
determine whether work in a new area is related to subjects
they are already publishing or, if not, whether it is worth
expanding into. Usually it is younger scholars, often without
commitments to a particular publishing house, who are doing
research in these new areas. Hence they represent "a new
field to mine." Editors realize that if all their time is spent on
authors whom they have already published, their lists can
become stale and inbred. Depending on their position in the
market vis-à-vis their competitors, editors will spend more or
less time scouting new fields. Apple Press devoted some
attention to this but not nearly as much as Plum Press, whose
social science authors were generally much younger than
those published by Apple.[3]

The primary means for editors to keep *au courant* of the
professional disciplines in which they work is through building and maintaining a wide and active personal network or, as
one Apple Press editor dubbed it, a "stable" of advisers
whom she could readily call on for good advice—for "objective comments about the merits and marketability of a particular project." Advisers can also be counted upon to refer
promising manuscripts. Boundary-spanning activities are not
unique to scholarly publishing, but in many important respects they are more crucial for scholarly editors than for their
editorial counterparts in trade houses, who can rely on literary agents for referrals, or those in textbook houses, who rely
on the lure of cash rather than reciprocity to attract authors.

Active "networking" outside the confines of the publishing
house is rewarding in a variety of ways. Advisers and friends
in academia are accessible sources of advice and information
about who is doing what, who recently received a large research grant, and what new journal articles are worth reading. A good network is also invaluable when it comes to

traveling. Despite the avalanche of unsolicited materials received by both Apple and Plum, all the editors agreed that "getting out and knocking on doors" was both the best way to find good books and the most rewarding. Senior editors at both houses favored an active style and enjoyed traveling to college campuses, to think tanks, to public policy institutes in Washington, and to the meetings of scholarly associations. Editors with a wide network are also more productive travelers. Friends in various universities can be dinner companions or provide a place to stay, both of which are preferable to spending a lonely night in a motel. Such contacts also enable an editor to be in the right place at the right time: an invitation to a small departmental party can be the occasion for a serendipitous find. Discovering a promising manuscript at a dinner party may seem accidental, but it is the result of maintaining a good network. Obviously, networks are not only good for business leads, they are also personally rewarding for an editor who combines scouting trips with a number of enjoyable social occasions. The comments of a senior editor, who had recently joined the staff of a major university press after a distinguished career in trade publishing, underscore the importance of traveling. He had just returned from a trip to a number of midwest campuses.

> Can you imagine: here it was, the dead of winter, snowing like mad, and I'm knocking on people's doors. Suffice it to say, most people were very flattered that I paid them a call. Not many editors make the rounds out there, certainly not in January. Publishing is a crazy business. We receive so many unsolicited manuscripts . . . and there is always work to be done, paper to push, manuscripts to read, forms to fill out . . . It's like anything else, I guess; if you let yourself, you can become nailed to your desk. You have to force yourself to get away. It is imperative that an editor be well informed. To do this you have to get out and knock on doors. I wrote the "big names" in advance and set up lunches and dinners. You can learn something, however, from all sorts of people. You can't ignore librarians, junior faculty, or graduate students if you

want to keep up with a discipline's fads and fashions . . . to learn what's going on . . . where a field is growing. You don't always learn these things from senior faculty. Traveling is an essential part of an editor's work.

Networks are formed by traveling, by "hanging out" wherever scholars gather, and by maintaining a large volume of correspondence. There can, however, be costs in having an extensive personal network. Every social relationship is constrained and shaped by its own history. Strong tensions can develop when editors feel more strongly committed to their authors and network members than to the firm for which they currently work. From an organizational point of view, editors are persons trapped in the middle. They are the author's only friend and voice within the publishing house. At the same time that they must represent the house in negotiations with authors, they are the firm's liaison with an author. Such competing demands of craft and commerce frequently create problems for editors in determining where their loyalties lie.[4] These competing demands can be particularly problematic when an editor moves to another publishing house. In such cases, authors often feel that the editor has abandoned them.

Editors also have many in-house responsibilities. They must act as an information resource for their books, advising the sales department on promotional plans or writing or overseeing the preparation of jacket copy. They also oversee the production process for the books they have acquired. They see that schedules are kept to, possibly recommend a free-lance copyeditor whom they know and trust, and act as intermediaries when authors are dissatisfied with the services rendered by other departments. In short, editors must be managers and promoters of their books within the house. As one editor put it, "You have to sell your colleagues—convince them that a book deserves care."

With all these responsibilities, plus the work involved in guiding and helping authors in the preparation of their books, it is no surprise that none of the editors find the job boring. Quite to the contrary, they worry that their work load prevents them from becoming sufficiently knowledgeable to make good decisions. Although they may be well informed about several fields, editors are essentially amateurs in a world of professionals. No doubt some scholars view editors as dilettantes. The editor-in-chief at Apple Press recalled a comment someone made many years ago that "a bookman's knowledge is as wide as the Amazon and about an inch deep." Another editor at Apple mentioned that "an editor could talk about any subject in the world for two minutes." One editor said, "It is the nature of an editor's job to get interested in an area, locate promising manuscripts by authors with some claim to fame in that field, build up a list in that subject, drop it, and get started on something else." Editorial work involves close association with an author for a relatively brief period of time. Then the editor must move on to other authors and other topics. Moreover, editors work with authors in different fields; however, it is fair to say that at any one time there are only a few topics with which an editor is deeply involved.

Some comments made by the president of Apple Press touch on the manner in which editors move from one subject to another:

> What my editors talk about is what they are doing at the moment. Talk to ——— and he will mention social work or criminal justice; six months from now it may be research in the area of stratification, while six months ago it was the sociology of education. At the moment, ——— is into organizational studies and administrative science. A month ago she was working with a number of psychologists. That's the nature of an editor's job. You get into topics, follow your leads, develop contacts, accomplish something, then move on to another topic. If your work bears fruit, you'll return to that subject in the future.

In this chapter I explore two main questions: How do editors, despite their limited knowledge of the fields in which they work, make reasonable decisions about which books to publish? and How do they balance the problems created by competing loyalties and conflicting values? In focusing on editorial decision-making, I analyze both the formal decision process within the house and the more informal choices that are made by editors as they acquire and evaluate manuscripts and work with authors and reviewers.

The Formal Process of Contracting for a Book

The key question to ask in any study of organizational gatekeepers is How do decision-makers narrow down a large number of competing items and decide which few to devote some attention to in order to select an even smaller number for eventual sponsorship? To answer this question, I initially studied the formal decision-making process within each of the two publishing houses. I quickly learned that the formal process of obtaining approval to publish a book involved little actual decision-making. The important decisions about what to publish are made by editors well in advance of the formal process of securing a contract.[5]

At Apple Press, the standard procedure for obtaining a contract was for an editor to solicit one or two outside reviews of a promising manuscript. Once these had been obtained, and if they were generally favorable, the editor would notify the author that Apple wanted to publish his or her book. A proposal-to-publish form was then filled out (a rough version is usually drafted prior to sending a manuscript out for review). This is a standard form that editors in every house must submit for each book they wish to publish. The form contains information about an author's professional background; a description of the manuscript and the reasons for publishing it (this usually contains several quotes from the reviewers' reports); contractual information, such as royalty terms; preliminary information about the manuscript's length and estimated production costs; a sales estimate; and a timetable for recouping the costs of publication. The editor sends this form to the editor-in-chief, who, on occasion, will return it with questions. It is then referred to the president of the company; after he signs it, the form is forwarded to the contract officer of the parent corporation, who draws up a contract. The entire process usually takes from four to six weeks.

During my fieldwork at Apple Press, I came across only two instances in which a proposal advanced by either of the two senior editors was turned down. In about 10 percent of the cases, the editor-in-chief would return a proposal to the originating editor with comments such as "Tell me less about the book and more about its marketabliity or sales potential." After a proposal had passed the editor-in-chief's scrutiny, it was uncommon for further discussion to occur. Once in a while, the president of Apple would raise questions about a book's sales prospects. If a proposal met with approval at Apple, it was extremely rare for an officer of the parent company to question it; if he did raise questions, they usually had to do with the suggested list price, not the feasibility of the project.[6] With a book that the editor-in-chief wished to publish, the decision-making process was even more routine. In the case of the beginning assistant editor, the process differed somewhat: she would discuss projects in detail with the editor-in-chief before drawing up a proposal-to-publish form.

One of the senior editors at Apple Press described the procedure in the following manner: "If I like a manuscript, I propose it to the editor-in-chief; if he concurs, it goes on to the president. Then we wait for the parent company to draw up a contract. If the editor-in-chief doesn't like my proposal, I may or may not choose to argue with him; if I do, he lets me have my way."

At Plum Press, the formal process was somewhat different; nevertheless, the outcome was the same. The social science editor could recall only one proposal of his that had been rejected over a four-year period. This was a translation of a Polish monograph; the reason for the rejection was that it was deemed to involve too much work. The behavioral science editor could not remember any of his proposals being turned down. The procedure at Plum Press was for an editor to complete a proposal-to-publish form after having obtained a favorable review by a scholar in the relevant discipline. The proposal form was more detailed than the one used at Apple Press, but the forms were seldom completely filled out. Once the review was in, the editor would contact the author and convey an interest in publishing his or her book. If the author agreed to certain deadline stipulations, the editor would tell the author that he would submit the book to Plum's editorial committee and that a contract should be in the mail very soon.

The editor would then send the proposal-to-publish form to the appropriate editorial vice-president and to the sales department, where the editor's estimates were checked to see if they were "in the ballpark," to use the words of the sales vice-president. Only once did I observe that a question was raised by the sales department, and this was due to the fact that a secretary had inadvertently typed 15,000 instead of 1,500 for a book's projected sales. After the proper signatures were obtained, the proposal was routed to the editorial committee for consideration at its weekly meeting. The committee could be called to meet more frequently in special cases—for instance, if other publishing houses were interested in a manuscript and a quick decision was needed. The editor-in-chief commented, "We probably approve 99.8 percent of the proposals that our editors submit." The entire process could be executed expeditiously within a week, or it could take as long as a month. Once the editorial committee's approval was secured, a contract was drawn up. The parent corporation of Plum Press had no involvement in this process or any knowledge of what books Plum Press was publishing.

In many respects, the formal decision-making process was ceremonial (see Meyer and Rowan 1977). At neither house was it likely that questions would be raised about a proposal, and it was even more unusual for a proposal to be turned down. At Plum Press, the process was both routine and prompt. At Apple Press, although the steps were routine, they were seldom prompt. This was because the last step involved sending the proposal "upstairs" for approval. The parent corporation was responsible for issuing all contracts. The contract officer dealt with proposals from each division of the parent company, and, as a result, there was a great deal of paperwork involved. A lengthy delay for a contract was not uncommon. This could create problems if Apple Press was competing with another house for an author or if the author did not have full confidence in the editor and began to worry about the cause of the delay. Eventually an executive at the parent company recognized the need for Apple to issue contracts more expeditiously. A new policy was established which required obtaining corporate approval only for projects that involved a sizable outlay of funds; otherwise, the president of Apple Press could grant final approval.

The Process of Deciding What to Decide Upon

Clearly, the process of winnowing out manuscripts occurred prior to the formal decision-making stage. Bachrach and Baratz (1962; 1963), in their critique of methods of community-power research, argue that an important "face of power"—the power tactics that prevent a decision from being made at all—is often ignored. This is the power of nondecision, the forces that influence whether an issue ever becomes part of the agenda. Many issues die before they ever gain access to the decision-making arena. Researchers who accept that nondecisions are an important part of decision-making must therefore be concerned with the process by which social actors determine what to decide upon.

At Apple Press, I studied these issues in two ways. First, I examined all the manuscripts, proposals, and prospectuses that had been submitted to the press for evaluation. I sought to learn which projects attracted the attention of editors and what features distinguished these few from the many others that received scant attention. Second, I repeatedly asked the editors to explain how they ascertained whether a manuscript had commercial potential. During this period most of my time was spent in the editors' offices reading manuscripts and going through correspondence.

The editors were not particularly helpful in accounting for how they determined whether a manuscript had commercial possibilities. Editors repeatedly claimed that the ingredients for a successful scholarly book are not well known in advance. "You have to take your chances . . . go with your sense of smell, and learn how to hedge your bets. And, as you know," they would continue, "these books aren't terribly expensive; so if you make a few mistakes, it doesn't matter that much, just as long as you don't make a habit of it."

While sitting in the offices at Apple Press, I observed what were, to me, anomalous situations. In one instance, a manuscript came in over the transom, and, to judge from its tattered condition and the marks on it, it had already been rejected by several other publishing houses. The psychology editor at Apple Press, once he finally got around to reading it, liked the manuscript a great deal. He decided it would best be divided into two books, and he thought up snappy titles to replace the drab ones selected by the author. The editor sent the manuscript to a prominent sociologist to review, who concurred with the editor that the material was very worthy of publication. The editor decided to start off by publishing only the first part of the manuscript; then, if it was a failure, he could refrain from publishing the second part. The book did very well and caught Apple Press completely off guard. It was surprised by a review in the daily *New York Times*, a review column that is normally reserved for trade books. The book went on to win a Pulitzer Prize and sell over 100,000 copies in a mass-market paperback edition. The editor was unable to articulate what it was that initially attracted him to this manuscript.

There were other things that puzzled me initially. One was the rejection of a book even though it was well regarded. Another was the signing of books that were noncommercial, that is, books that would not sell well or, for that matter, break even. The editor-in-chief would never openly acknowledge that these things occurred. He said, "We publish only the best material, and the brightest scholars, in the social sciences. Sometimes we may err, but our goal is to produce good scholarship and make a profit. I firmly believe that good books sell well. . . . Nobody published Max Weber because they thought they were doing a service for humanity; they did it to make money!"

The other editors resisted such generalities and pointed to a number of compelling reasons for rejecting what appeared to be "good" books and for signing "marginal" ones. For example, an editor might turn down a promising manuscript because it was outside the competence or interests of the house. This is not unusual; authors do detailed research on their subject matter but seldom do any at all on which publishing house is appropriate for their work.[7] For example, neither Apple Press nor Plum Press was interested in introductory textbooks or anthologies, yet hardly a day passed when proposals for these types of books were not received. Neither house published books in the humanities or did popular trade books, but proposals for such books arrived frequently.

I discuss in more detail in chapter 4 the way in which a house's tradition and backlist influence choices; for now it should be noted that the size and strength of a house's list strongly affect consideration of a manuscript, regardless of its merits. For example, an editor may have on his or her desk five excellent manuscripts dealing with deviance, but, if you publish only fifteen or so sociology books in a year, you are severely restricting your coverage of the whole field if you publish all five. In the interests of balance, it is more sensible to publish a "so-so" book on the topic of ethnic relations.

Editors may also reject promising manuscripts because they cover the same ground as another book that was recently published or soon will be. For example, I found that one editor was reluctant to sign a book on the history of the black family until Herbert Gutman's research on the topic had been published and reviewed. The editor was worried that other projects would pale in comparison with Gutman's work, and he also wanted to see the reviews of Gutman's book so that he might better gauge the market for this topic.

Manuscripts are also turned down because they will demand too much of an editor's time and energy. An important consideration for an editor is whether he or she has sufficient time to devote to a manuscript and wants to spend it on that particular manuscript. If an editor is expected to sign between twenty-five and thirty-five books a year, there is no way that every book can be a major book, for that involves a great deal of effort.[8] Editors occasionally turn down big books by well-known academics because they think these will involve more work than they can handle. Manuscripts of considerable appeal by cantankerous authors may be rejected because the editor would prefer not to relive previous unpleasant experiences. Projects may also be declined because they require too large a financial commitment. Such an investment could create cash-flow problems, and the editor may decide that it is preferable to do several less expensive books instead. There are also cases when an author's status has risen to the point where the house can no longer afford him or her. The author's name now commands an advance or royalty terms that are outside the house's normal range, and it is unwilling to spend that much money.

Not surprisingly, editors reject material that they do not understand. As one Apple editor noted, "Unfortunately, I tend to turn down things that are too difficult for me, such as a highly theoretical manuscript as opposed to something about voting behavior, political machines, or an interesting political biography." To some extent this practice reflects good business sense, for dense, complex books are not as likely to sell as well as intriguing case studies or engaging political analyses, but at Apple Press there was some reluctance to tackle highly abstract theoretical material simply because the editors did not feel competent to evaluate it. At Plum, demanding manuscripts could be referred to the series editors for review.

As for commercial considerations, cases in which editors signed books that were not expected to make money were not uncommon. Not making money and losing money are, however, separate issues. An editor at a commercial house very rarely publishes a book that he or she *expects* will lose money, and, on the rare occasion that he or she decides to publish such a book, the losses can be minimized by keeping the print run small and the production costs low. Of course, there are decisions where an editor's judgment, experience, or intuition is incorrect. Or an editor may rely on the advice of a noted scholar and the advice turns out to be commercially unsound. Publishers can also "miss" with books; that is, a popular topic may be played out by the time they publish a book about it. In trade publishing, timeliness is a major concern. It is less of an issue in scholarly publishing, although one means of reducing uncertainty is to "run with the crowd" and publish topics that other houses have found to be successful. As one university press director remarked:

> Some publishers will be smart enough to publish books that help set the agenda of our nation's culture, that capture our intellectual pulse. Other publishers will merely imitate that success until it is a tired old story. Look at the lists of houses— you name the fad, and every company has as least one book on it. The successful publisher—and whether it is the result of acumen or luck is difficult to say—is the publisher who got there first.

Of particular interest are the books that were deemed worthy of publication even though their commercial prospects were not bullish. It is important not to view publication of this kind as wholly charitable; rather, the publisher is concerned with, in the words of Pierre Bourdieu (1977:177–83), "symbolic capital" as opposed to economic capital. For example, I once mentioned to the social science editor at Plum Press that a particular author had taken a very novel approach to his subject. The editor responded enthusiastically, "You just have to publish books like that one. I doubt that we've made a penny on it, but I wouldn't hesitate to do it again. I personally enjoyed reading it; it's an important book. Besides, books like this don't cost that much, and they are worth doing."

The publication of books that maximize symbolic capital can also be viewed as a public relations strategy, designed to maintain the loyalty of house authors and attract others. The editor-in-chief at Apple Press spent a considerable amount of time "wooing several distinguished scholars back into the fold." These academics had published with Apple in the 1950s; they grew dissatisfied with the editorial staff in the 1960s and moved to other houses. The editor-in-chief made it one of his top priorities to regain these authors. He felt that their return would help signal Apple's resurgence in the 1970s. The press published books of essays, with limited commercial prospects, by these eminent scholars and vigorously pursued younger academics who were collaborators with the well-known scholars. In one case a younger colleague was offered a lucrative contract for his most recent book. This person promptly canceled his contract with another publishing house that he felt had not been particularly hospitable. A senior editor at Apple noted that this book should be well received, but then he remarked, "You can't live on prestige alone, and, given the financial terms, we haven't a prayer of making any money on it." This was an atypical example, and it involved the editor-in-chief; it would have been unlikely that any of the other editors could have done something quite like this. The example does illustrate, however, the way in which decisions can be based on nonfinancial criteria. In a similar vein, the editor-in-chief at a publishing house that was one of Apple Press's chief competitors described the publication of two books by a leading young British social scientist in the following manner: "We considered these books to be our research and development costs. We don't expect either of them to make any profit, but they are important books, and we anticipate that his third book will be a significant success."

A publisher with a well-known author under contract may also want to keep as much of that author's *oeuvre* in print as possible. This is one means of keeping authors happy and preventing them from moving to another house. If the author is highly regarded, it certainly pays, in the long run, to allow his or her less successful books to remain in print. There is always the possibility that, if the author's latest work is acclaimed, the earlier work will also attract attention.

Decisions about books that will add to symbolic capital can be vexing, and the evaluation process is complicated by the fact that editors usually must evaluate projects on the basis of a short synopsis and perhaps one or two sample chapters. Very few authors submit completed manuscripts. Several factors explain this. In the opinion of a senior editor at Apple Press, "Most of those who send in the entire manuscript are young people who don't know any better. They finish their work, which is probably their dissertation, and then look for a publisher." At the other end of the prestige pendulum are prominent scholars who are confident that any number of publishing houses would jump at the opportunity to publish their work. As one editor remarked, "Well-known, esteemed academics do not always want an editor telling them they have to change certain things. So they submit completed manuscripts and expect the publisher to either take on the project or pass on it." "It permits them to call their own shots," is the way another editor at Apple Press explained a prestigious author's submission of a completed manuscript. However, the great majority of authors submit only a prospectus and a sample chapter; they do not wish to invest a great deal of time and energy in preparing a manuscript unless they can first secure the interest of an editor and, ideally, a contract and a small advance to defray the costs involved in writing the book.

The need to make a quick decision on the basis of a small amount of material means that an editor must be a fast learner, one who can quickly acquire sufficient knowledge of a topic in order to discuss an author's proposal intelligently. This also means that editors must become proficient at finding experts who can evaluate projects. (The use and cultivation of outside readers is discussed more fully later in this chapter.) Knowing who will be able to ascertain the merits and value of a proposed manuscript is a special talent in itself. The editors must evaluate outside readers, not on the basis of their professional expertise, since that is assumed, but rather on their competence to assess an author's arguments without a great deal of bias. Editors become judges of others' judgments.

In theory, giving an author a contract on the basis of a proposal, which can be a very slim example of their skills, seems somewhat risky. In practice, however, all publishers' contracts state that the final manuscript must be "acceptable" to the publisher in form and content. This provision gives the publisher an out, permitting cancellation of the contract if he is dissatisfied with what the author delivers. Coser (1979) analyzes the asymmetrical nature of this relationship, which permits publishers to say no after they have initially said yes.[9] From a publisher's perspective, the house must retain the right to reject a manuscript that turns out not to be up to reasonable standards. The investment in reputation as well as money is too large a risk. However, a standard contract does bind an author to a publisher without imposing a parallel claim on the publishing house. One good reason for an author to ask for an advance is that the money helps cement the publisher's commitment. Of course, authors can and do break publishing contracts.

The Acquisition of Manuscripts

Although a voluminous amount of unsolicited material was received by editors at both Plum and Apple, their work involved much more than reacting to what arrived in the mail. An editor cannot decide that he or she does not want to publish any books in a particular season just because the manuscripts that have been sent in are not good enough. Sitting back at one's desk and waiting for materials to arrive is a poor way to do one's job. To begin with, some houses are more respected than others and receive much more promising material. Even editors with a list of renowned authors cannot afford to rest on their laurels. If they do, someone else will surely try to lure their authors way from them. A good scholarly editor must actively search for manuscripts.

One of the more remarkable features of the editorial search process is the extreme variation in the amount of time that this effort involves. I watched editors at both houses reject projects in less than fifteen seconds. On other occasions an editor would agonize over a manuscript for as much as six months, then set it aside, then agonize some more before finally deciding against publication. For some projects that were eventually accepted, the process lasted months and involved obtaining several readings from well-known academics, who frequently had contradictory opinions. Other projects were handled more routinely, with the editor reading the material, becoming excited about it, doing a very rough cost analysis on a pocket calculator, deciding the book wouldn't have to be priced at $35, and then sending the project out for evaluation by a person, knowledgeable in the field, whom the editor could count on to provide a favorable review. Normally the reader would reply within four to six weeks, and, if the response was favorable, the editor would propose a contract. Finally, some deals are concluded over a lunch or on the telephone; in these the project seems so obviously a winner and the author's track record is so successful that any subsequent consideration by the house is merely *pro forma*—the book is going to be signed.

It is common knowledge that unsolicited manuscripts have very slim chances of being published. (The acceptance rates at Apple and Plum are presented in chapter 5. For the acceptance rate for unsolicited materials in other branches of book publishing, see Coser, Kadushin, and Powell 1982:129–32.) Authors who send materials in "over the transom" had somewhat better odds of being published at Plum than at Apple. Yet, even at Apple, there were a few occasions when an editor responded favorably to a well-written cover letter and read the enclosed unsolicited manuscript. One such letter went as follows:

Dear ———:
I know that many new Ph.D.'s clutter up your desk with badly written typescripts on obscure subjects, and I've heard it is hard to break into a large and prestigious house such as ———. But I thought I'd give it a go anyhow. The few people who *have* read the book have either described it as "fascinating" or said that it may change the course of the sociology of religion for the next ten years. I myself am so familiar with the work that I no longer feel competent to judge either its intellectual worth or its readability.

So, enclosed in this envelope you will find the introductory pages and the first chapter of my dissertation, along with the Abstract prepared for the oral defense, which, although very stilted in style, gives more information about the basic argument of the work than does the first chapter. If you shudder at the thought of even having to look at the first chapter of a dissertation, let me just say that my dissertation adviser has already made me revise it five times, and it seems pretty presentable to me for right now.

My main reason for going to a house such as ——— is that I'm convinced that [my book] can appeal not only to an academic market but to the wider one of religionists as well. There are maybe twenty-five million people going to church these days, and some of them I feel sure will be curious about a book which says it knows why they do that. If you do like the first chapter, and feel the book might appeal to a wide audience, I am ready to put considerable energy into the extensive revisions I know will be necessary. With good feedback and being sure of publication, I know I can smooth out the rough places.

Sincerely yours,

———

Instances in which editors played such a reactive role were unusual; much of their time is spent gathering information and building intelligence networks. Each of the editors had his or her own way of doing this. The editor at Apple Press who handled the disciplines of sociology, anthropology, and social work actively socialized with scholars in these fields, and her circle of close friends consisted not only of academics but of editors in other scholarly houses. "I call them all the time, I lunch with them," she said; "it's terribly useful to talk frequently with your competitors." She attended parties regularly and liked to go to small conventions or lectures, where she was often the only editor in attendance. In developing a social-work list, her initial step was to make personal calls on the authors of the leading social-work titles that Apple had published prior to her joining the firm. She spoke with them at considerable length and persuaded one to edit a series for her. Her next step was to have lunch with the editor of a major social-work journal. She soon became close friends with both the author and the journal editor.

The Apple editor responsible for the fields of psychology, economics, and law pursued a different strategy. He would telephone people he did not know and say, "I'm looking for a book about [some particular topic], and I've heard you are the person to write it." He constantly fired off letters to prospective authors, frequently writing professors who had recently received research grants or awards. Two of his more successful books resulted from his dogged determination during a trip to Harvard. It was late one afternoon and snowing heavily. The editor-in-chief, who was traveling with him, wanted to call it a day, but the editor wanted to drop in, unannounced, on someone his sources had recommended that he talk to. He located this young scholar and found that he was at work on two books. Both were later published by Apple to much critical acclaim.

This editor spent a good deal of time corresponding with the contributors to the various reference books or anthologies that Apple Press had published. In the following entry in my field notes, I recorded his description of this process:

> This book [of ours] is a presidential commission report that has around sixty contributors. I sent a list of the contributors to a top scholar who knows the areas of law and psychiatry. He will evaluate the list for me and choose the top people. So when I send each author a copy of the book, I'll include a special letter to these people and ask if they have anything in the works. I've been doing the same thing for the Encyclopedia we're publishing, as well as that Handbook we did. Not only did I write to all the contributors, but I went through the bibliography. There were some very productive people, like ———, who was referenced over a dozen times. You know people like this have ideas for books.

The editor-in-chief at Apple Press pursued overseas contacts by staying in touch with editors at scholarly houses in Great Britain. Whenever he was abroad or British editors were in New York, he would dine with them. He would often purchase the American rights to British books and, on occasion, sell the British rights to his books.

The editor-in-chief was also a strong believer in staying in close personal contact with his authors. He commonly used them as a sounding board for his ideas. The following letter is a good example.

Dear ———:

I thought of you on your vacation up there and tried to figure out a way to disturb you. Here it is!

Please look over all the introductory material and as much of the manuscript as you wish in order to make a decision. Is this really a first-class piece of work which political scientists would buy in cloth and/or adopt in paper? Is this original and well written, and does he know what he is talking about?

If you really get into this, find it very interesting, and wish to read the whole thing, just let me know how much we owe you.

I received an excellent response to my letter regarding ———, and I will be ready to move into the next phase soon. I appreciate your kind offer of help and I will embark on this important project feeling much better because of it.

Where does your next book stand? I desperately need an excuse to get away. Isn't there some pressing business we must discuss?

Under separate cover I am sending you a very interesting book. After you have had a chance to look it over, I would like to know what you would think of a similar book on political scientists.

Best wishes,

———

At Plum Press, all of the editors stayed in close contact with their series editors. Each of them maintained a busy travel schedule.[10] The behavioral sciences editor kept an index file that listed all of his authors by geographical area so that, when he traveled to a certain city, he could get in touch with them. He also went to numerous professional conventions and, unlike many scholarly editors, attended most of the sessions;

he would then contact the speakers whose work he found promising. The social sciences editor at Plum felt that "the key to this business is to surround yourself with the right people, develop your own sense of taste, and let the opportunities present themselves." He also kept on the lookout for translation possibilities and the opportunity to reprint government reports. But most of all he liked to travel, more so than any other editor I spoke with. He described his job in this manner:

> I have about ten series editors, and I try to stay in constant touch with them. I want to hear what they are doing, as well as keep them informed about what's going on at my end. I visit my series editors personally at least once a year and preferably more. I love to travel. I probably travel a week out of every month. I spend between $7,000 and $9,000 a year on travel expenses. Some of it has to do with the fact that we are neophytes in the social sciences. But it is also a matter of personal taste. I like for a publishing relationship to be a personal one.

Analysis of Search Behavior

The relationship between an editor's preconceptions about what he or she is looking for and the eventual outcome of a particular search procedure is loosely coupled. The term "loose coupling" is used to describe the disconnectedness of behavior and its consequences (see Weick 1976). Organization theorists have come to question the assumption that individual and organizational decision-making is necessarily purposive and goal-directed. Initial work in this direction began with March and Simon's (1958) ideas on the cognitive limits on rationality and Charles Lindblom's (1959) notion of the science of muddling through, wherein organizations muddle through because of the proliferation of preference orderings and the complexity of cause-effect relations. Weick's (1969) discussion of rationality as "post hoc dissonance reduction" conveys a marked skepticism about calculated, instrumental behavior. To these theorists, organizations have

many competing distractions, and they labor under such formidable constraints as bounded rationality (March and
Simon 1958), uncertain or contested goals (Perrow 1961), and
unclear technologies (Cohen and March 1974).

The efforts by Apple Press editors to procure manuscripts
vividly illustrate loose coupling. A few examples will suffice.
In the process of looking for someone to write a book on
medical experimentation on dependent populations, an editor found a book on the shady and fraudulent practices that
retail stores engage in to exploit consumers. On another
occasion, when the same editor asked a noted academic to
review a manuscript that his house was considering, he
learned that the reviewer was finishing his own *magnum opus*
and was planning to look for a publisher in a few weeks; he
did not need to look further. Another editor, who attended a
conference called "Sociologists for Women in Society" in the
hope of finding several books in women's studies, met several
women who were currently engaged in research projects that
she felt were worthy of publication, though none of the projects dealt with women per se. Finally, while the editor-in-
chief was scanning the ads of competing houses in scholarly
journals and trade publications, he decided he wanted a book
on a new "hot" topic; without making any effort in this
direction, he received, three days later, a manuscript that
filled this newly found need. In short, the choices made at
Apple frequently depended on the order in which alternatives
presented themselves.

Other examples were perhaps not as serendipitous, though
they resulted from unexpected or unplanned personal contacts. It often happened that editors working at other houses
referred projects to Apple that they felt were not right for
them. These referrals were welcomed, but it is important to
realize that the editor usually had no prior knowledge that the
project was on its way and rarely had any preexisting desire
for a manuscript on that specific subject.

What I am arguing is that some decisions were made by
doing very little or by following a course of action that at its

outset was aimed in a different direction. Decisions at Apple Press are not analyzable as a discrete choice among various alternatives. Faced with five good manuscripts, an editor may decide to publish one, two, three, four, five, or none, depending on their subject matter, the authors' academic status, the house's financial situation, and the editor's current work load. The steps in a decision sequence are rarely clear in the beginning and are sometimes difficult to reconstruct in retrospect. The particular problem an editor is working on changes as new information and gossip reveal new problems. External events constrain possible alternatives and shape outcomes, yet often go unanalyzed within the organization. The fate of a manuscript at Apple Press depended on the support and interest that it generated within the house, the extent to which it avoided bottlenecks, where personnel or operating capital were tied down on other projects, and on how well the manuscript fit with the track record of the respective editor and the house's overall list.

Thus the decision to publish a book at Apple took place within a complex swirl of simultaneous occurrences that involved other individuals besides the author and editor, other firms than Apple, other projects besides the book in question, and other developments that were as yet unresolved. This results in part from the fact that the acquisition of "raw materials" took place on a highly personal, idiosyncratic basis, as in the following example. The editor-in-chief of Apple Press frequently voiced his "folk wisdom" that "people in the best schools write the best books." "If I received," he once said, "a manuscript on sociological theory from someone at East Delta State University, I would not consider it for a minute. If the manuscript is any good, why isn't the author at Berkeley or somewhere?" Nevertheless, what was preached was not always practiced. A number of Apple Press authors are from colleges and universities that have little claim to elite status. When I asked the editor-in-chief why he had published two books by a previously unknown academic from a small school, he responded, "I met him at a convention and we had a few drinks; he was a friendly and interesting guy. I had his work reviewed, and people liked it. Besides, I wanted to publish a couple of short ethnographies anyway."

Time and again, editors at Apple Press would comment, "I was dubious about that one when I received it; I never expected it to turn out so well," or "I had never heard of the author, and I knew little about the topic, so I didn't think we would want to publish it," or "It's pleasant surprises that arrive like this that make life enjoyable." My point is not that things always occur by accident but that precisely how a manuscript will be obtained cannot be planned or calculated. Editors do know, however, what are useful methods for acquiring manuscripts. Closeness and familiarity with academics on the part of editors is expected to be productive. This is why publishing houses allow editors generous expense accounts for travel and meals. We should also recognize that, at the same time that editors are looking for manuscripts, authors are looking for someone to publish their work.

In some important respects, the process of acquiring manuscripts at Apple Press resembled what James March and his colleagues (Cohen, March, and Olsen 1972; Cohen and March 1974; March and Olsen 1975, 1976) have termed the "garbage-can model of choice." Tossed into a garbage can is a loosely coupled mix of (1) problems or issues looking for solutions; (2) solutions looking for problems to resolve; (3) participants with different amounts of time and energy; and (4) choice situations waiting to be actualized. The term "loosely coupled" is meant to underscore the independence of these various streams and the lack of temporal ordering; that is, solutions may precede problems, and both solutions and problems can await appropriate choice opportunities.

In garbage-can situations the social structure of the organization influences each stream's arrival and departure times, the allocation of participants' attention to the choice opportunity, and the set of possible links among the various streams. In publishing, the cast of participants changes over time as both editors and authors come and go. Timing is a crucial element. Opportunities are the result of a particular blend of situations, problems, and participant availability. The dynamics of acquiring manuscripts include chance elements that appear to have been rationally calculated only after a manuscript has been secured; rationales are then constructed to explain events. Beliefs or preferences may appear to be the results of behavior at least as much as they are determinants of it (see March 1978); motives and intentions are then discovered after the fact. March and Olsen (1976:15) argue that we must recognize the "possibility that there may be attitudes and beliefs without behavioral implications, that there may even be behavior without any basis in individual preferences, and that there may be an interplay between behavior and the definition of self-interest."

I am not arguing that decision-making at Apple Press was irrational or totally dictated by chance. In fact, it is important to recognize that Weick (1976) is probably correct in arguing that, because loose coupling lowers the probability that an organization will have to respond to each little change in its environment, a loosely coupled organization probably devises more novel solutions than a tightly coupled organization would devise. Moreover, there were editorial decisions that were clearly intelligent, calculated moves, such as publishing the latest work of a well-known scholar whose previous books had sold well, or buying the American rights for a book originally published in England to considerable acclaim and purchasing the rights for a price that means you have to sell only a thousand copies to recoup your investment. As one editor quipped, "With a deal like that, you can't miss!"

There were, however, many situations in which the participants were faced with too many things to attend to, and decisions seem to have been made by flight or oversight. Here is one illustration:

> I asked an editor about the status of a particular project that had arrived in the house several months before. He responded, "Oh, I had forgotten all about it." He hunted around the cluttered office, found it, and glanced at it for a few minutes. He then said, "You've helped me to make up my mind for me. I'll reject it."

Situations such as these were not uncommon. Fortunately, the projects were not always rejected. Sometimes the editor would say that he would send the lost project out for review as soon as he had had time to think about who would be appropriate. Then the project would be placed on top of another pile of papers, and, if it wasn't attended to that day, it would once again be buried in the stacks of undecided projects.

The key element at Apple was not the informality or haphazardness of the decision-making process but the fact that an editor usually did not know when—or whether—his or her search activities would pay off. Quite often the process of acquisition did not appear to be strongly related to making a decision. Feldman and March (1981:177–78) assert that the main point of a decision process may not be an outcome; the central purpose may be the process itself. In such a view, decision-making is an arena for exercising social values, for displaying authority, and for expressing and discovering self-interest. Choice processes of this type are probably most common in organizations where goals are either unclear or inoperative, technologies are imperfectly understood, history is difficult to interpret, boundaries are not fixed, and participation is fluid. The last factor is particularly important because most theories of decision-making do not recognize that attention varies, decision-makers have competing distractions, and participants wander in and out of the choice process. March and his coauthors argue that decision-making is rarely a discrete event; it is far more likely to be a stream of activities with multiple inputs. Nor does all the ambiguity come from the external environment, for these authors also see the decision-making process as a receptacle into which many kinds of personal and organizational problems are dumped: group relations, departmental conflicts, and career frustrations are all played out in the process of making decisions.

Garbage-can decision processes no doubt occur in most organizations under certain kinds of circumstances. More generally, organizations that cope with diverse points of view about appropriate technologies, rapid technological innovation, divergent consumer demands, multiple or mixed goals, and a disparate and/or irregular labor supply seem particularly ripe for garbage-can situations. Thus garbage-can theory is likely to be applicable to organizations other than the "exotic" ones, such as universities, free schools, and voluntary associations, that have been studied thus far. One could argue that the more contact points, at both the input and output boundaries, an organization has, the more divergent is the information it receives. As a result, competing views develop about what would be an appropriate course of action, and internal consensus declines. Such a condition characterizes not only much government policymaking (Pressman and Wildavsky 1973; March and Olsen 1983) but policymaking by business firms that operate in uncertain international markets or in intensively competitive and innovative fields.

Garbage-can choice processes are also likely to be common in service organizations that employ a professional labor force. This is due, in part, to the fact that professionals differ among themselves about what the organization should be doing. Indeed, organizations can become an arena for the clash of different reference groups and ideologies. In publishing, for example, to assert that acquiring and signing books is a talent not subject to quantification or empirical analysis is, in part, a form of mystification that serves the self-interest of editors. Such an assertion by editors can be viewed as an ideological justification of their craft, a means for fending off the demands of accountants, corporate executives, and sales directors. The claim that the craft of editing is a special skill is part of the culture of publishing professionalism. It is a part of the struggle of the members of an occupation to define the conditions and methods of their work or, in Larson's words (1977:49–52), to control "the production of producers" and to establish a cognitive base and legitimation for their occupational autonomy (Collins 1979). As Larson shows, the professional project is rarely achieved with complete success. Nevertheless, the ambiguity and variability that typify such organizations as publishing houses, advertising agencies, universities, law firms, research institutes, and other culture-producing industries indicate that the resident professionals are attempting to define their work in a manner that does not lend itself to routinization and formal standards.

The terms "organized anarchy" and "garbage can" suggest a choice process that is quite different from what a rational model of choice would imply. The difference, however, should not be exaggerated. I would argue, and I suspect March would agree, that there are regular patterns in the apparent disorderly process of decision-making. All organizations have rules of evidence, that is, standard operating assumptions about what information is relevant to a particular decision and how past history should be interpreted in the light of current choices. For example, the history and traditions of a publishing house have a major impact on the amount and quality of attention that a particular author receives. Organizations also have decision structures that determine who is permitted to participate in a decision. Such subtle forms of control are discussed in the next chapter.

The search behavior of editors at Plum Press contrasted sharply with the more free-wheeling style of Apple Press editors. The editorial staff at Plum relied heavily on their various series editors for advice and used the suggestions of their other academic advisers as a means of reducing uncertainty and problems of information overload. Some of the uncertainty faced by editors has to do with not knowing which new areas of scholarly research are likely to be "growth industries" and which scholars can be counted on to provide high-quality, marketable books. To cope with these concerns, Plum editors routinely used series editors as "trail scouts." For instance, the social science editor met with one of his series editors and went over the list of faculty members at every major sociology department in the country. The series editor checked off the names of the people he knew personally. The social science editor then sent each of them a letter, informing them about Plum's series and inquiring about their research in progress. This process was repeated with series editors in other fields. Another Plum Press editor made it a regular practice to dine with his series editors. He always asked his academic advisers to invite their colleagues to join them. The editor used these occasions to learn about recent academic developments.

At Apple Press the editor was assumed to be the resident expert in a given field. It was very rare for anyone else to ask to see what an author had submitted; other members of the house relied on the editor's evaluation. At Plum Press, editors were not considered experts; instead, the series editors served this function. The primary responsibility of editors was to locate hard-working series editors who had extensive academic contacts and exercised good judgment. The selection of appropriate series editors was extremely important. An inappropriate choice—that is, someone who would use the position to repay debts to colleagues, or to reward students, or to push his or her own particular view to the exclusion of other approaches—not only would be a financial loss but could seriously harm the house's reputation. And, in time, the series editor's reputation would suffer as well. The prestige system of science serves to attenuate self-aggrandizing behavior on the part of series editors.

Pfeffer and Salancik (1978:145–47) have demonstrated that, when situations of exchange are uncertain, organizations may attempt to establish linkages with key elements in their environment and use such linkages to acquire needed resources. Linkages can expedite the search for information; they are a means of social coordination that reduces uncertainty and increases predictability. The establishment of links to the academic community in the form of series editors also provided Plum Press with a forum for communicating its intentions and for generating exposure. Moreover, prestigious series editors were a sign of support; their reputations enhanced the legitimacy of the press's publishing program.

In several relevant ways, the search for scholarly books by Plum editors resembled shopping in a Moroccan bazaar, where information also is scarce, maldistributed, inefficiently communicated, and intensely valued. As Clifford Geertz (1978) has shown, the village bazaar is marked by uncertainty

about the quality and reliability of goods; he describes
(1978:30–31) "clientelization" as a means of coping with the
uncertainty that pervades the Moroccan bazaar in Sefrou.
This is the "tendency for repetitive purchasers of particular
goods and services to establish continuing relationships with
particular purveyors of them, rather than search widely
through the market at each occasion of need." Clientelization
partitions the bazaar crowd into those who are genuine candidates for attention and those who are merely theoretically
such. It is a means of personalizing the exchange relationship
in order to limit the search process. This mechanism narrows
the relevant field and permits in-depth, intensive search
rather than broad, but superficial, extensive search. Geertz
(1978:32) shows that:

> Search is primarily intensive because the sort of information
> needed most cannot be acquired by asking a handful of index
> questions of a large number of people but only by asking a
> large number of diagnostic questions of a handful of people. It
> is this kind of questioning, exploring nuances rather than
> canvassing populations, that bazaar bargaining represents.

Search behavior at Plum Press resembled the strategy of
clientelization in that, instead of casting their nets widely,
Plum editors utilized a few series editors to guide them in
their efforts to locate new authors. There was a strong preference for a few repeated dealings; thus the search process
employed by Plum Press editors was purposive and highly
targeted. The uncertainty of the search was reduced through
the assistance of the series editors. It is worth noting the
parallels between the Plum strategy and that of a business
firm facing an uncertain market for its products. One response to such a state of affairs is for the sales department to
sign long-term purchase agreements with various customers.
By doing so, the sales force eliminates some of the uncertainty faced by the firm, but it also sharply reduces the organization's dependence on the sales department. In the same
manner, the use of series editors greatly lessened the problems of information overload and information impactedness

commonly faced by editors. Yet this practice also reduced the editors' power within the house and rendered them less irreplaceable. Indeed, as long as a series editor's loyalty was to the house and not to an individual editor, an editor at Plum could be replaced and the new editor would not have to build a new network of advisers. The differences in the hiring process at the two houses aptly demonstrate this. At Apple Press, editorial positions remained vacant for long periods of time—in some cases for as much as six to nine months. Job candidates were asked to provide letters of reference from authors with whom they had worked. In contrast, editorial vacancies at Plum were quickly filled, and outside candidates were evaluated on the basis of the sales records of the titles they had published at other houses.

Evaluating Manuscripts and the Use of Outside Reviewers

Once a manuscript is under consideration, an editor must evaluate it. (The speed, or lack of it, with which a manuscript is reviewed is discussed in chapter 5.) Editors have a list of questions that they ask of each manuscript under serious review. They want to know what groups of scholars will be attracted to a book. They must judge whether a book has adoption possibilities for graduate or upper-level undergraduate courses and whether it has book club or foreign sales potential. An editor must also determine how well written a book is and how much work will be involved in publishing it. An editor has to decide whether to spend his or her time on a particular book. Finally, and most important, the editor must determine whether the manuscript makes a substantial intellectual contribution; for assistance in deciding whether the scholarship is respectable, editors frequently turn to outsiders.

To help them solve some of these questions, or if these questions have been answered affirmatively, editors will "cost out" a manuscript—that is, estimate, at least roughly, the costs of producing and manufacturing the book. To do this, the editor must decide on the number of copies to print.

In making this decision, the editors at Apple Press "take the most pessimistic view possible and try to make it work." At Plum Press the strategy is similar, except that the social science editor often feels that his books have greater sales potential than the other books the house publishes. This generally has been true, and his outlook is usually more optimistic than that of his more conservative colleagues. At this point, all of the figuring is very speculative; the editor is concerned, in a general way, with whether the project is "doable."

If these preliminary computations (they will be revised at a later stage) demonstrate that a project is worth undertaking, the editor must then decide whether the book should be sent to someone who can provide an authoritative judgment on its merits. Editors cannot send every manuscript out for review, nor need they. Unlike university-press editors, commercial scholarly editors are not required to obtain outside assessments in order to sign a book. If a book is by a well-known author, an Apple Press editor may not bother with obtaining a review. Or the editor might seek an independent judgment, after the book has been contracted for, as a service to the author to aid him or her in the revision process. At Plum Press, if a manuscript was strongly supported by a series editor, no further review was considered necessary. However, if an editor had questions about the material, the market, or comparable books on the same topic, an outside review could help answer these concerns. In addition, if a Plum editor felt particularly enthusiastic about a project, he or she might obtain an outside review in order to bolster the case for publication.

One simple reason why every manuscript under serious consideration cannot be sent out for review is the cost, in both time and money, that is involved. Equally important is that, in sending a manuscript out for review, an editor is making demands on the reviewer's time. The honorarium that is paid for evaluating a manuscript is rather small compensation. Scholars review manuscripts out of loyalty to a house and because they are interested in reading new material. If an editor sends a reviewer several poor manuscripts, the reviewer's enthusiasm will naturally wane, and he or she will begin to question the editor's ability. No editor wants a reviewer to think, "Why is this stupid person sending me this junk?" Any manuscript that passes in-house screening should be presumed to include new work that will need to be read by others in the field when it is eventually published.

Harman and Schoeffel (1975:333) state, "The care of readers [i.e., manuscript reviewers] is . . . central to the work of an editorial department—locating them, ensuring that their time is not wasted on evident dross, persuading them to tackle yet one more manuscript, and shielding them from direct confrontation with the author." Editors select reviewers in several ways. Here is one editor's strategy:

> Ask the author if he can recommend anyone, or if there's somebody he does *not* want it sent to, because there may be cases where he attacked somebody in the book, or something like that, or he knows somebody is down on him—it's only fair to do that, sometimes. Often I will say, "Can you name two or three people—people you do not personally know—as reviewers for the manuscript?"

Editors may also select reviewers from an author's bibliography. But the largest source of potential reviewers are the authors who have already been published by the house. Becoming an author is often the start of a long-term relationship with a publisher. If a book is a commercial or critical success, an editor will then freely call on the author for advice and for assistance in evaluating manuscripts. The relationship between a scholarly press and its authors can be close and long-lasting. It is of paramount importance that editors sustain these relationships. At Apple Press, the editors frequently called on their authors for assistance in reviewing manuscripts. Following are three examples of cover letters that accompanied manuscripts sent out for review by Apple Press.

Dear Professor ———:

Under separate cover, I have sent you the complete manuscript of ———. I very much appreciate your agreeing to read it for me in view of the incredible demands on your time now.

You need not read it all, because the book is not yet under contract and I want only your general impressions of his work at this stage. I fully believe it will be an important book, and, as I said, my major question is, how important. What are the chief books already published on this subject, and how do they compare?

I am enclosing with this letter the table of contents and the 56-page introduction to the author's first book, ———, on which the manuscript in question builds. It may be of help.

I'll send you $—— for your brief overview, as we agreed. I fully appreciate your time problems. Whatever you can do will be most welcome.

Sincerely,

———

Dear ———:

Although, as you will see from the enclosed, I received this letter and proposal some months ago, I have spoken to the author several times since, most recently in ———.

May I please have your comments on the need for such a book, its potential market, and his ability to do it properly? Is this a work that will be used widely? To what audience will it appeal? Is the material suitably organized?

I am really quite hesitant to send you too much material, knowing how busy you are, but you and I have discussed projects like this in the past, and I do not feel it would take up too much of your time.

Regards,

———

Dear ———:

Please excuse my inordinate delay in getting you a contract. Suffice it to say that we will be very proud to publish another book by you and that I will put a contract in your hands as soon as I dig out far enough to do the detestable paperwork. Let me add to my excuse by telling you that I just returned from a

combination business trip–vacation to England. It was, need-
less to say, an unforgettable trip. However, I know that you
are a patient man, and I promise to get you a contract soon.

I will now add insult to injury by asking you to do me a
favor. I enclose the uncorrected proof of ———. You will see
that it is from ——— in England, and they want to know if we
are interested.

We recently published ———, and it is selling exceptionally well. Is this the same kind of book? In a word, do you
recommend we publish it in the U.S.? Why, or why not? Is it a
respectable work of scholarship? Is the research sound?
Could the manuscript be cut without loss of effectiveness?

Upon receipt of your review, I will send you an honorarium. Thanking you in advance, I very much appreciate your
help.

Best wishes,

The responses of reviewers play an important role determining the fate of a manuscript. Unless the editor feels
strongly about a manuscript, one negative review may kill its
chances. Yet there are also times when an editor overlooks
unfavorable reports. Responding to a negative review, the
editor-in-chief at Apple Press quipped, "I wasted $—— on
that." In other cases, when a manuscript was already under
contract, a sharply critical review served only to dampen an
editor's enthusiasm. As a rule, if the editor did not have a very
strong opinion about a manuscript, the reviewer's comments
weighed heavily; if the editor was favorably inclined, he or
she would be likely to select a reviewer who would be interested in the work.

Reviewers' reports varied considerably, in both length and
substance. This was due partly to the style of an individual
reviewer, but it was also a consequence of the editor's having
provided an indication of whether he or she wanted the
manuscript "sniffed" or thoroughly read. The comments re-
produced below are typical reviewer responses.

Dear ———:

This is written confirmation of my earlier oral report to you concluding that the manuscript, ———, should not be accepted for publication. I think the book is at most superficial, and frequently downright misleading. This is due to the authors' abortive attempt at viewing both criminal and civil law simultaneously. The result is enormous distortion. Even had they succeeded in eliminating the distortion, I see very little need for such a work. There are a host of books which cover this area that are better written and more soundly conceived than this one.

Please let me know if you desire further details.

Sincerely,

———

Dear ———:

The manuscript is an impressive piece of work. He manages to present in this rather smallish book the essentials of the notion of verstehen (understanding) as it developed from its origins in German classical philosophy to such luminaries as Rickert, Dilthey, Simmel, Weber, to more recent discussions in the Frankfurt School (Habermas), in phenomenology and ethnomethodology and in British linguistic philosophy (Wittgenstein and his successors). It is a very remarkable job of critical discussion and tight logical argumentation. In fact, this is probably the best thing on the topic that exists in English.

However, this was written with a British audience in mind. British social scientists are much more sophisticated when it comes to philosophical or epistemological issues than their American counterparts, who are often totally innocent of any philosophical knowledge. This would raise issues as to how widely a book of this kind would be used here. A counterargument is, on the other hand, that with the rise of ethnomethodology, phenomenology, and Frankfurt-style Marxism there has emerged a younger group of social scientists who are interested in these questions. (And you know that the ethnomethodological studies you have published have done pretty well, even when couched in esoteric language.

Summa summarum: I think that you should probably take this little book. Not only has it considerable intrinsic merit, but the overall series of which it is a part looks promising enough to warrant an initial outlay on the first of the series, so as to have an option on later volumes.

One last thought: You probably won't sell much of that book in the Middle West, but it might do quite well in quality schools on both coasts, and it might also do well in smaller places, where one now can find instructors of phenomenological or Marxist persuasion. There will also be some interest in certain departments of philosophy.

Cordially,

In a few cases, the comments of reviewers were extensive. The following summary concluded a detailed eight-page review of a work of diplomatic history:

> The reader believes the work to be unusually attractive, both as scholarship and as literature. I recommend publication enthusiastically and without reservation. No major revision is required. The authors do not hesitate to come to clear and authoritative conclusions when evidence permits. In situations when evidence is not complete and where previous authors have indulged in speculation the authors review those speculations. They provide both judicious and bold statements. Readers will like the book; it seems destined to enjoy a market well beyond most efforts of comparable scholarly quality.

At Plum Press, the editors utilized their authors considerably less than was the case at Apple Press. As I have noted, they relied much more heavily on the opinions of their series editors. The following entry from my field notes captures the workings of this relationship:

> Upon returning from lunch, an editor discovered that a manuscript had arrived in the mail, referred by one of the series editors. The accompanying letter from the series editor stated that "this book will grace our list." The series editor instructed the editor "not to send it out for review, as it has already been favorably commented upon by a noted demographer." The editor at Plum Press stated that this manuscript represented several years of work on the part of the series

editor——making suggestions, reviewing drafts, editing, etc. I asked the editor if he would get another outside review. "In cases like this, where the manuscript is right up my editor's alley, generally not, especially since he has worked so hard on it. If it was outside of his immediate area of expertise, I might get it reviewed and then tell him about it afterwards."

The series editors at Plum Press functioned as minipublishers—scouting for manuscripts, evaluating them, making suggestions, and even editing in some cases. Thus, when the series editors referred material to the house editor, the chances of its being published were quite good but certainly not automatic. As one Plum Press editor commented,

> No, we don't publish just anything that a series editor recommends. For sure, everything they submit gets serious attention. Anyway, you don't want to upset them. But you have to bullshit them from time to time. You don't want to say that you don't like the manuscript, so you blame its rejection on your supervisor or the editorial committee.

Saying No Gracefully

Declining to publish an author's manuscript is a part of every editor's job. Many of the rejections are handled mechanically. The editor writes "reject" on a sheet of paper and attaches it to the letter or manuscript and turns it over to his or her secretary, who then sends out a fairly standard rejection letter. Two of the most common lines in rejection letters are "publishing is not an exact science" and "given the nature of our publishing program." A typical letter of this sort often goes as follows:

> Dear Dr. ———:
> I regret to tell you that we have decided against publication of your book on ———. This decision in no way reflects on the quality of your work but has to do with the nature of our publishing program and our appraisal of the needs of the market.
> Publishers differ, of course, in their programs and evalua-

tions, and we hope that you are successful in finding a suitable publisher for your book. Thank you for giving us the opportunity to consider it.

Sincerely,

———

Some rejection letters, on the other hand, are handled quite thoughtfully and with great tact. The sociology editor at Apple Press exhibited much concern over rejection letters, as her comments to me attest:

I feel I owe it to authors who have submitted reasonably good ideas to make a serious effort. If we decide not to publish, I always try to write a helpful rejection letter. When I think it's appropriate, I'll provide the names of friends in other houses who might react more favorably. If I do not know anyone right off, I may still suggest other houses that might be interested. Taking the time to write a well-thought-out rejection letter can mean that the author will think of you for their next manuscript.

The following letter is an example of this editor's consideration for an author she is currently declining to publish:

Dear ———:

You write awfully well, and you've done a remarkably good job of integrating work by several authors so that the book reads as an integrated whole—but I'm afraid I don't think it's for us. Our list as a whole is small, as you know; my personal list is overwhelmingly large, as you also know; and the reason for the rejection boils down to a matter of triage. I don't think the manuscript holds sufficient commerical promise to vanquish some among the flood of others awaiting a yea or nay. I certainly think it's publishable and interesting, but not a big potential money-maker. Maybe try ——— at ———? If he doesn't bite, you could send it to ——— and tell them I suggested it.

I'm sorry, but please don't rule us out for your next product.

Best,

———

The psychology editor at Apple Press remarked that you never know what can happen as a result of a poorly conceived, perfunctory rejection letter. "They may tell their colleagues you treated them cavalierly." The unanticipated consequences of tactfully declining an author's work were demonstrated when this editor received a job offer from another publishing house as a result of his having treated an author in a straightforward manner. As he commented to me:

> Remember last fall, when I was talking with you about ———? Well, I had his manuscript reviewed; the reviews were so-so at best. The thing needed a *lot* of work, but I assumed we would sign him because he is a big name. Then we would try to improve the manuscript after the contract was signed. I submitted the proposal and told him that things looked good. Much to my surprise, the editor-in-chief kicked the proposal back to me; he wasn't enthusiastic about signing the book unless we could get a promising review. So I had to get back to the author and break the news. I figured I had made an enemy for life. I called him, and yes, he was upset. But he mentioned that ——— had offered him a contract. I doubted that he wanted to revise the manuscript for us, so I suggested he sign with them; I made a number of recommendations to him, and I figured that was that. Now it turns out that it was ——— [the author] who had recommended me to the executives at ——— [the other publishing house]. An unusual way to get put up for a job, isn't it?

An inappropriate or thoughtless rejection letter can, by the same token, have dire consequences. As the psychology editor noted, "Academics have well-organized grapevines; word gets around the academic community very quickly."

The social science editor at Plum Press spoke of the inherent difficulties in rejecting manuscripts from certain people. As he explained:

> This is the outline of a book that was referred to me by ——— [one of the editor's favorite authors, whose latest book is a critical success]. This is the second project that he has referred to me that I will can. I just can't see where the audience is for this book. It's a real problem, though; I'd love for him to refer

something to me that I could accept. In this case I'll write a nice personal rejection letter to the author of the manuscript and send the recommender a copy of it too.

The decision to reject books by important people or by "friends and supporters" of the house is often a very trying experience. These are what editors call "political problems." In certain cases it is simply unwise to disappoint an important scholar because of the danger that he or she will move to another house. For example, a distinguished author or the editor of a series published by the house may wish to publish a collection of his or her own papers or may highly recommend another person's manuscript. The editor must weigh the risks involved in turning down either the scholar or his protégé. The risks may not be worth taking. Editors who work for university presses encounter similar problems. Sometimes they receive manuscripts that have been recommended by a member of their board of directors or publications committee. When this occurs, they are quite naturally concerned with the possible consequences of rejecting these manuscripts. As August Frugé (1976:5), former director of the University of California Press, recalls, "We once rejected, and with no repercussions, a manuscript by the then president of the university. We also passed up two manuscripts by the dean of a school in Los Angeles, but it is not so clear about the repercussions; our offices were in his building, and we had to move not long thereafter."

I do not wish to contend that well-known authors who have prior associations with a house have *carte blanche*. Their manuscripts may on occasion be rejected, but this is done with great discretion. A "regular" author may submit a project that the editor is not favorably predisposed toward; however, the editor does not want to personally say no. In such cases the editor will go through the review process and then point to a reviewer's lack of enthusiasm or raise a question about the potential market. These are acceptable reasons for rejecting the project. Or, at a university press, the editor may take the project before the publications committee, knowing full well that the committee rarely approves anything that has received a negative review. The editor is then able to tell the author that it was the committee that turned the project down.

In the final analysis, the rejection of a manuscript—whether it presents a "political problem" or not—can be a troubling decision for an editor. Every editor with whom I have spoken can recount an extraordinary "one that got away" story. They each can remember at least one manuscript that they rejected, secure in their opinion that it lacked commercial appeal or intellectual promise, only to have another house publish it with great success. Editors also recalled turning authors down, firm in the belief that their work had little potential; they would later watch with dismay as another firm published the author's *next* book to critical acclaim.

The Publishing of Journals

The editors at Plum Press spent between 10 and 20 percent of their time either working on the various journals that the press published or evaluating proposals for new journals. Deciding whether to start a journal or, alternately, assuming the responsibility from a professional society for publishing its journal, is handled in the same manner as a proposal for a new book, but the stakes are higher. As the social science editor remarked: "Publishing a journal is a most serious responsibility. A bad book is one thing, but a bad journal can be a major embarrassment."

The social science editor at Plum would ask the following questions about a journal proposal: What are the competing journals? Can this journal attract material away from them? Is there a community of scholars large enough to support it? Who is the journal editor going to be, and what are his credentials? If a journal proposal was of interest to the editor, he would get reviews of the person who had proposed the journal. The editor would also ask the house's authors in the relevant discipline about their impression of the need for a new journal. The editor would also try to speak with the editors of existing journals in the area to learn whether any other publishers were planning a similar journal. The sales department would assist in the whole evaluation process.

In some cases successful journals will spin off a monograph series. There was one case where a journal editor had received a number of articles that were too long for his journal. He mentioned this to the editor at Plum, and they agreed to develop a monograph series. The journal editor then contacted the authors of the lengthy articles and attempted to persuade them to expand their articles into books. The social science editor noted that "journals generally play an important role in aiding the acquisition of manuscripts."

The editors at Plum Press assist in the selection of a journal's editorial board and, on occasion, provide ideas if an issue of the journal is to focus on a special topic. Once the journal is on its feet, the editor of the journal is usually left to his own devices. There is an annual financial evaluation. However, two editors and the editor-in-chief each remarked, "Plum would never discontinue a journal. If things were terribly bad, we might merge two journals if that would help." The behavioral sciences editor said, "It would look very bad if we stopped publishing a journal, even if it was unprofitable. Even though we can't count its profitability in pennies, journals bring in and maintain a clientele. They are often very prestigious."

The vice-president of the sales department pointed out that, although the academic editors run the journals on their own, his department helps them as much as it can. He commented:

Developing journals is like developing books, but it is much more difficult. These days you have to be very careful. In 1976 we will not begin any new journals, nor do we have any plans for 1977 at this time. In 1975 we started two, and they first appeared in print in 1976. Both look to be coming along well, but it takes two to three years to tell. Some of our journals aren't all that great, but by no means would we ever quit doing one. That could be a fatal mistake.

Journal publishing was another strategy used by Plum Press to cover a particular discipline effectively and fully exploit all the available opportunities. The sales department's vice-president describes the "dynamics of our publishing program" in this manner:

> You approach a scientific area this way: you try to set up a primary journal first, then begin publishing advances, reviews, serial, or continuation lines. Then you bring out a multivolume state of the art. After all this, a monograph series can be spun off. Then you tie it in with a reprint line, particularly if the reprints in this area date back before 1900 and are in the public domain. At the end of each year, our journal subscriptions bring in hundreds of thousands of dollars of income, on which we don't have to deliver any goods immediately. The orders for the serial publications build up in advance. We have large standing orders for many of our books. We try to send out promotion mailings prior to publication, and then we get a number of advance orders. We can use our journals to advertise our books. It's a very effective program; it's really the classical European approach to scientific publishing.

Apple Press publishes no journals. It has, however, recently had success with handbooks, annual reviews, and encyclopedias. The Apple management wants to publish more of these, for not only are they profitable in themselves, but reference works of this type are useful for establishing contacts with, and acquiring manuscripts from, the various contributors.

Relations with Authors

The editors at Apple Press were very supportive of their authors. As one of them remarked, "Authors like to know they are appreciated; they have to be stroked and curried." This particular editor would explain a contract in detail to each author, warning about clauses that were strongly to the publisher's advantage. These clauses were rarely removed from the contract, but the authors were at least informed, and this might prevent disagreements at a later date. Another editor noted that "in our kind of publishing we don't compete on the basis of money. We can't give authors big advances or outlandish royalty rates and still publish profitable books. Instead, we go all out in trying to assist our authors every step of the way." In marked contrast to trade and textbook publishing, negotiating a contract for a scholarly book is generally a simple matter. In part this is because advances are low and royalty rates are standard at almost every scholarly house. An added factor is the absence of costly competition among houses for an author. Scholarly houses certainly compete with each other, but rarely does this competition lead to lucrative contracts for authors. Instead, the competition revolves around editorial services and the comparative prestige of the houses. Scholarly houses are all competing for roughly the same market, and authors are aware of this and usually do not expect that their books will make them rich.

Many authors relished the attention they received from the editors at Apple Press. Yet there were a few who felt that such attention was unnecessary; they were, in fact, suspicious of the press's solicitousness, particularly after their book had been published and they were unhappy with the marketing campaign. One author commented that what he liked most about Apple Press was the "cheerfulness and enthusiasm for his work" but that he "distrusted it."

The editor-in-chief went to great lengths to keep distinguished Apple Press authors content. He would send birthday and seasonal greeting cards. For "one of the deans of American history," he went to an out-of-print bookstore and purchased several books, which he sent to the historian with a note saying, "Please accept these with my gratitude for your having published with us . . . ; if you already have copies, you can donate them to your university's library." Whenever an Apple Press author visited New York, the editors would try to take him or her out to lunch. Authors who lived in the New York metropolitan area were fortunate to receive such treat-

ment frequently. When one long-time author was hospital-
ized, the editor-in-chief took the time to send a card and a
lovely plant, as well as the following letter:

> Dear ———:
>   I was very sorry to hear that you are not feeling well. After
> a long and very pleasant meeting with your colleagues yester-
> day, however, I was glad to find that you are in the hands of
> such talented doctors.
>   Please let me know if there is anything I can do for you or if
> there are any errands you would like taken care of. You know
> that I will be delighted to help in any way possible.
>   Get well soon! I won't know what to sign up until you get
> well and back to work. Please don't hesitate to call me if I can
> do anything. I really mean it.
>   Best wishes,
>   ———

Efforts such as these reflect genuine concern. Such policies
at Apple Press stemmed from its high regard for its successful
authors. Problems sometimes developed when authors came
to expect exceptional treatment as a matter of routine and the
editors were too busy working on acquiring books to attend to
already published authors. While editors were genuinely interested in their authors, they naturally expected the authors
to reciprocate. In return for the services that were provided to
particular authors, the editors felt that they could call on
these people for advice, to "pick their brains," or for assistance in promoting a particular book. One example of this
type of request goes as follows:

> Dear Professor ———:
>   In January, 197—, we will publish ———, by ———. The
> reviewers who have already read this material in an earlier
> form report that it is a magnificent piece of work on an
> important subject and that it should take its place as one of the
> two or three most important books in legal philosophy in the
> twentieth century.
>   It is very well written, and it examines the literature in

depth in at least five languages without ever bogging down in too much detail.

I enclose a copy of the uncorrected bound proof of this work. I would very much appreciate it if you would look through this work and, assuming that you like it, send me your reaction, from which I may glean a prepublication "quotable quote." I would then, of course, send you a copy of the bound book upon publication in January.

Thank you very much for your help; I hope to hear from you.

Yours truly,

It is common in all branches of publishing for editors or promotion personnel to write to well-known people and ask them to read a manuscript and provide a "quotable quote." Our research has shown that the success rate for such queries is normally rather low unless the person being asked is a close friend or admirer of the author. At Apple Press, however, the rate of response to requests for quotable "blurbs" is very high, and this is in part attributable to the "stroking and currying" of successful authors.

One of the most upsetting things for an author is to have his or her meaning changed by editing. The author often feels that no one has the right to tamper with his or her thoughts. Many authors fail to see that an editor is trying to understand and clarify what they have written. Few authors stop to consider that, if a reasonably intelligent editor finds a certain idea ambiguous, other readers will probably be puzzled by it also. An editor must feel confident that he or she can work with an author and produce a publishable manuscript. This process can take months, sometimes years. Editors must be sympathetic; yet they have to be capable of saying that they dislike something. The timing of suggestions can also be important. As a senior editor at another scholarly house observed, "Occasionally there may be a really important book being written by someone who hasn't got hold of it, and you need to keep intervening . . . and then there are people who simply sit down and write a book, and the manuscript requires only a few internal changes." It is important for editors to be able to "read" their authors and judge how they react to criticism. Some writers look to the rewriting, polishing, editing, or changing stage as a major step in the development of their work. Other authors are literally uneditable; they may react vehemently to even the slightest suggestion of alterations. Once their thoughts are down on paper, their book becomes so real for them that they cannot conceive of it any other way.

The editors at Apple Press often found themselves caught in the middle of disagreements between authors and the production department. Such cases were often no-win situations for editors, although they usually intervened on behalf of their authors at the expense of making the production staff angry. This created extra work for the editors. Going out on a limb for an author or spending a great deal of time working on a manuscript was not considered an important part of an editor's job. As one editor noted, "Editors win points, raises, promotions, etc., on how many books they sign and how many they get out. If you don't feel obliged to work on manuscripts yourself, then it's no problem. If you do, it's another matter, and it means you lug your work with you everywhere—to home, on vacation, on trips, etc."

One editor faced serious problems as a result of the attention she lavished on manuscripts. It took her longer to process paperwork, and this created a bottleneck. She found herself retyping material that had been copyedited and then editing it herself so that the author would not be upset by the original poor copyediting. Her relations with the production department deteriorated. Eventually the president approved of her extra efforts when he spoke with several authors who were extremely enthusiastic about her work. But another problem arose: word spread about this editor's skills. Her fine editorial hand was a major plus in acquiring manuscripts. In addition, the editor-in-chief would turn over to her the manuscripts that he considered very important but in need of polishing. It soon became a vicious cycle. As she confessed to me:

I'm having real trouble with my work load. I've been signing
lots of books; then I have to find time to give each of them my
personal touch, which is one reason authors are attracted to
me and I sign so many books. Now if I don't provide them with
excellent comments, they get upset. I'm going to have to ask if
I can work at home one or two days a week.

A senior editor who worked for a scholarly house that was
one of Apple Press's major competitors also felt the conflict
between the demands of signing manuscripts and her personal feelings that doing line-by-line editing was something
her authors valued:

If I think a really big difference could be made, then I'll
copyedit the manuscript myself. Sometimes the author requests this of you. I feel that I would prefer to do the copyediting myself, because I am infinitely better at it than anyone we
would hire. We still use a lot of free-lance copyeditors. Frequently, then, when my manuscripts come back from having
been farmed out, I go over them to remove what I consider
asinine . . . so that the author shouldn't be driven to a frenzy.
It is a painful process to get a manuscript back with all these
pink flags all over it, and marked up, even if it is done well. It is
always painful, even if you are edited by the very best. Because it hurts your vanity and makes you anxious. . . . But to
be copyedited by an incompetent is the most anxiety- and
rage-producing experience. But there isn't time to copyedit as
many books as I would like. The trick, of course, is to get good
writers. Then you can say to the copyeditor, "This person
knows more about writing than you. Leave them alone. Just
make sure that there are no spelling errors and that all the
numbers are spelled out or written out, or whatever."

On occasion there were manuscripts that needed work,
and the editors at Apple approved of the extensive revisions
made by the copyeditors. In one special case the editor-in-
chief had hired a free-lance person to add more "punch" to
what he regarded as a "dry" treatment of a subject that
potentially had a wide audience. The editor-in-chief knew
that he had a lot of tough negotiating to do with the author
over these additions, as the tone of his letter indicates:

Dear ———:

Before you scream, I implore you read through the entire manuscript. I believe that our helper, whose name is ———, has done exactly what I asked her to do, which was to write a new introduction, to plug in material on prisoner labor, food, behavior modification, the use of prisoners in experimentation, punitive transfer, and other points, as well as adding some punch to the manuscript throughout.

I believe that you will find that she has done what I asked and more. I don't expect that you will accept 100% of what she has done, but I frankly would be disappointed if you rejected more than 10%. I went through the entire manuscript, and you will see my notes throughout. Often I kicked myself for not seeing and recommending what she did.

Call me as soon as you have looked over this, and we will talk about it.

Best wishes,

———

Finally, there were those unusual cases in which the editors at Apple Press did not intervene on an author's behalf when disputes arose over copyediting. In one instance the author wanted to rewrite his manuscript while it was in the galley stage. He was told that if he did so his contract would be canceled. Another author wrote the press, saying, "Please restore the pre-penciled purity of the text." He had erased the 700 pages of copyediting that had been done on his manuscript. His contract was promptly canceled.

There were two other problem areas in author-publisher relations at Apple Press. One concerned the marketing department. As I have noted, this was Apple's weakest link, and the authors I interviewed consistently gave low marks to its sales and marketing efforts. The psychology editor took it upon himself to try to remedy this situation. He would send complimentary copies of recent books to noted academics, and he contacted the editors of various journals and magazines and alerted them to a new book that he was enthusiastic about. When he traveled to college campuses, he would stop in and chat with the manager of the campus bookstore. In short, he did everything he possibly could to increase his books' exposure. Not surprisingly, the sales staff did not always applaud his efforts. Moreover, as word spread through academic networks about the editor's promotional efforts, authors would contact him, rather than the marketing department, to suggest additional ideas for promoting their books.

Another perennial problem is the "stepchild" book: manuscripts signed by predecessors and passed on to the next person hired. Editors felt some responsibility toward these books, but they were seldom enthusiastic about them. This was particularly true when completed manuscripts suddenly arrived unannounced. If the author first contacted the new editor and a relationship was initiated, there was usually more enthusiasm on the editor's part.

At Plum Press, none of the acquiring editors did any line-by-line editing. It was generally felt by editors not only at Plum but at competing houses that editors simply cannot meticulously edit detailed, specialized monographs. On the rare occasion when a book was thought to have some appeal to a broader audience, the sponsoring editor would spend some time going over it. However, few books of this sort were published by Plum Press, and it was even more unusual for the book to be regarded in this manner prior to publication. More often than not, the fact that a book appealed to a larger audience came as a surprise, and it was not until a book received reviews in such magazines as the *New Republic* that the people at Plum Press realized what they had on their hands.

A constant problem for editors at Plum Press was delay in the publication of multiauthored books that reported on the latest advances in a field. Prompt publication is essential for such books. However, the job of selecting authors and persuading them to get their chapters in on time was the responsibility of the volume editor. A Plum Press editor could intervene but had to do so cautiously, so as not to affront the editor of the volume. Considerable delays, which created many difficulties, were not uncommon. Too long a delay in publication could mean that the reports on the "latest" advances or developments in the fields would be embarrassingly out of date. Often there were awkward situations when punctual contributors were being penalized by those who were less prompt. Delays were frustrating for Plum, since they upset all the planning and budgeting for printing, advertising, and promotion.

The following letter to overdue authors illustrates the problems inherent in multiauthored works. In this case there was a real danger that the annual review for the following year would be in print before the work in question was published. This would not only be most embarrassing but could seriously hurt sales as well.

Dear ——:

In my capacity as sponsoring editor of ——, I met this week with the volume editor, Dr. ——. As you know, all chapter authors agreed to submit their final manuscripts to the volume editor by September of last year. In truth, only some of the chapters were submitted at that time. However, the overwhelming majority of the chapters are now in the editor's hands, and I am sorry to have to write you as one of the very few overdue authors.

From the publisher's point of view, there is very little we can do in terms of production work until we have a complete manuscript. We are, of course, disappointed, for had we received the manuscript on schedule, the book would now be nearing publication.

More important, however, is the situation regarding your colleagues in the field, whose chapters have been in the hands of the editor for some time. They feel rather put upon, since their work is now lying dormant and going out of date as time passes.

Dr. —— has informed me that he will be required to present a report on the volume's progress to the membership of the association at the business meeting, during the annual convention. He wants to be able to report that all chapters are in his hands at that time.

As you know, other volumes, designed along similar lines, are planned for the future. In fact, the next one is now being organized. I would hope that we will not see this book preceded by the aforementioned work!

Dr. ———, your coauthors, and I expect that you will respond to this letter by the 30th of May, hopefully enclosing your chapter. At the very least, we ask for a realistic indication of a final submission date. Considering the amount of time we have lost, I feel that June 15th is not an unrealistic target for receipt of a final manuscript.

We look forward to hearing from you, and to a rapid solution to this problem.

Sincerely yours,

———

The Plum editors did not exert as much effort in "stroking and currying" authors as the Apple editors did. Nor were they as concerned with whether an author remained loyal and published all of his or her future work with Plum. Both the nature of the publishing program at Plum and the sheer size of its operations meant that author-publisher relations were less personal. Although individual authors were seldom personally catered to at Plum, the press was exceedingly diligent at maintaining good working relationships with their series and journal editors. Plum authors did, however, receive some special attention. At most publishing houses, many steps in the publishing process are delegated to free-lance outsiders; such services as copyediting, artwork and design, and even promotional work are entrusted to them. As we have seen from Apple Press examples, this can lead to problems for authors. At Plum Press, very little use was made of outsiders. In-house staff handled most of the steps in the production process. In particular, Plum was very capable of doing first-rate work with highly technical, heavily statistical manuscripts. Moreover, every book was promoted and marketed in the same fashion. There were no favorites or multitiered lists, which are common at other houses. Every book was promoted through journal ads and direct mailings; hence, although authors were treated with more distance and less affection, the product of their work was produced by Plum Press with considerable professionalism.

Summary

The editors at both Plum Press and Apple Press enjoyed considerable latitude in executing their work. This was particularly evident in the acquisition of manuscripts, but the editors also had a great deal of discretionary power in other parts of their jobs as well. They also had a substantial amount of influence over the activities of other departments. There is a considerable literature demonstrating that the higher one's rank in a hierarchy, the greater one's time advantages (Coser 1961; Merton 1957; Mintzberg 1973). Publishing represents a partial exception to this observation. While editors are not at the very top of publishing hierarchies, in their role as boundary-spanners they have considerable freedom of movement, lowered observability, and greater choice in the use of their time. In this regard, time can be viewed as a resource for social control (Schwartz 1975; Zerubavel 1979). Editors work on their "own" time, devoting their attention to the pursuit of their own interests. Other members of the publishing house do not have this freedom; they work according to the directives and desires of others. Moreover, their work pace is largely determined by the acquisition efforts of editors. Of course, editors usually devote a greater amount of their time on behalf of the firm, but they have considerable leeway about when and where to do so. As Merton (1957:76–77) has argued, lowered observability and greater choice in the use of time can be viewed as evidence of trust that the individual will live up to organizational values or goals without overt supervision.

Editors exhibited not only considerable freedom of movement within houses but a good deal of mobility across houses. David Jacobs' perceptive analysis (1981) of the relationship between individual performance and organizational success helps us to understand the underlying basis of this mobility; it also suggests that editorial freedom may depend on an editor's track record. Jacobs argues that there are three types of relationships between individual performance and organizational success: (1) an exemplary individual performance in some positions adds a significant increment to an organization's total performance; (2) an exemplary individual performance has little effect on the total performance of the organization; (3) an exemplary individual performance adds little to overall performance, but the occasional mistake will reduce the total performance of the organization by a significant amount. Editorial positions fit category one, for successful books can make a significant contribution to a firm's annual performance. In addition, editorial failures are not all that costly. Jacobs (1981:693) goes on to show that when poor performance is not very damaging and stellar performance has a big impact, firms will engage in a continuous search for new talent, and "lateral movements between such organizations should be common."

In the following chapter I examine in some detail the rationales offered by editors to account for their autonomy; I then go on to suggest some reasons why editorial discretion may be more apparent than real. In the present chapter I have illustrated how editorial duties are embedded in a network of personal relations that extend across houses and backward in time. In the next one I examine how these boundary-spanning ties influence the allocation of power within firms. I also introduce what I take to be an equally crucial observation: just as individual networks are embedded in personal career histories, so the structure of authority within organizations is embedded in social relations that extend backward in time, well beyond the individual tenures of particular editors, and outward in scope, in a manner that is far more dense than the associational contacts of any one editor.

4

DISCRETIONARY POWER AND UNOBTRUSIVE CONTROLS

At both Plum Press and Apple Press the senior editors worked under their own direction, with apparent immunity from supervision by others. If they needed to go on the road for a few days or spend the afternoon with an author, they did so, letting their secretary or the editor-in-chief—depending on how long they would be out of the office—know their intended whereabouts. Members of other departments had little voice in editorial decisions. Such freedom is largely limited to scholarly publishing. Trade-book editors are far more likely to discuss projects with members of other departments—most commonly, subsidiary-rights directors and the promotion and marketing staff. Whether such discussion takes place informally, in the hallways, or requires a formal presentation by an editor to an editorial board, composed of executives, differs from house to house. Trade houses vary as to who attends editorial meetings and whether an actual vote is taken. Moreover, editors may have enough influence to prevail in spite of general skepticism on the part of the others in attendance. Editors in textbook houses are even more likely than trade editors to be required to obtain formal approval for their projects from top executives in other departments. In addition, textbook editors spend a great deal of time in meetings, coordinating the production of their books with the staff members of other departments. Finally, in both trade and text houses the approval rate for projects proposed by editors is considerably lower than the 99 percent enjoyed by editors at Apple and Plum.

In this chapter I analyze, and provide illustrations of, the discretionary power that is apparently enjoyed by the editors at Apple and Plum. There are several strong theoretical traditions that help to account for editorial autonomy. Nevertheless, it is important to realize, as Weick (1969:40) does, that the basic raw materials with which many organizations operate are ambiguous, uncertain, and equivocal bits of information. A focus on individual choices is much more likely to capture this uncertainty, for it is only when we look at a population of choices made over time that we recognize that most organizational activities are directed at establishing a tolerable level of certainty. The answer obtained thus depends on the question that is posed; the focus—on individual decisions or on a population of decisions—will shape the reality that is observed. The format of this chapter reflects my learning curve about editorial choices. At first I was struck by the amount of apparent freedom that editors had. I was also impressed by the strong craft elements that typify editorial work. It was only after many months of fieldwork that I began to ask, Where do decision rules and performance programs come from? The answer to that question is that editorial work is subject to a number of powerful, if unobtrusive, controls.

The Case for Editorial Autonomy

The editors at Apple and Plum made frequent reference to the autonomous nature of their work, claiming that they knew their fields best and that it would be both impractical and unprofitable for their supervisors to dictate how they should go about doing their jobs. The editors were subject to little, if any, formal evaluation, and no attempts were made to hold them accountable for each book they signed. Editors at both houses felt that they worked best without guidance. As one Apple Press editor put it:

I work under my own direction. Sure I have disagreements
with the editor-in-chief, but rarely is it over whether to do a
book or not; instead, it's a question about pricing or sales
potential. We don't have editorial meetings here. The editors
are left on their own. No one here knows my fields better than
I do. It stands to reason, then, that I should be the one to
decide which books to publish.

Another Apple editor strongly concurred that editors are
best left to their own devices and that good editors must be
permitted flexibility:

As you know, I feel that the individual editor has much more
personal clout than is generally believed, even by most editors. There are editors who are in high favor (usually this
depends on their track record, but it sometimes applies to new
employees who come from the right backgrounds, have the
right connections, or for other reasons are able to impress
people); they have very little trouble getting approval of
anything they submit, whereas editors lower in the pecking
order may be required to submit more documentation, pare
down their royalty proposals, etc., in order to get the go-
ahead.

There's also an element of personal salesmanship involved.
In almost every house that I've worked for, the top brass
never sees the manuscript or proposal on which the editor's
initial decision is based but instead depends on the editor's
highly selective presentation of the gist of the book and often
on a highly selective assortment of reviews. Sometimes an
editor gets a proposal or a manuscript that is not really up to
snuff but feels pretty certain that the author can pull off a good
book, with lots of help, and in essence the editor writes a
proposal describing the book he or she would *like* to have. I'm
well aware that this is a kind of cheating. I feel guilty, and
anxious, about it, but I've done it.

The editor-in-chief at Apple felt that his senior editors
"didn't need telling how to do their jobs." Moreover, he
certainly expected to be the judge of what he himself should
be doing. As for the young assistant editor, he said: "This is
her first editorial job, so naturally she needs help. But if she'd

go out there and start lining up authors on her own, I'd be overjoyed."

Members of the noneditorial staff of Apple Press commented about how "editors run the show" and that the other departments had little influence over what books were signed. The head of the production department grumbled, "The usual hardcover print run is around 2,500 copies. Even when they do a hot item, then it's only 10,000. I don't know why they do such small stuff. But I don't have any say. It's all up to the editors. Me, I just work here." And the marketing director at Apple Press remarked, "An editor is interested in how a book sells over the long haul. They may also be satisfied if a book wins a prize or gets good reviews even if it doesn't sell well. I don't have that luxury. I'm evaluated on a more short term basis—the amount of annual sales." On another occasion when I spoke with the marketing director about how she determined which books have good sales potential, she responded:

> Presumably they wouldn't have been signed up if they wouldn't sell, although sometimes I look at a book and I'm not at all sure why it was signed. But, once I have them, it's my job to sell them. I certainly have no voice in whether or not they are signed . . . I see the proposal, which has the suggested price of a book, but I have no say as to what the books will cost. If books aren't selling well, it isn't up to me to suggest that they shouldn't have been published or that they be revised or updated. That's up to the editors.

The president of Apple Press, echoing these comments of the marketing director, noted that:

> A formal profit-and-loss statement is not prepared for each book. The editors do have access to all the pertinent records, but I guess they are too busy to keep tabs on the past. Editors will tell you it's their job to sign books, not sell them. They are oriented toward the future, and sales records serve only to tie them to the past.

At Plum Press, too, the editors had a great deal of discretion in the execution of their duties. Not only did they make the decisions as to which books to sign, with very little input from other members of the house, but most of the services performed by other departments required the final approval of the sponsoring editor. The editor-in-chief described the responsibilities of Plum editors the following way:

> The sponsoring editor has the broadest, most general responsibility for each book, from the time it is signed to the time it is declared out of print. To a very unusual degree, our editors work with other departments. Almost everything done by other departments, from ad copy to the jacket design, *has* to be approved by the book's sponsoring editor.

The social sciences editor at Plum alluded to the free rein his job afforded him in the following comment: "As for the company's editorial committee—I know what they get their jollies on. I've had only one contract rejected since I have been here, and it was a translation. Often I commit the company to a contract before the editorial committee has approved the idea." The behavioral sciences editor maintained, "There's no quota or understanding as to the minimum or maximum number of titles an editor must sign. I honestly couldn't tell you how many books I signed last year. Nobody tells us, 'Thou must produce.' I work on my own, doing what I think is necessary."

I asked the director of the sales department what input his department contributed to the editorial process, and he replied:

> Very, very little . . . and what little there is really comes after a book is signed. Oh, sure, we're asked to check every proposal; but we don't give comments unless we think a particular project is very badly conceived . . . like, if it's an immunology book projected for 3,000 sales, and the professional association has only 700 members . . . then we would wonder where the audience is coming from. But it remains entirely up to editorial to decide what is or is not signed. We can't even give any specific figures about promotion costs until we see the actual book, and by then the contract has long been signed.

Having observed that sales had no influence on the decision to publish, I still assumed that editors would, at the very least, receive feedback from sales regarding the performance of books that had already been published. The vice-president of sales pointed out that this was rarely the case:

> Well, there are weekly and monthly stock-status reports, but very few editors pay any attention to them. Most [editors] are uninterested in checking the sales records, probably because they are sure of what they publish. The only exception is —––––– [the social sciences editor], and that's because (1) his publishing program is the youngest and (2) his books have the greatest potential to take off and reach larger markets. I'm well aware that, in trade and text houses, sales departments have much more influence. Here the power lies in editorial . . . I used to be an editorial vice-president before I moved up here . . . it's an unusual career pattern, I know . . . but, given my background, I approve of our setup.

I followed up on the comments by members of the sales staff in a later conversation with the social sciences editor:

> Q: The head of sales tells me that you keep a closer eye on the sales of your books than the other editors. He claims that you check on your books while none of the other editors do. He seemed to appreciate your concern. Could you tell me why you are more interested?
>
> A: Sure. It's because my publishing program is new. I'm trying to get an idea how it's doing. Also, I anticipate more sales of my books than do others, and I push for lower prices; that means I'm cutting it closer, and the books have to sell more to make it.
>
> Q: What happens when they don't?
>
> A: Nothing. Oh, on occasion the editor-in-chief might stop by and say, "That book was a bomb. Well, how come?" I'll say, "I'll look into it," and that's that. He usually forgets to check back. Or I might say, "I blew that one. It doesn't look as if that subfield is a growth area."
>
> Q: So you don't lose any sleep over it?
>
> A: Oh, no; it's part of the job.

In discussions with editors at both houses I suggested that, despite their seeming autonomy within the firm, they ulti-mately were forced to rely on outside reviewers for the final judgment of a manuscript. Every editor disagreed, many pointing out that not all books receive an outside review. Moreover, one editor compared the use of reviewers' reports to the way film companies make use of negative reviews by well-known film critics. "Few reviews are ever totally negative, so it's always possible to excerpt a few favorable lines if you really want to do the book."

The psychology editor at Plum Press noted that, if a manuscript comes in under contract (that is, it has already been signed on the basis of a proposal or a sample chapter), he never seeks an outside review. As he said, "We already own the book, so why spend money on a review?" At Apple Press, on the other hand, the editor-in-chief frequently sent manuscripts out for review even if they were already under contract. "It doesn't have anything to do with the decision to publish," he said; "we've already bought the manuscript. But I want to find out what we've got on our hands. The reviewer can tell us that and maybe provide suggestions for improvement." Another editor said, "I use outside reviewers for questionable books; for manuscripts that I lack the qualifications to evaluate properly; for books that I like, but I'm unsure of the market; and when I want to build support for signing a book that I really like and I don't want my proposal questioned."

Control over Uncertain Aspects of the Work Process

One explanation of why editors have so much discretion would stress that their power is a structural phenomenon. Because their role spans organizational boundaries and attempts to deal with an uncertain environment, editors are in a strategic position. A report to the Board of Governors of Yale University Press by the university's Ad Hoc Committee on What to Publish begins with this statement: "One of the greatest joys and griefs associated with publishing springs from an inability to predict with precision the success or failure of a book" (Kerr 1974:212). In short, editors work in a situation where the origin of conventions about what is or is not commercially feasible remains something of a mystery.

Given the uncertainty about the acquisition of manuscripts, editors are permitted considerable leeway. Their work requires flexibility.

What do we mean by uncertainty? Decision theorists such as Knight (1921) and Luce and Raiffa (1957) have defined as uncertain those situations where the probable outcome of events is unknown. Lawrence and Lorsch (1967:27) argue that uncertainty consists of three components: (1) a lack of clarity of information, (2) a long time period before definitive feedback can be obtained, and (3) ambiguity concerning casual relationships. More generally, uncertainty can result when (1) the flow of resources to an organization is unpredictable, (2) the technology utilized to transform the resources is complex or nonroutine, and (3) the organizational field in which a firm competes is dynamic, diverse, or hostile.

External environments that change in ways that are difficult to analyze or predict create problems for organizations for which there are no easy and ready solutions (Thompson 1967). Perrow (1967) has illustrated the various ways in which a complex and changing environment poses special problems for organizational personnel: the exceptions to organizational routine are many; established procedures for problem-solving cannot be developed; and "no formal search is undertaken, but instead one draws upon the residue of unanalyzed experience or intuition, or relies upon chance and guesswork." The greater the variability of the "raw materials" that arrive as inputs from the environment, the greater is the need for adaptiveness and worker autonomy. Thus, an appropriate organizational design depends on matching internal structure to the requirements of an organization's environment.

Editors maintain that their jobs cannot be standardized because each case with which they deal is unique. Many researchers, in particular Hage and Aiken (1967) and Pugh and his associates (1968), have shown that, in organizations where work is repetitive, work roles can be formalized. Rules, procedures, instructions, and communications are specified, and employees are clear as to what is expected of them. In highly formalized situations, work behavior is very routine, and there are few options as to how a job can be carried out. On the other hand, where work is nonroutine and variable, organizational roles are not formalized, and employees are permitted considerable autonomy in dealing with the problems they encounter.

The literature is replete with studies that illustrate the thesis that organizations operating in uncertain environments are more successful if they adopt flexible and adaptive internal structures rather than more formal, bureaucratic arrangements (see, e.g., Burns and Stalker 1961; Lawrence and Lorsch 1967; Duncan 1972; Lorsch and Morse 1974). Thompson and Tuden (1959) contend that universalistic standards are likely to be used in circumstances where there is agreement on the connection between actions and results. However, in the face of uncertainty, it becomes far more likely that particularistic criteria will be used, simply because no criteria are universally accepted. This permits the employee to determine which criteria he or she deems relevant. Peterson and Berger (1971) argue in similar vein when they show that in cultural organizations, where there is widespread uncertainty over the precise ingredients of a successful product, administrators must rely on the experienced judgments of their employees. Close supervision in the product sector is impeded by ignorance of the relations between cause and effect.

Thompson (1967) has maintained that organizations seek to cope with uncertainty by allowing the segment of the organization that directly interacts with the turbulent elements of the environment to be loosely organized, so that it can adapt to the continuous changes in the market. The other parts of the organization, which make up the technical core, are thus segregated, or "buffered," from the environment and can be organized in a more routine, hierarchical manner. From Thompson's perspective, editorial autonomy is an efficient structural arrangement. The assumption is made that editors have been hired because they are fluent and skilled in their tasks. They know their work and how to go about it.

Hickson and his associates, in their study of intergroup

power within organizations (1971), maintain that the distribution of power within organizations is related to (1) a subunit's ability to cope with situational uncertainties and (2) the extent to which those who perform these activities are replaceable. Salancik and Pfeffer (1974) found that departmental power at the University of Illinois was best predicted by the amount of outside grant and contract money a department brought in; the power of a department was a function of the amount of important resources it controlled. More generally, Pfeffer and Salancik (1978) argue that the differential ability of different sections of an organization to deal with environmental contingencies determines the internal arrangement of power within an organization.

From a resource-dependence perspective, the autonomy of editors is derived from their control over the most uncertain aspect of the publishing process: the acquisition of commercially and critically successful "products." Power in organizations is related to the ability to solve critical uncertainties (Crozier 1964; Hickson et al. 1971; Pfeffer and Salancik 1978). Thus it is no surprise that other departments in scholarly and monograph houses are in a dependent position vis-à-vis editors, for it is the editors who have the skills that are necessary to procure the products the others in the house need in order to perform their jobs.

Craft and Occupational Control

The concept of occupational control refers to "the collective capability of members of an occupation to preserve unique authority in the definition, conduct, and evaluation of their work" (Child and Fulk 1982:155). My conversations with the editors at Apple and Plum, quoted at the beginning of this chapter, show that they had this capability. Child and Fulk (1982) go on to argue that occupational control includes the capacity to "determine the conditions of entry to and exit from the practice" of an occupation. Such control is exercised by only a handful of professions, such as medicine and law, that are able to restrict access to the profession's knowledge base. Both law and medicine provide services based on the authority of expertise—on keeping their professional knowledge at arm's length from their clients. This practice differs both from "people-working" professionals, who share their knowledge with clients, and from other professionals, such as accountants, whose work activities are directed toward serving the goals of the administration of the organization that employs them.

Editors generally do not possess a monopoly of access to the knowledge that is needed to perform their tasks. In publishing, the management of the firm controls the process of hiring and firing. Career and income progression for editors requires meeting the general goals established by management. An important distinction that is relevant to the question of occupational versus organizational control is made by Jamous and Peloille (1970). They describe two types of occupational knowledge and draw a distinction between "technicality" and "indetermination." Technicality refers to a rationalized, systematized, and hence transferable body of occupational knowledge; indetermination refers to the tacit, esoteric elements of occupational knowledge that defy rules and rationalization and are possessed by individual practitioners. It is over this special, personal, and indeterminate knowledge about writers and networks that editors attempt to maintain exclusive control.

There is much disagreement over who or what is "professional."[1] The established professions, such as law, medicine, engineering, architecture, and accounting, are undergoing a process of routinization of their professional knowledge and are increasingly subject to outside definition (Oppenheimer 1973). Computer technology serves to hasten the codification of professional knowledge and has the potential for permitting outsiders to carry out some of the tasks formerly reserved for members of the profession (Haug 1977). In addition, Scott (1965) has shown that many professionals work in "heteronomous organizations"—organizations over which they do not exercise strategic control and within which they are constrained by an administrative framework. At the same time, many occupations are lobbying for professional status. Despite the diminution of the term "professional" through the decline in the power of the traditional professions and through the success of practitioners of what were once regarded as nonprofessional work activities in having their professional aspirations legitimated by the state (DiMaggio and Powell 1983), editors cannot, by most standards, be considered professionals. Even in comparison to practitioners in the somewhat related fields of journalism and library science, editors receive far less systematic training and preparation for their eventual work.[2]

The Association of American Publishers (AAP), concerned over the lack of available training for careers in publishing, has organized a committee to develop educational standards and criteria for such careers and to establish reasonably uniform descriptions of the various jobs in the industry.[3] In the committee's report, issued in 1977, the president of the AAP, Townsend Hoopes, is quoted as saying, "If we are honest, we will admit that publishing is only beginning to address the question of whether it constitutes a body of attitudes and practices sufficiently tangible and delimited to be defined in a coherent curriculum" (AAP Education for Publishing Committee 1977:6).

I asked the two senior editors at Apple Press whether they regarded themselves as professionals. Their comments are illuminating. One of them said:

> No, I guess I am a practitioner of a certain skill. My job doesn't require an advanced degree. Certain things I do are the same every day. My job is to sign up books and turn them over to production. That's my job description. I don't do original research—nothing far-reaching, anyway. I am supposed to estimate trends. I read scholarly journals, but I read them first for publishing ideas and second for my own knowledge.
>
> I'm more of a custodian. There are ideas that deserve to be made public, and I help to do that. My primary self-interest, of course, is to publish good books. I don't see myself as a censor. I am a selector . . . I look at numerous ideas that

people offer and choose certain ones because I think they are important and will sell. I'm not interested in influencing our foreign or domestic policy. I have no illusions about leaving a legacy. Even books that are important contributions won't change the world.

The other editor said:

I'm very evasive about that term . . . anyway I'm not [a professional]. I'm a skilled worker, plying my trade. Education is irrelevant to a career in publishing. What is essential is social and professional contacts, experience, and gut smarts. The ability to work with people and having worked in the same area for a number of years also help. You have got to know whom to ask for help. You must understand what the author is trying to say and help him or her to say it better. The mistake many young people in publishing make is to try to change what the author is saying.

Many editors pride themselves on their sense of "smell"— their flair for finding just the right book. They contend that the traits of a good editor—judgment, expertise, intuition, and character—cannot be taught. Editors argued that success is a combination of luck, hard work, and timing. It was most difficult to get editors to be precise about how they reach decisions. One editor said, "You have to be a reader of the culture. If it's something you like and you think it is a good book, you supply the reason to publish it. If it's something you don't necessarily like and you reject it, then you are reading the culture."

Editing can best be viewed as a skilled craft. Becker (1978:864–65) states that a "craft consists of a body of knowledge and skill which can be used to produce useful objects, or . . . from a slightly different point of view, it consists of the ability to perform in a useful way." Editorial skills are developed through a process of technical socialization, characterized by an apprenticeship system. Editors learn on the job, beginning as either editorial assistants, promotional assistants, sales representatives, or secretaries. Learning to be an editor is a gradual process. As one first-rate editor commented, "You can learn all the technical stuff in six months; the rest takes a lifetime." Editors move through a series of positions, from assistant to associate to senior editor. If they attain senior-editor status, they are at the top of the editorial job ladder and their income is maximized. The only career alternatives for senior editors are in administration, as editors-in-chief or editorial directors, or in top management, where the acquisition of manuscripts is no longer the primary part of the job.[4]

Both Stinchcombe (1959) and Hall (1975:188–201) have shown that skilled craftsmen and professionals exhibit a number of similar characteristics. They are alike in that both have a strong sense of autonomy. They differ in that professionals lay claim to possession of a body of theoretical knowledge, while the skilled craft workers claim mastery of techniques, practical knowledge, and creative intuition. Due to their lack of powerful professional associations, the crafts have much less status the professions. Although both exert some occupational control over recruitment, the professions are much more powerful in this regard.

Craft occupations are characterized by occupational communities with extensive social interaction and informal ties. Indeed, for many editors, editing is much more than a job; it is a way of life. Most editors' jobs spill over into their private lives. Their circle of personal friends often consists of other publishing people and authors. As one scholarly editor commented, "Many of my authors and reviewers can also be considered personal friends, with easy and informal access to me and I to them." I often observed editors doing special favors for their authors and friends (e.g., editing an encyclopedia article for a friend, informally acting as an agent for an author's manuscript, advising authors about points in their contracts, and editing a friend's manuscript that was being published by another house).

There are strong informal ties and interaction between people in different scholarly houses. Socializing and collegiality are important; a good reputation enhances one's chances for occupational mobility. Publishing is characterized by an extremely high rate of turnover. Lateral movement from house to house is frequent, and manuscripts are often referred through networks that link houses through previous employment ties.[5] The standard editorial career ladder permits only limited mobility; this, along with the craft features discussed above, encourages turnover. Turnover and promotion chances are inextricably linked: turnover is more likely when upward mobility and the challenges associated with it are not available. If a senior editor does not wish to move into a managerial position, taking a job in another house is the only option open. As the psychology editor at Apple Press reflected, when offered a job by a competing house, "Actually I wouldn't want to advance; I couldn't stand being in a management position. Keeping track of how many paper clips are used is not for me. But another house would mean new faces, new vistas." Another aspect of editorial work that encourages turnover is that many scholarly editors find it challenging to start a publishing program from the ground floor or to revitalize a list that has seen better days. But once a list is established and the normal routine of exploiting existing contacts sets in, much of the excitement vanishes, and an editor may decide it is time to move on.[6] And even though editors may have substantial discretion in terms of how they acquire manuscripts, every editor I've spoken with knows that the selection of repeated "failures" is grounds for dismissal. There are no tenured appointments in publishing.[7]

In scholarly and monograph publishing, editors are solitary workers. That is to say, while an editor may have personal ties to other editors at their press, their in-house colleagues work in different disciplines. It is rare for a house to employ two editors to work in the same area. This kind of specialization is also the rule in textbook publishing, but it is not found in trade houses, where editors handle books on a wide variety of subjects. At scholarly, monograph, and textbook houses, as well as university presses, editors find that it is editors in competing houses, working in the same field, who share their interests, problems, and concerns. As the editors at both Apple and Plum pointed out, they are more likely to know and be interested in what an editor with the same specialty in a competing house is involved in than in what their own editorial colleagues are up to. An editor's reference group is thus scattered across many publishing houses rather than within his or her own house. Like university faculty members who work in different departments and have little contact with each other, editors in nontrade publishing houses work in different disciplines and engage in little in-house collaboration. An editor's key ties are extraorganizational: they are to authors, to reviewers, to free-lancers they regularly work with, and to editors in other houses who work in similar fields.

Informal interaction between editors in different houses is further promoted by the fact that, although most individuals in publishing have at least a college degree and many scholarly editors have advanced degrees, they are paid comparatively low salaries. Starting annual salaries in publishing are often under $10,000. Senior editors in scholarly and monograph houses, with many years of experience, seldom earn more than $30,000 a year.[8] In 1975, *Publishers Weekly* reported the results of a nineteen-industry survey which showed that executives at publishing houses received the lowest salaries of all the industries in the sample. Positive evaluation of one's work by others in the industry helps to compensate somewhat for the lack of financial remuneration.

The changes described in chapter 1 have left their mark on trade and textbook publishing (see also Powell 1982b), but changes in corporate ownership and editorial policies have not had a comparable effect on scholarly publishing. The scholarly sector has had to cope with inflation, declining library budgets, and many of the same general problems currently facing higher education, but pressures from top management to change the decision process at scholarly houses are not common. In this sector of the industry, editors still appear to have more discretion than their counterparts elsewhere. Because scholarly publishing is highly specialized and lacks mass appeal, a scholarly house does not need an expensive publicity, marketing, or subsidiary-rights staff. Much of the information that is systematically collected by these departments in trade and text houses is informally gathered by scholarly editors. As one editor explained, "One of the reasons scholarly editors tend to get mystical when asked how they make their decisions is that they don't really think about, much less quantify, what goes into seat-of-the-pants judgment." Another scholarly editor noted that "the craft of editing is a combination of many things—experience, including many discussions with colleagues in other houses and academics in your network, awareness of the histories of other books, and gut feelings. We don't have time to be systematic about these things, but they figure into any decision."

Watson (1980:147) has argued that "the history of Western occupations has been very much one of the rise and fall of the degree of occupational self-control maintained by various groups." Scholarly editors are clearly aware of the discretion they possess, and they are naturally reluctant to lose it. They are quick to resist any effort to impose on them an administrative framework for the conduct and evaluation of their duties. It is to an editor's personal and occupational self-interest to assert that choosing books is a talent not subject to market analysis. The comments of editors that the skills required to be a good editor cannot be taught reflect an effort to maintain possession of the knowledge required to do their jobs. Control over such knowledge can provide scholarly editors with an enduring basis for the maintenance of their discretionary power.

The Power of Informal Controls

As I spent more time at Apple and Plum, I came to question the amount of discretion that editors actually exercised. A number of factors were responsible for this skepticism.[9] First, the editors had a strong sense of priorities. They knew which authors should receive prompt service and which ones could be put off without penalty. Second, editors never proposed publishing certain kinds of atypical books, such as a 2,000-page manuscript, a novel written by a social scientist, or a

book replete with photographs. There clearly were boundaries around what was permissible. Third, I found it hard to
reconcile high editorial turnover with the view that editors
were the dominant group within the firm. Bluedorn
(1982:108–9) points out that, in organizations where turnover
is variable among units, the departments with less turnover
should reap some advantages, in terms of influence, from
their greater insight into the operation of the firm. I began to
wonder how editors could understand and manipulate the
internal decision process within publishing houses if they
frequently moved from house to house. Finally, I personally
became very adept at predicting which manuscripts would be
accepted and which ones would be rejected. The choice process was no longer mysterious to me. I had learned that
editorial decision-making is guided by a number of informal
control processes. In one sense, a statement that decisions are
guided by conventions or informal premises is almost a
sociological truism. The key question is where such conventions come from; as the philosopher Croce (1968:31) puts it,
"But if there are to be conventions, something must exist
which is no convention but is itself the author of convention."
In the remainder of this chapter I analyze the genesis, persis-
tence, and operation of unobtrusive control processes.

Direct bureaucratic controls are commonly used at the
lower levels of an organization, but such obtrusive controls do
not work well with a highly educated or professionally trained
staff. (Indeed, recent work suggests that bureaucratic controls are counterproductive *whenever* they are used [Hack-
man and Oldham 1980].) Professionals and other highly
skilled workers object to rules and tight control. Moreover,
organizations stifle innovation when they attempt to direct all
aspects of work behavior (Kanter 1983). Formal controls also
require constant surveillance and monitoring, and neither is
feasible in organizations where tasks are nonroutine. Even
professional employees, however, do not like complete freedom of choice. An endless range of choices can lead to chaos
and confusion. An effective way for an organization to exercise control is to channel and shape behavior unobtrusively.

A number of organization theorists suggest that the predominant form of control in many modern organizations has shifted from formal, obtrusive supervision to a process that relies on the internalization of organizational values and preferences (Edwards 1979; Perrow 1976; Ouchi 1980; Williamson 1975). This change is a profound one, yet there is little consensus on what has caused it. Williamson (1975) argues that the creation of internal labor markets and reward systems is more efficient than contracting through market mechanisms. Ouchi (1980) contends that goal congruence, achieved through socialization, affords efficiency advantages because of the reduced need for supervision. For theorists in the transaction cost tradition, the problem is to discover how work can best be organized under conditions of idiosyncratic or firm-specific knowledge. Edwards (1979) and Perrow (1976) see this change less benignly; they suggest that a different problem is being solved: unobtrusive controls represent a sophisticated means of maintaining control over the labor force. Such a shift makes the exercise of arbitrary power less necessary; unobtrusive controls are viewed as more legitimate and tolerable.

When behavioral boundaries are well defined, employees can be permitted a good deal of latitude. They will voluntarily restrict their range of alternative behaviors, relieving superiors of the need to process routine information and make minor decisions. Decision-making authority can be delegated to the persons most immediately involved, who thereby learn from the experience and develop special skills. Because such delegation requires a particular model of authority, organizations rely on inconspicuous controls and effective socialization so that employees will perform in a manner that is not injurious to the organization.

According to Herbert Simon (1957), the superior can structure the perceptions of subordinates so that the latter see things in the manner the superior wants them to be seen. Such a model fits well with recent ethnographic research that shows that managers give few direct orders; instead, they set priorities and channel behavior (Mintzberg 1973; Peters 1978).

Simon has argued that the decision-making process can be deliberately modified. He states (1957:79): "Individual choice takes place in an environment of 'givens'—premises that are accepted by the subject as bases for his choice; and behavior is adaptive only within the limits set by these 'givens.'" He then goes on to show that, once attention and behavior are initiated in a particular direction, they tend to continue in the same direction for a considerable period of time because psychological "sunk costs" limit the range of future options. Williamson (1975:121) also notes the tendency for organizational activities to persist, regardless of their utility. These sunk costs "insulate existing projects from displacement by alternatives which, were the program not already in place, might otherwise be preferred."

Crucial to Simon's model of authority is the distinction between the premises that underlie decisions and the decisions themselves. Simon argues that, in all choice situations, attention is paid to only a fraction of the possible stimuli, meanings, and responses. Individuals are capable of coping with uncertainty only because they have acquired premises that interpret the meanings of various stimuli and the possible responses to them. When premises are controlled and shaped by others, the range of behavior is more predictable. Premises provide order in uncertain situations and allow employees to feel independent. Perrow (1976) has argued that, as long as an organization can control the premises that are used to make choices among alternatives, it can leave the actual choices up to subordinates. In other words, when policy is centralized, its execution can be decentralized. Mechanic (1962) recognized this when he stated that "an effective organization can control its participants in such a way as to make it hardly perceivable that it exercises the control that it does." One of the principal means of establishing organizational premises is through socialization.

Most adult socialization entails little attempt to change closely held values or to influence basic motivations. Instead, it involves the learning of new role expectations and performances as newcomers try to meet the demands of significant others. Indeed, it can be argued that most occupants of middle- and upper-class work roles have sufficiently internalized, both cognitively and effectively, the norms of appropriate behavior so that they are likely to perform competently, or at least try to do so, when placed in appropriate work settings. One reason for this is, as Inkeles (1969:629) has observed, that each organization is a "consumer" of the products of prior socialization by other organizations. Perrow (1974) recognizes this when he argues that professionals are the ultimate eunuchs: because of their extensive socialization, they can be turned loose in an organization and relied on to properly discipline themselves.[10]

Socialization theory argues that "scripts" are laid down for an individual by the groups to which he or she belongs. Both the person's social self and the behavior of others will influence how he or she will act out the script, but the script determines most of the appropriate behavior. This argument holds up well for occupations in which there is formal schooling or training, extensive anticipatory socialization, or processes of mortification or conversion.[11] In publishing, the "scripts" provided for new employees are largely blank. They are filled in on the job, through trial and error and through assimilation. Much of what is learned is not explicitly taught but is derived, rather, from casual and unscheduled contacts. New employees must learn to "sink or swim" on their own. This type of socialization is informal and often unexamined. Yet it must be recognized that it can be costly: failures in apprenticeships or new senior appointments are extremely expensive to the organization.

Organizational socialization refers to the manner in which the experiences of people learning the ropes in a new position are structured for them by other members of the organization (Van Maanen 1978). Socialization strategies may be intentional or unconscious. As Van Maanen (1978) has shown, different forms of organizational socialization produce remarkably divergent results. Socialization processes are most overt when employees first join an organization or when they are promoted or demoted; however, the process of socialization goes on continuously.

How are editors socialized into the mores of a publishing house? The following entries from my field notes illustrate one unobtrusive, yet effective, method. One day, not long after she had been hired, I found the sociology editor going through a stack of a dozen or so previously published books. I asked her what she was doing. She responded,

> These are books that the president asked me to look at. He's exceptionally clever, always looking for old areas that can continue to be mined. This is exceptionally rare in publishing; most houses couldn't care less about books they published ten years ago. He wants me to look these books over to see if any of them could be revised or brought out in a new edition or if the author has continued this line of research. It's a good idea for using old information in new ways. There are two or three here that look promising. I'll contact some friends and ask them to look them over and tell me if they think a revision is in order and what new material should be added.

I later spoke with the president of Apple Press and mentioned that one of his editors felt he was very adept at exploiting the past. I asked if he did this frequently. Did he regularly pore over sales data from previous years or study the performance of particular titles? He responded:

> Oh, no, that isn't an important part of my job at all. You see, [the sociology editor] is new here and unfamiliar with our backlist. This was just a way to help her become acquainted . . . to let her learn on her own the type of books we do around here. It shows her the importance we attach to our backlist. For us, many of our bestsellers are backlist titles. We publish with a conscious notion that every book should become part of a backlist. I just thought that would be a good way for her to become comfortable with our image of the type of books we do.

The result of the editor's research was that two books were brought out in new editions, and one author was encouraged to update and expand an earlier volume.

A similar example can be gleaned from an interview with a woman who had recently been hired as a senior editor at a scholarly house that was one of Apple Press's principal competitors. I inquired how she had learned to make an assessment of what the audience was for a particular book. She responded:

> Mostly by seeing what the books that were being published did. And when I got here, I had no authors of my own and no books that I had commissioned. And so, as frequently happens—certainly in a small house like this—I became a house editor. I was given manuscripts to handle that had already been signed. So that, very quickly, I had books that were my books—book that I was looking after—and I got a lot of experience seeing what happened to them—or didn't happen to them. Also, it was mostly from sitting in on meetings and listening to the conversation . . . Let's see, if you have to actually describe the learning process, it's very hard to do . . . Now, you know, we are a very big backlist house. So we often have reprint meetings. Sometimes the meetings are once a week, sometimes every two weeks. All the editors are there . . . and the business manager and her assistant. She says, "We are getting low on inventory on this book and that book." And of course the essence of good backlist publishing is to have just the right amount . . . never to run out but never to be overstocked. That's why we do this frequently; it's a sort of fine tuning process. So, by sitting in on those meetings, by hearing about whether we should reprint and how many, what the book did last year, what we expect it to do now . . . all this dealing with the old books gave me a much better sense of how to go about my work.[12]

These examples illustrate how simple reinforcement and reassurance can lead to patterns of recurrent behavior on the part of editors. An editor who learns which of his or her behaviors is rewarded in certain situations will repeat those behaviors in situations that are perceived to be similar. Cognitive social learning theory (Mischel 1973; Bandura 1977) suggests that an individual learns behavior-outcome expectancies, or contingency rules, that lead him or her to generate the response pattern perceived as most likely to obtain the outcome that is subjectively most valuable for a particular situation. Behavior is a function of previous organizational experience: choices that were approved or rewarded tend to be repeated, while efforts that did not bear fruit are replaced in favor of more approved behavior.

Previous educational and occupational experiences are also important elements in the socialization process. Many occupational career ladders are so closely guarded, both at the entry level and throughout the career progression, that individuals who make it to the top are virtually indistinguishable. For example, March and March (1977) found that individuals who attained the position of school superintendent in Wisconsin were so alike in background and orientation as to make further career advancement random and unpredictable. They attributed this randomness to the existence of a filtering process, common to all Wisconsin school systems, that ensured a high degree of similarity among acting superintendents. Barnard (1938) and Kanter (1977) both describe the same kind of filtering of aspirants to top management positions in American corporations; Kelsell (1955) notes the homogeneity of entrants into the higher civil service in Great Britain; and Hirsch and Whisler (1982) contend that there is very little variation among the directors of the boards of the Fortune 500 companies. DiMaggio and Powell (1983) argue that to the extent that key staff members of an organization are drawn from the same universities and filtered by a common set of attributes, they will tend to view problems in a similar fashion, see the same policies, procedures, and structures as normatively sanctioned and legitimated, and approach problems and decisions in much the same way. Filtering may even be more personal and subtle. Driscoll (1980) maintains that almost all new hires in business are made by informal means—word of mouth, personal contacts, and special school-employer relationships built up over time (see also Granovetter 1974; Lin et al. 1981).

Organizational vocabularies are another means of premise-setting. Organizational "lexicons" (Cicourel 1970) are important in directing attention to types of behavior and attitudes that are regarded as appropriate. C. Wright Mills (1963:433) recognized that "a vocabulary is not merely a string of words; immanent within it are social textures—institutional and political coordinates. Back of a vocabulary lie sets of collective action." Perrow (1976:14) suggests that there are even more subtle symbols: "a superior may simply give signals, such as frowns, impatience, blue-pencilling memos or highlighting words and repeating them, to show what distinctions are no longer important and which are." In this manner, employees learn that certain things are simply not done, while other behavior is considered normal and is taken for granted. Individuals in an organization are also socialized into common expectations about their personal behavior, appropriate style of dress, and standard methods of speaking, joking, or addressing others (Ouchi 1980). Peters (1978) has suggested that there are numerous "mundane tools" that managers use to influence their organizations. He views managers as transmitters of signals, and he notes that signals take on meaning as they are reiterated. Frequent and consistent positive reinforcement is a primary shaper of expectations. Employees are also attentive to what kinds of questions managers ask of them. Through various mechanisms—agenda management, the interpretation of an organization's history, modeling behavior—managers provide a sense of direction that permits latitude for employee discretion.[13] Pfeffer (1981) argues that the most important managerial function is to interpret organizational action for participants so that they will develop a shared system of meaning.

I observed the hiring and socialization of a new editor at Apple Press. In her first weeks on the job, she was terribly conscious that the customs there were very different from ones she had known at the press where she had formerly been employed. She worried that she would not be permitted to work closely with authors. None of the other editors did careful line-by-line editing. She found the company to be bureaucratic and its people blunt and gruff. She felt that there were forms to fill out for everything. She said she just knew "that the red tape would be incredible." She complained that editors had to do all the computing of the costs of their books. Within a short while, however, she fitted in very nicely. She learned that, although other editors did not edit manuscripts, they labored long and hard to satisfy the whims of their authors. She found that her colleagues' bluntness was their style of humor and openness. The forms and computations that she had feared turned out to be routine and easy to do with a pocket calculator.

Caplow (1964:171–72) has observed that "even a small organization has an intricate complex of ideals and ideologies, of norms and standards, of beliefs and prejudices, and of expectations and myths." The force of tradition and the constraints imposed by social structure do not control so much as they enforce limits. They restrict the range of options and lead to a commitment to doing things in a certain way. Naturally, organizations differ in the amount of their commitment to the past. Some become superstitious, believing that what worked for them before will be successful in the future. Most constraints on organizational behavior are the result of prior decision-making or the resolution of conflicts between competing groups.

Just as organizations may take on a life of their own, so do the lists of publishing houses. Books can endure longer than those who wrote or published them. When editors are in the process of signing books, the list that is already in print will impose its own logic on them, in both obvious and imperceptible ways. Editors-in-chief from all sectors of publishing have told me they believe that editors are attracted to a particular house more because of their affinity for a house's image, style, or list than because of the salary and other emoluments they are offered.

As Tuchman and Fortin (1980) note, both literary critics and historians of the publishing industry suggest that publishing houses have personalities. Editors maintain that their lists have a certain character or identity, that they are able to describe the quintessential type of book for their house. The house's identity, or tradition, finds expression in its backlist, which constitutes those wise choices of previous years that continue to sell well today. I argue that in houses such as Apple Press and Plum Press, where the sales from the backlist constitute at least 60 percent, and in some years a much higher percentage, of total sales, there is an ever-present consideration of how well the material currently under review "fits" with the previous books done by the house.[14]

The social sciences editor at Plum Press mentioned that, after you have worked there long enough, "you tend to acquire a kind of cognitive map—you know what goes and what doesn't." An Apple Press editor remarked that "each house has its own image that no one can quite specifically define. It may take several weeks or many months to learn it, but, once you do, you've got it, and you know what will float and what won't."

A crucial premise-setting characteristic at both Apple and Plum was complementarity. Certain subjects, regardless of how well they are treated, are considered outside the competence of the house and are seldom considered for publication. Editors select manuscripts that are appealingly compatible with previously published books. In scholarly and monograph publishing, the lists of houses are, in effect, statements to academics about what particular domains the publishers are involved in. Marketing capability is also a concern. One editor at Plum Press commented, and his editor-in-chief nodded vigorously in agreement,

> We couldn't publish a book in philosophy, even if it was the greatest book of the century on its topic. We've never published in philosophy; we lack the knowledge of the field, the mailing lists, and other related books to advertise along with it. We just wouldn't have the ability to do that kind of book.

The president of Apple Press voiced these related sentiments:

> You simply cannot sign just one book in an area. How in the world would you promote it? If you are going to move into a field, you have to sign three or four books; otherwise you don't stand a chance of breaking in and becoming noticed.

That is one reason why publishers like to do the kinds of books that they have done before. It's safer to work in an area that you are familiar with.

A good number of Plum Press publications were part of a series, and editors were always on the lookout for manuscripts that would complement earlier books in a series. It is much easier to market serial publications, since there is a ready-made audience consisting of those who have purchased previous books in the series. There were certain fields in which the house was well-established and for which it therefore showed a predilection. Editors at both houses were constrained by the types of books their firms had previously published. They would not suggest projects that would be considered out of bounds. Apple Press would not publish a resounding critique of the established authors whom they had published. Nor did they go in for "polemics or very speculative works."[15] Editors were able to bend the house's tradition, but they did so covertly. For example, when an editor wanted to publish a leading Marxist, the editor did not mention the author's politics but instead touted his academic credentials.

At Plum Press, the publishing program in the social sciences was less than a decade old. Plum had delayed moving into the social sciences because the firm's executives had doubts about the scientific respectability of these disciplines. Such concerns still loom large at Plum Press. The editor-in-chief continues to refuse to publish in the field of history because he maintains that "history is not a science." Hence, when the social sciences editor wanted to do a social-history book, he "advertised" it to the editor-in-chief as a work of comparative political economy.

The traditions of the two houses also put boundaries around the decision-making process in other ways. It was hard for editors to judge the significance of new subfields in which their house lacked good connections, so if they decided to publish a book in a new subject area and the book fared poorly, their interest in the subject waned sharply. They did not consider that what was responsible for the book's lack of success may have been not its subject matter but simply the fact that it was a very poor book. In addition, authors directly influence the future of a publisher's list. Authors who are satisfied with the publication of their books frequently act as informal scouts, referring others to the house. It stands to reason that authors are most likely to refer manuscripts by those who share their intellectual interests; hence they ultimately contribute to the maintenance of the house's tradition. Satisfied authors also continue to submit their own writings to the house. The editor-in-chief at Apple Press demonstrated his satisfaction with this arrangement by remarking, "One thing that can make your work a lot easier is to get a person's books throughout their life. That's quite an accomplishment, and, if you can do it, you can even count on them to have a new book for you every three years or so." The recurrence of a transaction reduces uncertainty and the need for search. Recurrent exchanges lead to familiarity between actors, the development of personalized exchange relationships, and a dependence of each actor on the other, resulting in a need to continue the exchange (Cook 1977).

Another way in which the premises of a house influence its decision-making is in the selection of outside reviewers. The most common source of reviewers at both Apple and Plum was their own authors and series editors. As a result, authors were called on to uphold the standards that they themselves had helped to establish. As one reader's report at Plum Press put it: "This manuscript is well written and probably publishable. But it is not as good as previous books in our series . . . I do not think it advisable that it be included . . . You might consider publishing it anyway, but not as a part of our series." And at Apple a reader's report said: "An intelligent and engaging study . . . from what I gather, however, this highly speculative, meta-theoretical treatment is not the sort of thing Apple usually does."

In their study of submissions to the British house of Macmillan between 1866 and 1887, Tuchman and Fortin (1980; also see Tuchman 1982 and 1984) found that the readers' reports strove to protect "the sanctity of their image of Macmillan and Company." Readers would comment that certain nonfiction books would bring no profit but would "be a credit to your list," and they commonly disparaged popular novels as "not suitable" for Macmillan. John Morley, one of the firm's primary readers, commented that a mysterious novel, "with blood and madness and dead men's bones . . . ought to be published and would sell—but [it is] certainly not of your style of publications."

Premise-setting is enhanced by standard operating procedures (March and Simon 1958). At both Plum and Apple, the print runs and prices of books were relatively fixed. The same forms, requiring the same information for each book, had to be filled out each time an editor wanted to propose signing a book. The process of obtaining approval was the same for every book. In cases where an editor wanted a larger advance for an author or a larger print run, he or she had to wage a special campaign to obtain approval. As the psychology editor at Apple Press told me after he had landed two very prestigious, popular authors within one week, "Publishing these guys is a real coup for us, but they do require a much bigger than normal investment. I had to anticipate the questions that the editor-in-chief would pose." This reflects a more general organization process, noted previously by Becker (1974): one can do things differently if one is prepared to pay the price in increased effort.

An organization's control over its operating premises is never perfect or total. Premises are not terribly useful during periods of rapid change or when organizations are faced with a string of unpredictable events. Premises are more likely to be resistant to change than supportive of it. Premises may be superstitious and contain the seeds of organizational obsolescence. They can even be viewed as part of the liability of aging (Aldrich and Fish 1982). Along with outdated premises, we commonly find a hardening of vested interests, an encrusting of tradition, and a homogeneity of perceptions. Continued poor performance by an organization may lead its members to question the value and nature of premises. Nevertheless, when successfully used, as they were at both

Apple and Plum, premises effectively guide behavior by providing reasonable and coherent boundaries. As long as the behavior of editors remained within these boundaries, they were free to carry out their duties in their own manner. Premises serve cognitive, ideological, and social-control functions, and they help management reduce uncertainty about employee performance.

Summary

In contrast to perspectives that emphasize the autonomy of craftsmen or the strategic power of the individuals who resolve critical uncertainties, I prefer a view that attends to the constraints faced by both an organization and the occupants of particular roles within it. In this chapter I have emphasized how patterns of exchange, the force of tradition, and an emphasis on complementarity serve as unobtrusive premises that guide editorial behavior. These situational, structural, and historical elements dispose editors to act in a particular manner. However, not only are editors socialized in an unobtrusive manner; publishing houses also are subject to both formal and informal pressures to adopt particular courses of action. Goal congruence is seldom individually tailored. There is ample borrowing of practices from other organizations that are viewed as legitimate role models. And, in turn, many less prestigious publishers tried to copy the successful policies of Apple and Plum. Moreover, as I shall maintain in chapter 6, publishers and highly productive members of the scholarly community at times engage in both subtle and not so subtle coercive efforts at furthering their own goals.

Editorial discretion is a negotiated order, a continual process of interaction and redefinition between an editor's preferences and the house's tradition and operating premises. Executives feel that, with proper socialization, editors acquire built-in regulatory mechanisms that shape their selection of manuscripts. Effective socialization and informal controls obviate the necessity of expensive and onerous surveillance. Editors, however, learn to use the premises and traditions for their own purposes. They know that unique situations become routine if repeated over time. Editors also have personal likes and dislikes, and these prejudices influence their work. Younger editors at both houses were more conformist. They did things by the book and were unlikely to intentionally take on books outside the house's tradition. Older, more experienced editors at Apple and Plum were more familiar with informal expectations; they knew, in addition to what were the "musts" of their role, what the "mays" were (Thornton and Nardi 1975). They had the ability to impose on their role their own personal style, modified in certain ways by their particular house. If they were successful, and their performance was accepted by others, they were in a position to create and expand the house's tradition in the course of their daily tasks.[16] Through them, the house published in new fields and, in a short time, incorporated these into the house's area of competence. More experienced editors also had their own "stable" of contacts and did not need to be wholly reliant on house authors as outside readers.

The individual initiative of editors is thus curbed and shaped but not stifled. Editors are never completely integrated into a fully cohesive order. Crozier (1981), in an analysis of a hospital, describes the balancing and managing of complex internal tensions within an organizational system as a game. The game must have rules so that collective association can continue, but, within the rules for playing it, different strategies are possible. In publishing, the rules can, on occasion, be broken. This is because decisions about which books to publish are significant events in an editor's professional career. Editorial performance of a high caliber must be rewarded in some fashion, because an editor-in-chief has to consider not only an author's career but the editor's as well— in particular, his or her recent track record. One senior editor at Apple felt that "one of the main criteria of a good house to work for is the extent to which an editor can debate an executive decision." If an editor had frequently been correct about books that others in the house were dubious about or had done several very successful books, then the editor-in-chief might decide it was "wise" to approve a manuscript proposed by this editor, even though his own judgment told him otherwise. An editor at Plum felt that an important consideration for him was how much "rope" he was given by his editor-in-chief. He recalled one instance where he received very poor reviewers' reports on a book for which he had recently proposed a contract. The editor-in-chief was disturbed and considered terminating the contract. The editor asked for patience and gambled on past experience with the author that he could turn the book around. He did, and the book did well.

An editor-in-chief must consider the morale of his editors when evaluating their proposals. An executive wants editors to be committed to the books they publish; therefore an editor-in-chief must think long and hard about the internal consequences of rejecting an editor's proposal. If a proposed book is very expensive, or if the author or manuscript will take up too much of an editor's time for what will be a modest return, the editor-in-chief may turn these projects down. It required careful combing of the editors' correspondence for me to find an occasional case where a proposal had been vetoed. This contrasted with the editors' frequent comments that their propsals were never turned down. The discrepancy comes from a selective memory: a project that an editor is passionate about is very rarely turned down; when an editor's commitment is weak, the possibility of rejection is higher. There are also a few proposals that editors are willing to use as tradeoffs or hostages to the future; when such projects are axed, the editors discount it, because these are not "real" proposals.

One of the most important influences on editorial behavior is work load. The decision process is very sensitive to decision load, hence editors must develop informal rules of thumb for managing their daily work load. In the next chapter I analyze the factors involved in the evaluation of manuscripts and discuss the consequences that information overload has on the process of making choices.

5

DECISION-MAKING AS A MEANS
FOR ORGANIZING OBLIGATIONS

Making decisions, as everyone knows from personal experience, can be burdensome. In publishing, the burden is greatly increased by the fact that editors are inundated with "raw materials." At both Apple and Plum, editors received or acquired many more proposals, prospectuses, and manuscripts to evaluate than they could ever publish. Over the course of a two-year period (1975 and 1976), Apple Press received approximately 4,680 projects to consider. Fewer than 140 of them were accepted for publication. Such figures are by no means unusual. Editors at other houses also report that they receive a large number of "raw materials." In the fall of 1976, Columbia University Press noted in their brochure "The Pleasures of Publishing" that in 1975 they received 1,321 manuscripts and rejected all but 71 of them.[1] In 1981, Princeton University Press received 1,129 manuscripts and accepted 118. The Princeton data reflect steady growth over the previous decade, although submissions, which had risen by 52 percent since 1972, outpaced acceptances, which had increased by 42 percent (Darnton, 1983:533). Such low rates of acceptance are not unique to scholarly publishing (see Coser, Kadushin, and Powell 1982 for comparable data on other sectors of the book industry). Nor are high rejection rates merely a contemporary phenomenon. In the April, 1913, issue of the *Atlantic Monthly*, George Brett, who was then the president of Macmillan, asserted that "the number of books that appear in print is usually only about two percent of the total number of manuscripts submitted to the publishers for examination." Simon Michael Bessie, a distinguished editor, stated in 1958 that less than 3 percent of the novels written in America are published.[2]

For each of the editors at Apple and Plum, time was a scarce resource. The demand for editorial time far exceeded the available supply. Scarcity, whether of time, energy, or money, makes allocation decisions necessary. Editors cannot give each potential "product" an equal amount of attention. Only a small percentage of submitted manuscripts receives serious attention. This act of gatekeeping is an organizational necessity. In chapter 4, I emphasized how, at each house, both the backlist and the editors' network ties shaped editorial opinions. In this chapter I analyze how editors allocate their attention. What methods do they use to achieve an economy of effort, and how do they determine what are the most rewarding and morally demanding tasks? Editors manage these concerns through the use of a queue discipline. These rules for allocating attention are crucial, as the data on the numbers of manuscript submissions will vividly demonstrate. Yet location in queues is not the sole determinant of editorial attention; other factors—finances, an author's academic status, and the overall work load at the house—also influence the expenditure of an editor's time and ultimately determine the fate of manuscripts under review.

In a few cases, acquiring a manuscript and accepting it are one and the same. In the majority of cases, however, acquisition and evaluation are two separate and distinct processes. As we know from chapter 3, editors must keep track of many different streams of activity. There is a steady flow of unsolicited materials and referrals from people known by the editor, while other manuscripts are obtained as a result of editorial initiative or luck. At the same time that manuscripts arrive at the house, additional manuscripts are under review. Each manuscript is evaluated, and, if necessary, the editor will locate an appropriate reviewer to assess it. Once convinced of a manuscript's merit and marketability, the editor will "sell" the project to his or her superiors. Faced with so many demands and responsibilities, editors must develop strategies to cope with information overload. I found that most editors had personal rules of thumb. They conserved their energy by taking on projects that were either politically or financially expedient; or projects that were simple, meaning that the book did not require a great investment of time or energy; or projects that were enjoyable to work on—that is, the book dealt with a topic they were interested in. Therefore, one key to learning how decisions are made is to understand how an editor's attention is allocated. It seems logical to argue that the greater the amount of time that goes into evaluating a project, the more likely it is that the project will be published.[3] Even if we discount theories of cognitive consistency, we are left with the simple fact that spending time on some projects precludes giving attention to others.

I tried to map the various ways in which manuscripts are acquired by asking the editors at Apple Press to keep a record of all the materials they received.[4] This was a difficult request to comply with, because Apple did not keep records of submitted projects that were not published. Only rejection letters were kept on file. The editors were divided as to the utility of keeping these records for me. One editor said that now, for the first time, he felt organized. Another grumbled, saying, "Most of this stuff will never be published, so what's the use?" I abandoned this procedure after several months because it required too much of the editors' time. I decided that a more workable method would be to trace the manner in which all the books published during 1975 and 1976 had been acquired and to gather comparable information for all the books that were contracted for during 1975. In addition, I contacted the authors of the books that were published in 1975 and 1976 and obtained their version of how their manuscripts had come to be accepted. For projects that were signed while I was present, I was able to observe the evaluation process and ask questions as the acquisition took place. This research strategy was later partly replicated at Plum Press.[5]

Access and Waiting: Differential Chances of Being Published

The decision to perform one act before another implies an assignment of priorities. This does not mean that choices are necessarily purposive or based on stable preferences and expectations. Research suggests that preferences develop over time while decisions are being made, through a combination of education, socialization, and experience (March and Olsen 1976). My analysis of unobtrusive controls in chapter 4 suggests that decision-making most commonly represents the fulfillment of obligations and the maintenance of loyalties. Editors employ a variety of tactics to bring the supply of manuscripts and the demands on their time into a workable equilibrium. As Barry Schwartz (1975:80) contends, every organization that processes people or the "things" created by people must in some way make use of a queue discipline, a set of rules that govern the order in which service in rendered. In many organizations the standard policy is first come, first served; however, this is not the case everywhere. Queues can serve as a means of organizing obligations.

In some organizations there is a recognition of special circumstances or privileges that entitle a person to faster service. These preemptive priorities allow some clients to displace earlier arrivals. Schwartz (1975:78) also maintains that, in institutions as varied as hospitals and scientific journals, the longer the queue is, the less attention it gets. Effort expended on small queues produces a more visible impact than an identical amount of effort expended on longer ones. Moreover, as Schwartz (1975) and Schwartz and Dubin (1978) have shown in the case of academic journals, the reward that a journal editor experiences in finding papers to accept, and arranging to get the final drafts of each in hand in order to get the issue out on time, is very different from the reward he gets for rejecting papers on time. Thus, correspondence about rejections not only waits in a longer queue and takes more time than correspondence about acceptances; it is accorded a much lower priority.

A queue discipline is not the only way an organization can accommodate conflicting and competing claims. Excess demand may be responded to by omission or by cutting categories of discrimination, that is, by responding to tasks with less precision than would be the case at lower rates of input. One example would be for editors to rely on the institutional affiliation of an author as a way of reducing processing time. As Schwartz (1975, 1978a) points out, a client whose status is low cannot offer much to reward the service-provider for prompt service; this client will therefore wait. A high-status author of course has more to offer an editor in a reciprocal relationship. I was particularly attentive to the advantages in terms of access that were afforded to academics from prestigious institutions; however, as I discuss below, although academic status has a significant effect on network location, status alone is not a primary determinant in editorial decision-making.

Staffan Linder (1970) points out that under conditions of work overload or time scarcity, low-quality decision-making is the most sensible way to achieve organizational efficiency. A more effective decision-making process would be too time-consuming. For instance, a rational choice about a manuscript's value would require considerable information about both its intellectual contribution and its market potential. But to obtain that kind of information, an editor would have to read each and every manuscript, solicit reviews, investigate sales potential, and so on. To do so would mean that the editor was functioning very unintelligently, because such behavior would be an uneconomic way to allocate one's time. All editors recognize that decisions must be made in the absence of complete information. Nor is this a cause for great worry, as the comments of one editor vividly illustrate: "There are a lot of fish out there to be fried; if one gets away, you can't lose sleep over it. Everybody in publishing can tell you stories about great books that got away or were turned down." Linder's analysis helps account for this seemingly arbitrary aspect of the publication process.

In general, waiting time is reduced when there is financial competition between service-providers. But, as mentioned earlier, frenetic competition for authors, which is commonplace in trade publishing and to a lesser degree characterizes the college textbook field, is largely absent from the world of scholarly publishing. Competition for an author among scholarly houses usually involves high-quality service, the prestige of a house, and the author's affinity for the editor. The norms of peer review and first-rate scholarship are not typically associated with financial reward; therefore, waiting time is seldom reduced because of competition among scholarly presses.[6]

In an organizational society, delays in getting administrative decisions are a problem in a wide variety of settings (see Stinchcombe 1980). A pure case of red tape occurs when bureaucratic rewards are incongruent with bureaucratic purpose. In some cases there is neither a reward for prompt service nor any penalty for delay. Many service-rendering organizations do not lose clients by requiring them to wait a long time, because clients seldom have alternative services to which they may turn. The causes of delay at Apple Press, however, were not due to rule-bound behavior or to lack of reward for speed. Delays were caused by work overload; as a result, most manuscripts spent more time waiting in the queue than in being evaluated. The exceptions to this rule were those written by authors who had had some prior contact with Apple Press.

I argue that the time an editor spends on a project and hence its chances of being published are largely determined by the manner in which the project comes to the editor's attention. The data that I collected at Apple on manuscript acquisition yielded a list of approximately thirty means of obtaining manuscripts. These ranged from materials that arrived unsolicited to situations where the author was a personal friend of the editor. (The complete list is presented in an Appendix as the Manuscript Acquisition Code for Apple Press.) I collapsed these various methods of acquisition into three main categories:

1. The author initiates the contact with the publishing house. This category includes projects that come in over the transom or through an author's approaching a representative of the house at a convention or a meeting. In these cases the author has had no prior contact with the house.

2. The author has had some previous association with the house or with a person who has had such an association and is willing to act as a broker for the author or the house. This category includes both referrals from other publishers or from informal advisers to the house and also situations where the house has an informal arrangement with particular institutions to publish their materials.

3. The editor acquires a project as a result of his or her efforts or contacts. This category includes referrals from an editor's close personal friends and cases where the editor searches for projects.

The volume of materials received through these different channels varied considerably. The data I collected enabled me to place in one of these three categories all of the projects and manuscripts Apple received in the two-year period (1975 and 1976). Most fell into the first category; in fact, Apple Press was commonly swamped with over-the-transom materials. With some seasonal fluctuations, the house received an average of about thirty-five unsolicited projects a week. One editor noted that the sheer quantity of over-the-transom materials affected the quality of his work life; noting that most of his time was spent going over his mail, he lamented that "signing a book is actually something that happens rarely." The second category was less typical; approximately eight to ten projects a week arrived in this manner. The third category was the least frequently represented; during some weeks, no projects were obtained in this way, but at other times, especially if an editor was on the road, several projects could develop in a single week. I estimate that fewer than fifty projects a year were acquired in this fashion.[7]

After ascertaining the number of projects that were submitted to Apple, I spoke with both editors and authors to determine how the books that were published in 1975 and 1976 had been obtained. As the information presented in table 4 indicates, there clearly was a preemptive queuing system by which prospective authors' projects were processed in accordance with the extent of their previous association with the house or with a particular editor. Last to be processed were projects whose authors were unknown to the house and its editors, i.e., those who sent in unsolicited materials. The general result of this queuing system was that efficiency and short waiting times for one set of prospective authors resulted in ineffectiveness and long waiting times for unsolicited authors. This statement should be qualified somewhat by noting that, on occasion, an editor would scan an unsolicited project very quickly and then, if the manuscript was wholly inappropriate, reject it on the spot. A secretary would then return the author's materials. More commonly, unsolicited materials that had some appeal were added to the editor's pile of work and would, at some point, receive further scrutiny, although their chances of publication were quite slim.

The data presented in table 4 confirm the notion that the amount of attention an editor devotes to a manuscript depends on the manner in which it was acquired, and this attention subsequently affects its chances of being published. The more than 1,800 manuscripts submitted each year by authors who had had no prior contact with Apple Press had very small odds of getting published; in fact, their chances were considerably less than one in a hundred. Authors with some previous contact had chances of getting published of slightly less than one in ten. Projects that were obtained as a result of an Apple Press editor's efforts or connections—projects which averaged about fifty a year in number—had publication odds of about one in three.

Manuscripts that arrived as the result of a preexisting relationship with the house (category 2) illustrate how the house's previous history may influence editorial behavior. There are occasions when the relationship between the author and the house preceded a particular editor's tenure with the firm. The most common example was the "stepchild" manuscript, the

Table 4
Acceptance Rate for Books Published by Apple Press in 1975 and 1976

Acquisition Category	Estimated Number of Submissions	Books Published	Percentage of Submissions Published
1. Author had no prior contact with house	3,640	21	0.57
2. Author had previous contact with house	940	79*	8.4
3. Editor acquired materials personally	100	35	35.0
Insufficient information	—	2	—
Total	4,680	137	2.9

*Category 2 includes 32 titles that were revised editions, paperback editions of books that originally appeared in cloth, and old contracts, signed by the previous administration.

book that had been contracted for by a predecessor. There are also other relationships—with an author, an informal adviser, or an institution—that were established prior to an editor's employment with the house. In effect, a new editor inherits a complex network of contacts when he or she fills a position previously held by another editor. If the editor values these relationships or is strongly encouraged by management to cultivate them, he or she will pay attention to the material that is received as a result of these previous ties. This by no means ensures publication; but if the editor wants to continue the relationship, these materials must at the very least be attended to with care and some dispatch. Manuscripts that were directly acquired by an editor (category 3) obviously received the most immediate attention.[8]

It is important to note that authors in the high-priority queues (categories 2 and 3) would quite possibly transfer their allegiance to another house if they did not receive the prompt treatment and attention that their position in the queue merited. It is this priority service that creates the bonds of moral obligation and reciprocity that link authors to Apple Press. Editors gave their highest priority to what were morally their most demanding tasks—the tasks that gnaw at an editor's conscience when left undone. As Barry Schwartz (1978b:9) points out, "What this means is that the constraining elements in work are not altogether intrinsic to the task at hand but must be derived in part from its location in a queue."

I collected additional data from both Apple Press editors and authors for books that were signed, but not published, in 1975. This information appears in table 5. Both the means of acquisition and an author's chances for publication are quite comparable to the data presented in table 4.

Young unpublished academics will perhaps find some solace in the fact that their chances of publication are actually better than the odds facing unpublished authors of trade books (see Coser, Kadushin, and Powell 1982:128–35).[9] Some major trade houses will not even accept unsolicited materials. Menaker (1981) estimates the odds against pub-

Table 5

Acceptance Rate for Books Signed by Apple Press in 1975

Acquisition Category	Estimated Number of Submissions	Number of Books Signed	Percentage Published
1. Author had no prior contact with house	1,820	7	0.38
2. Author had previous contact with house	470	34*	7.2
3. Editor acquired materials personally	50	17	34.0
Insufficient information	—	2	—
Total	2,340	60	2.56

*Includes three revised editions

lication of unsolicited novels are approximately 15,000 to 1. The general prospects for unpublished writers who send in their materials over the transom are so poor that we advised:

> If the reader who is unfamiliar with publishing takes but one message away from this book, it should be that formal channels of manuscript submission are the very last resort of would-be authors. To get a book published, recommendation through an informal circle or network is close to being an absolute necessity. [Coser, Kadushin, and Powell 1982:73]

At Plum Press I was unable to collect data that were directly comparable to the data I had collected at Apple. I therefore solicited rough estimates from each of the editors and then fine-tuned their estimates by going through their correspondence files. I then asked the editors to go through their various methods of manuscript acquisition and tell me which manuscripts would receive the most serious attention. The Plum editors all accorded their highest priority to manuscripts that were directly referred to them by a series editor. They estimated that between 70 and 80 percent of these manuscripts were eventually published, although in a few cases a book did not appear in a specific series.

As I have noted, Plum Press was a relative newcomer to the social and behavioral sciences. Few Plum authors in these fields had done more than one book with the press. This is illustrated by the results of a questionnaire I sent to 58 randomly selected authors who had recently published a book in these fields with Plum. Of the 45 respondents, only 8 had had more than one book published by Plum. In the case of 22 authors, the book in question was the first one they had written. In contrast, Apple Press had many authors who had published four or five books with them and a few who had done eight or even more. Apple had a much larger circle of "friends and supporters" than Plum, and, as a result, far more manuscripts were referred to it by house authors than was the case at Plum. This was one reason why the behavioral and social science editors at Plum felt it was incumbent on them to travel and actively search for manuscripts, but, despite this additional effort, their traveling was slightly less productive than the search efforts of Apple editors. The Plum editors estimated that they eventually published one out of every three or four projects they acquired as a result of their travels—a somewhat lower percentage than at Apple. Because of Plum's late entry on the scene, its editors in the social and behavioral sciences devoted a good portion of their travels to spreading the word about Plum and their new publishing programs and were therefore less selective about the manuscripts they acquired. The editors wanted exposure for Plum, not just potential "products."

Plum also had other sources of manuscripts. They purchased several books each year from foreign publishers. They also had the option of publishing in the United States books that were originally published by their London branch office. In addition, Plum established ongoing relations with several research institutes, and they published most of the materials that were referred to them through these institutions.

At Plum, as at Apple, over-the-transom materials were not very likely to be published. A slight but important difference is that Plum was somewhat more hospitable toward over-the-transom materials because it received fewer of them. The editors at Plum estimated that "one out of every twenty-five or thirty" over-the-transom manuscripts was eventually published. Plum's late entry into the field and its resulting lower visibility among members of the social science community explain why it received fewer unsolicited submissions. The fact that its editors were not overwhelmed by over-the-transom projects meant that they could give more attention to them, and this increased these projects' chances of publication. In addition, the editors were buffered by the series editors, who handled many unsolicited manuscripts on their own. Often the series editors would reject unacceptable projects without contacting an editor at Plum.

I asked both the social sciences editor and the behavioral sciences editor at Plum Press to go over the list of their books that had been published during the two years 1975 and 1976 and describe how each had been acquired. The behavioral sciences editor begged off, claiming a very faulty memory. The social sciences editor was able to recall the way most of his books had been acquired, and, when he could not, his correspondence file was well-enough organized to enable me to track down the needed information. I then double-checked this information by contacting the authors and obtaining their accounts of how their books had been acquired. The summary results are shown in table 6. In effect, this is a shorter version of the manuscript acquisition code that I used at Apple Press.

In order to compare Plum Press data with Apple Press data, I assigned each of the methods of acquisition shown in table 6 to one of the three categories I had used for analyzing the Apple Press data. The results, shown in table 7, do not

Table 6
Methods of Acquisition of Social Science Books
Published by Plum Press in 1975 and 1976

Method of Acquisition	Number of Books Published	Percentage of Total Books Published
Editor's initiative	9	14.3
Recommended by a series editor	19	30.2
Originally published by Plum's London office	9	14.3
Arrangement with a research institute	4	6.3
Serial publication or proceedings of a symposium or conference	4	6.3
Signed by West Coast office	4	6.3
Import from a foreign publisher	3	4.8
Reprinted from a Plum Press journal or referred by journal editor	2	3.2
Author had previously published with Plum	2	3.2
Referred by well-known scholar because of Plum's backlist	1	1.6
Over the transom	4	6.3
Information not available	2	3.2
Total	63	100

Table 7
Social Science Books Published by Plum Press,
by Category of Acquisition, 1975 and 1976

Category of Acquisition	Number of Books Published	Percentage of Total Books Published
1. Author had no prior contact with house	4	6.4
2. Author had previous contact with house or one of its representatives	32	50.7
3. Editor acquired materials personally	21	33.3
Insufficient information*	6	9.5
Total	63	99.9

*Four titles were acquired by the West Coast office of Plum Press and could not be classified.

differ greatly from the Apple Press results. The overwhelming majority of Plum Press social science titles were acquired either through the direct efforts of a house editor or a series editor or through a preexisting relationship between the author and Plum Press. The data on the social science books, and the estimates provided by other editors, indicate that there is a preemptive queuing system in operation at Plum that influences how editors' attention is allocated and, ultimately, an author's chances of being published.

Manuscript queues operate as filtering systems. Not everyone in the high-priority queues gets published, nor is everyone in the lowly regarded queue rejected. As I observed above, a house's tradition and an editor's interests are important mediating influences. If a manuscript in the low-priority queue complemented books already published by the house and the editor found it to be interesting, its chances were naturally improved. On the other hand, if a manuscript in the highly regarded queue had these characteristics, its chances of publication were very high. There are other considerations editors must take into account in their decision-making, and in the next section I discuss these; but it must be kept in mind that location in the work queue differentially affects chances of publication.

Other Factors in the Decision to Publish: Inventory Considerations

From an author's point of view, timing must be viewed as pure chance. It is impossible for an author to know when a publishing house is short on "product" and is thus more likely to be receptive to new materials, and few authors will know whether or not an editor is looking for a manuscript on a particular subject. One reason why both Apple and Plum kept a backlog of materials was to ensure that there was ample "product." Editors are engaged in a delicate and continual balancing act in terms of scheduling; they must coordinate the signing of books with the release of new books, always checking to avoid periods of either inactivity or overproduction. At Plum Press it seemed that some books were signed so that a continual flow of product would keep their large work force busy. This opinion was routinely stated by production and manufacturing personnel. The following comments by a production editor touch on the issue of work flow:

> They often sign books just to keep us working . . . Oh, sure, the books fulfill other functions too—like they will sign up a guy's book even if they know it's not that good because he just got a big grant and they want to publish the results of the research . . . It's a big company . . . they want all these people to earn their money. [*How can you be sure of this? The editors don't tell you this, do they?*] Not in so many words, but they clue you in at transmittal meetings—where an editor turns a book over for production—by saying things like "This book is pretty dull, so don't bust your tail on it," or "There's not much you can do to improve this one; it's very dry, and we'll have to publish it as it is." The editor sort of lets you know when the book doesn't require the standard treatment.

At Apple Press, the twenty-odd employees were always busy, so there was no need to sign books just to keep the labor force working. However, maintaining a constant flow of materials is crucial to all organizations in order to avoid cash-flow problems. Thompson (1967:20) has suggested that "buffering on the input side" is essential and that organizations must stockpile materials acquired in an irregular market to maintain constancy in their service processes. This also explains why editors "sit" on manuscripts. I observed cases where manuscripts had been evaluated but editors held off on making a final decision, preferring to wait and see what the quality of forthcoming manuscripts would be. Such delays can be explained as protection against future contingencies. The concern with keeping up a constant flow of products is also a factor in relations between editors and management. The following entry in my fieldwork notes illustrates this:

> On the next-to-last day of the month, the editor-in-chief walked into a senior editor's office; he quite clearly looked worried. When asked what was wrong, he replied, "I'm wondering how the hell I can explain to the president why we didn't sign a single manuscript in the month of October." The senior editor responded that he had reached agreements with authors on at least seven projects during October but that the formality of the contract-signing probably wouldn't clear the parent company's bureaucracy until December. "It helps to know that," the editor-in-chief said, "but not that much. I'll just have to convince [the president] that this absence of projects won't create any scheduling problems for us sometime in the future. I just wish I had a book signed this month!"

Editors at several university presses reported that their presses have developed multitiered lists. This is a system for categorizing books based on their commercial potential. Each list has three types of books: C books are monographs on which the press expects to lose money; B books are expected to pay their own way; A books should earn money and pay for the Cs. These different categories of books receive dissimilar marketing attention. Obviously, in each season a university press will have to balance its mix of books. If a list needs to be cut back, a press may postpone some of the Cs. Another way of dealing with this problem, and of avoiding postponements, is for editors to defer making final decisions on C manuscripts. The rationale behind such a move is certainly reasonable; but, as I have argued elsewhere (Powell 1982a), it is incumbent on university presses to explain to their C authors—who are typically young and inexperienced—why a postponement or deferral is necessary. A key difference between university presses and Apple or Plum is that the latter will rarely knowingly publish a book on which they expect to lose money.

The Status of Authors

What effect does an author's location in the academic stratification system have on his or her chances of getting published? Hargens and Hagstrom (1967) demonstrated that having obtained one's Ph.D. at a major institution is a significant advantage to a scientist. Many of us are familiar with Merton's (1968) Matthew Effect, which echoes the gospel that unto him who hath shall be given, as when scientific recognition accrues to those who already have it. Merton argues that there is a continuing interplay between the status system, based on honor and esteem, and the academic class system, based on differential life-chances, which locates scientists in differing positions within the opportunity structure of science. Without deliberate intent, the Matthew Effect operates to penalize the young and the unknown, and, in the process, it reinforces the already unequal distribution of awards.

In deciding which books to publish, are editors reproducing the academic class system? If so, should this be cause for concern? Fulton and Trow (1974) suggest that only a limited number of academics are involved in research and that many American academics do little scholarly writing, opting instead for a teaching role. The Coles (1973) argue that the most talented scientists are located at the best schools and that science is a highly universalistic system that rewards merit. Clearly, scholars employed at elite colleges and universities have better facilities, greater research support, more release time, and lighter teaching loads. Such a system of accumulated advantages (Zuckerman 1970) would result in the rich getting richer at a rate that makes the poor become comparatively poorer.

Yet the amount of influence that accrues to an academic as a consequence of his or her affiliation with a prestigious department or university is not a simple thing to determine. It was certainly the case that authors from less prestigious universities were less likely to have contacts at Apple or Plum. My colleagues and I also found that writers affiliated with high-prestige schools were more frequently asked to review manuscripts (Coser, Kadushin, and Powell 1982).[11] In cases of multiple submissions of a manuscript by an author, we found that more than half of our sample of authors from top schools were offered a contract by more than one publisher, while only a third of the authors from nonelite schools enjoyed the opportunity to choose among several interested publishing houses. Authors from elite schools were also somewhat more likely to be offered larger advances. From a publisher's point of view, it is quite sensible to agree to publish the latest work of a widely known scholar. But to accept the work of a young Ph.D. candidate or an unpublished junior faculty member primarily on the basis of his or her university affiliation is a different matter. In his research on scientific reward systems, Stephen Cole (1978:176) found low correlations between measures of scientific output and the prestige rank of departments. He argues that this indicates that scientific talent is not concentrated in a handful of elite institutions.

Comments made by several editors revealed the importance they attached to academic reputation. For example, the psychology editor at Apple said, "Sure, if I get a project that has a Harvard letterhead, I'll handle it with dispatch . . . I might even take it home to read that night. There's no question but that someone from Harvard has an inherent advantage over others. Why shouldn't they?" The editor-in-chief at a competing scholarly house quipped, "People at good schools write good books, and people at poor schools write bad books or no books at all. It's that simple. You can't go wrong publishing the books of people at the elite schools."

The majority of editors at Apple and Plum nevertheless asserted that few decisions are made solely on the basis of where an author is currently employed. Most editors felt that academic credentials are increasingly difficult to evaluate. One editor noted that the majority of graduates who remain in academia received their Ph.D.s from elite schools. He commented, "It used to be the case that the best ones stayed at home or went to other top schools, but that's no longer the case. The academy is unable to properly reward young people these days. Heck, I know prize-winning authors teaching at unknown schools." The contraction of university faculties and the simultaneous increase in the number of new Ph.D.s have greatly affected the academic job market. As a consequence, some editors have adjusted their thinking about academic prestige. The following comments by the editor-in-chief of a major university press illustrate this:

> As a matter of fact, our director was asking me about that just yesterday, whether I paid attention to what college the letter came from. It used to be that that was a fairly good criterion of what you could expect, because obviously so many of these places . . . well, it isn't that they may not be good colleges, but many of these colleges are teaching institutions almost exclusively; and they may be fine teaching institutions, but they don't allow much time for, or do anything to encourage, research and writing, and so they don't support this kind of thing. But the way things are now, people are getting jobs where they can find them. So I am reading a lot more carefully something recommended to me that comes from some college I've never heard of.

Academic staus is important because both graduates and holders of positions in elite schools have much greater access to effective socialization; that is, they are more confident, they will probably write better letters of introduction, and they will have better contacts, all because they have learned the ropes from people who already know "what matters."

Caplovitz (1963) has made use of the concept "effective scope" in illustrating that the poor have a more restricted life-space; as consumers, for example, they are psychologically less mobile and more inhibited than well-to-do consumers; the latter, who can shop in a wider radius of stores, are not subjects of a captive market, to which sellers offer inferior goods at inflated prices. More generally, we know that, in the world at large, class position influences the degree of knowledge about, and the use people make of, labor- and money-saving opportunities. It is no accident that scholars in elite schools have a more "effective scope" than their counterparts at less prestigious schools, and they also develop a greater number of "weak ties" than do authors from the less elite schools. As Rose Coser (1984) argues, one's position in the social structure influences both the number and quality of opportunities one is afforded. Individuals with many weak ties (e.g., acquaintances as opposed to close friends) are far more likely to be involved in networks that enable them to contact an editor directly. Such individuals will have better access to information, and, as a result of their opportunities and enhanced awareness, they will gain experience and become more cosmopolitan (Granovetter 1974; Knoke and Burt 1982).[12]

Literary agents are little used in scholarly publishing. The stakes are small and unappealing, and agents lack the specialized knowledge needed to perform a bridging function between academic authors and scholarly editors. This function is served by a different group of intermediaries: an editor's friends; formal advisers to a house, who are paid an annual retainer; series editors; and senior academics, who play the roles of patron and broker. Just as authors located at the more prestigious universities are more likely to be called on to review manuscripts and to serve as formal advisers or series editors, so are brokers and patrons more likely to be located at top schools. Stephen Cole (1978) argues that academic sponsorship is primarily important in obtaining one's first job; from then on it has little effect. My observations at Apple and Plum made it clear that sponsorship can work in other ways as well. It enhances the contacts and access enjoyed by the graduate students and junior faculty who are members of the same department as a senior broker or patron. This, in turn, can raise the junior person's visibility and enhance the perceived quality of his or her work. This is critical for two reasons. First, the greater the collegial recognition of a scientist's early work, the greater is the probability that he or she will continue to be productive. Second, "successful scientists are more likely to have their work perceived favorably independent of the content of the work" (S. Cole 1978:174–81). Of course, sponsorship can be handled adroitly or poorly. Some high-placed academics try to use their connections with publishers as a way of paying off debts to students and colleagues. Others indiscriminately praise everything they refer. A good editor learns which academics are reliable and which ones' recommendations must be discounted.

The editors at Apple and Plum, who received unsolicited material from scholars at prestigious universities almost every day, were very selective; only a few of these projects were accepted for publication. This suggests that young academics at elite schools who, lacking contacts or connections, submit unsolicited materials are treated much the same as anyone else. A Chicago or Harvard letterhead alone does not guarantee publication. The social sciences editor at Plum, responding to a question I asked about a manuscript from a Harvard junior faculty member, said, "Something must be wrong with the guy. Doesn't he have any colleagues who think highly enough of his work to recommend it to me?" The psychology editor at Apple voices a similar concern in response to my query about a manuscript from a young scholar at a top school: "I know plenty of people there, and no one mentioned him to me; so I have to wonder."

Several things may limit an author's access to a high-quality publisher such as Apple or Plum. For the most part, the degree of access that authors enjoy depends on their location in social networks. Academic status is important because it enhances an author's ability to make personal contact with an editor. Interestingly, academics at nonelite schools in the

New York metropolitan area are also more likely to be personally acquainted with someone in book publishing. Although I did not collect data directly on this, it is my impression that authors who teach in schools in the New York area have better chances of getting published than do authors from top schools located in America's heartland. Academic status can be important, but first-name familiarity with an editor is even more advantageous. Yet it is not surprising that people from elite schools are more likely to be found in the "right" queues.

Commercial Concerns

Financial and marketing considerations are involved in all publishing decisions. However much authors may regret it, the fact is that publishing is not an eleemosynary institution. Nevertheless, pecuniary concerns were not paramount at Apple or Plum, for two reasons. First, a financial evaluation was frequently colored by an author's location in the queuing system. If an expensive project came in via the lowly regarded queue, its chances were nil; but if an expensive project came from the high-priority queues, it would not be rejected out of hand. Editors would look for various ways of reducing the costs. Second, in scholarly and monograph publishing, most of the books are relatively inexpensive to produce; thus, in contrast to other branches of publishing, a different set of considerations—academic merit, originality, the quality of the reviews—may ultimately determine a book's success in the marketplace. For scholarly publishers, a book that sells well is almost always a success. This is not typically the case in trade or text publishing, where the various costs of doing a book—author's advance, size or print run, and promotion budget—may be so large as to render even a book with healthy sales unprofitable.

In comparison with trade and text houses, members of the sales or marketing staff at scholarly presses have little voice in the decision to accept a manuscript. One university press editor, who was delighted with this state of affairs, said:

> I'd like to stress the fact that most university presses really
> care a lot more about the quality of a book than its sales. I
> think most people in university presses are really enjoying
> themselves . . . because our jobs aren't dependent in such a
> hard fashion on sales . . . we don't have that much pressure,
> and that makes me much more comfortable.[13]

The attitude that the staff of trade and text houses must
take is quite different. Some editors question whether it is
responsible of them to push for books that marketing or sales
personnel are opposed to publishing on commercial grounds.
Roger Straus III, once a director of marketing but now an
editorial director, states the problem as follows:

> To publish a book that a number of us are infatuated with
> without making any marketing commitment to it is a real
> problem. I think in the long run you aren't doing yourself or
> the author any favor. If you are going to publish a book, you
> have to put a certain amount of money behind it or it's going to
> be a problem. So very often what I will say is, "Hey, we love
> the book, but can we envision making the kind of effort that
> will be necessary to secure the audience, and, if we don't, are
> we just going to lose the author, who'll be angry that we didn't
> do an aggressive enough job on his or her work?"[14]

In the course of our general study of book publishing, my
colleagues and I asked a sample of some 130 editors how
important a criterion, in deciding to publish a book, was the
profit anticipated from its sales in its first year of publication.
Almost 60 percent of the college text editors said that this was
a critical factor in the decision to publish; approximately a
third of the trade editors noted that first-year sales were
critical, but less than 20 percent of the scholarly editors listed
this factor as important. Trade editors were most concerned
about a book's subsidiary-rights potential. In general, we
found university-press editors least concerned about commercial prospects and scholarly editors at for-profit presses
somewhat more concerned but not as markedly so as trade
and text editors. This does not mean that money is unimpor-
tant to scholarly editors but that, in defining commercial
success, they take a much more long-term view than their

counterparts in other sectors of the book trade. Given the steady backlist sales of houses like Apple, this view seems appropriate.

At both Apple and Plum, most financial determinations, such as royalty rate, print run, and advertising budget, are made according to a standard format. Advances were rarely larger than $2,000 at Apple; at Plum they were less than $500 when they were given at all.[15] As a result, books are not often rejected because they are too expensive to do. As one Apple editor stated, when I asked him how he handled financial negotiations with a prospective author:

> My experience is that it's harder to convince the house than the author. Almost every author is *delighted* to be published by Apple. I therefore do the best I think that I can for the author when I make the proposal. If the author objects when the contract arrives, I'll see what I can do. It's often easier for me to get a change through then than it would have been to propose higher terms initially. Some editors may work the other way—they find out what the author will take, then make the proposal accordingly. I'm interested in getting the books I want and minimizing in-house hassles.

Apple and Plum authors can—very occasionally—through their affiliation with private foundations or research institutes, offer subventions that will help defray the costs of publication.[16] Obviously, editors find these helpful. Editors also keep their eyes open for books that are inexpensive to produce. Sometimes, for example, British publishing houses will sell the foreign rights to books originally done in England, and the economies realized on these projects are often very inviting. A less common example involves books that are short and by authors who are without previous publishing experience. Generally these are young people, and the book in question is often their dissertation. They are happy to be published and not overly concerned if various economizing steps are taken. Such ways of cutting costs include a lower royalty rate; omitting a jacket for the book; and requiring the author to submit the manuscript on computer tape, coded for typesetting.

Summary

In many respects, Apple and Plum compete for the same audience; but the competition is not of the zero-sum kind. I know of no evidence that suggests that a consumer of scholarly books buys only x dollars' worth of them and so must compare the latest releases of Apple, Plum, and other scholarly presses in order to decide which books to purchase. I do not imagine that a potential consumer considers whether a new book from Apple at \$16.00 is a better buy than a new title by Plum at \$20.00. I assume that most scholarly readers are motivated to purchase a new book because they read a prominent review, receive a recommendation from a reliable friend, or peruse a publisher's catalogue or exhibit and find a book that interests them. Apple and Plum can pursue a similar audience (although, as noted in chapter 2, the houses point in different directions along a continuum of audience size: Apple aims more broadly; Plum has a more specialized focus), but there are important differences in how they choose to market their books and—what is more germane to the topic at hand—how they decide which books to publish.

So far I have drawn a comparison of the two houses: Apple is smaller and more informally organized, and its editorial search methods resemble a garbage-can process, although the "stuff" that enters the garbage can is strongly shaped by tradition, external ties, and network relations; Plum is much larger, more formal, and more routinized, and it uses a strategy of clientelization, or reliance on a few series editors, to reduce uncertainty and make key choices. In the operation of the queuing systems we see that similar differences crop up: the authors who receive the most attention at Apple have either a close personal relation with an editor or an ongoing contact with the house. At Plum, contact with an editor helps improve one's chances, but the highest priority is accorded to the recommendations of series editors. Most of Plum's publications result from the efforts of their series editors, who serve boundary-spanning roles by virtue of their positions of prominence in academia. Plum Press also frequently publishes the proceedings of conferences and symposia; it also makes use of its journals to help with the acquisition of manuscripts. Furthermore, no projects are ever published without at least one review by a scientist in the manuscript's field. In short, Plum has successfully worked out a publishing strategy in which a few academics are coopted and utilized to perform a great many tasks for the press. In return, these academics enhance their own status and influence, in addition to receiving a modest financial compensation.

At Apple Press, editors more frequently rely on their own contacts, and they consult with academics, who then evaluate how good a choice the editor has made. Reviewers play a less significant role in the decision to publish than they do at Plum Press. Nevertheless, Apple Press often calls on its own authors for advice and assistance in promoting its books. The publishing philosophy at Apple is to create strong and lasting associations with eminent scholars, who then "spread the gospel," in the editor-in-chief's words, by directing potential authors to the press and speaking favorably about the press's publications.

At each house the particular queuing process acted both as a sorting system and as a means for organizing obligations. The odds in favor of publication for those in the lowly regarded queue were very slim, although, as a result of the efforts of the series editors, Plum paid more attention to young unpublished authors. But even authors in the highly regarded queues had no guarantee of publication. It is at this point that timing, finances, and academic status come into play, along with the concerns, discussed in chapter 4, about how well a manuscript fits with the backlist and with the house's image. The queuing system allows certain manuscripts to receive more attention than others; but once they have been scrutinized, the fate of these manuscripts depends on a considerable range of historical, network, and financial factors.

We can see that many aspects of the editorial process—in particular, editorial search behavior, the employment of series and journals editors, the use of outside readers, and the operation of the queuing systems—are integrally tied to the structure of the American academy. The motives and career-related needs of academic authors form a fragile alliance with the organizational demands of scholarly publishers. In the final chapter, I will discuss some of the effects that the specific publishing practices of Apple and Plum have on developments in social science research. More generally, I will discuss the interrelations between scholarly publishers and academics and the reciprocal influences they have on each other. I will also draw several theoretical implications from this comparative case study and discuss their relevance in light of recent debates in organization theory.

6

IMPLICATIONS

This comparative case study has illustrated the many ways in which organizations interact with their environments. In this concluding chapter, I will suggest that much of contemporary organization theory is not very helpful in accounting for the kinds of behaviors I observed at Apple and Plum. All theories are, of course, abstractions from reality, and it might be argued that networks of cooperation and affiliation are too informal and complex to model. Theories typically simplify complex social realities in the interest of parsimony. But such simplification runs the risk of ignoring precisely the aspects of reality that are the most crucial. For example, the "balance of payments" between Apple or Plum and its environment is not an easily quantifiable one-way exchange. Transactions at both of these publishing houses are highly interdependent, embedded in a history of previous associations, and guided by norms of reciprocity. Prestige is frequently the currency of exchange, and at times it even seems that editors and authors form their own quasi-organization, which is linked to the market as well as to the production and business side of the house.

I will also argue that the case studies I have presented here have a broader relevance, beyond simply helping us to understand the operation of two scholarly publishing houses; for other kinds of industries exhibit similar patterns of embedded relationships with their environments. But we know very little about how the environments of organizations are organized. I will briefly compare scholarly publishing with public television in order to show how variation in the collective organization of environments influences the internal workings of firms. I will then conclude by discussing the ways in which the organization of scholarly publishing creates an opportunity structure for scholars and, in doing so, restricts access to some and opens doors for others.

The Shortcomings of Orthodoxy

To a certain extent, the editorial departments of publishing houses interpret and shape the environment in which they operate. They try to define the reality of the external world (this they do by searching for manuscripts in particular places, not universally), and they socially affirm its salient features (by publishing and promoting certain authors and by using them as reviewers, they reinforce the external world they have defined). Yet, from another perspective, these editorial departments represent exogenous social forces contained within the formal organization of the publishing house. This dialectical process, between editors as agents of the publishing house and editors as friends and supporters of authors, reflects the manner in which organizations incorporate certain aspects of their environment—certain techniques, knowledge, and skills. These aspects are not invented inside the organization but instead are brought within its purview, sometimes by someone occupying a formal role, such as a series editor or paid adviser, but, more commonly, by someone occupying an informal role, such as a talent scout or friend and supporter.

Ongoing affiliations of this kind reflect more than a web of resource dependencies. They are institutionally embedded, often dating back to the earliest days of a company's history. A good illustration of this historical linkage can be seen in the genesis of Apple Press. It was established in the 1950s when a noted academic contacted a friend who had an interest in book publishing and suggested that translations of classic works of European social science had a significant potential for college-course adoption. Less than a year later, Apple Press published its first list. Thus the recurring associations between publishing houses and their friends and supporters make it difficult to specify who is dictating what to whom. If it is the publishers who are doing the controlling, they—the controllers—routinely find themselves also being controlled.

I argue that close ties between a firm and its environment are commonplace, even though a good deal of contemporary organization theory downplays such ties.[1] The patterns of behavior at Apple and Plum have meanings that exceed the local circumstances that provide their occasion. Yet one would not necessarily expect this if one used current organization theory as a guide.[2] Much of the current research in organizational analysis is based on some or all of the following simplifying assumptions: (1) the typical firm is organized as if it were a single uncommonly intelligent individual; this implies a neat hierarchy, which can be modeled as a unitary actor; (2) organizational boundaries are clear and distinct, even though the actual line of demarcation between a firm and its environment may be problematic, and boundaries around task activities are drawn one way rather than another in order to maximize efficiency; and (3) rational actors make, in Simon's terminology, "intendedly rational," deliberate decisions (Simon 1957). These assumptions, however useful they have proved to be, may in fact not just simplify reality; they may distort it and lead researchers in the wrong direction.

Two major organizational processes—the organization and control of editorial activities and the making of editorial decisions—have been analyzed in this book. Neither process conforms to the neat assumptions of orthodox theory. With respect to the organization of work, we have long known that there is an informal organization that exists alongside the formal hierarchy. Akerlof (1984:80) succinctly summarizes decades of research on the sociology of work by noting that these studies suggest "a complex equilibrium in which official work rules are partially enforced, existing side by side with a set of customs in the workplace which are at partial variance with the work rules, and some individual deviance from both the official work rules and the informal work norms." The data I have presented in chapter 4 go further and show that the customs found in the workplace are part of a complex game, some of whose rules stem from obligations owed to external constituencies. Much of the time, editors behave as if they are optimizing not their organization's welfare but their own or the welfare of the social networks to which they belong. Publishing executives are naturally aware of this, and they try to shape editorial behavior with a variety of unobtrusive controls. This is an ancient problem: formal controls get in the way of the motivation and flexibility that are needed in pursuing specific strategies; yet unobtrusive controls are never a complete proxy for authority (see White 1983). The premises that underlie informal controls are tied to the relational contexts in which the houses operate. Premises not only reflect patterns of exchange but also the history of a firm's previous associations. Premises may even be superstitious; fallacious rules of inference can persist for long periods of time. As a consequence, unobtrusive controls are nearly always incomplete, and many decisions are the result of complicated negotiations.

The discussion in chapter 5, of editorial decision-making as a means for organizing obligations, illustrates that the main point of a decision process may not always be a final choice. The central purpose may be the process itself. Orthodox decision theory assumes that no interdependencies affect decisions. Yet, clearly, people are resources for one another, and editors value certain persons more than others. Moreover, the limited information-processing abilities of editors force them to restrict their search for authors. The number of potential authors, reviewers, and advisers is finite, and the choice of one particular network of authors and sponsors not only may preclude the choice of other aspirants; it may serve to restrict access—either intentionally or unintentionally—to other potential authors. Information and opportunity, far from being open, are systematically distorted, depending on one's location in the social structure. Both houses adopted mechanisms to reduce the costs of search and to cope with uncertainty. Editors at Apple Press relied on extensive personal networks and on the loyalty of Apple authors. At Plum, external networks were brought inside the house and formalized in the person of series editors. These different arrangements are, in a sense, functional equivalents: not only do they allow editors to economize on search efforts; they are also means for introducing continuity and trust into business relations.

Organizations were never the simple entities that our theories suggest, and they are decreasingly so. The boundaries between firms and their environments have become increasingly blurry. Internally, firms have become more complex by introducing into their formal structure such market processes as profit centers and transfer pricing (see Eccles and White 1984). Current theory is also poorly designed to deal with the interconnectedness that characterizes the reality of organizational life. More broadly, the institutional foundations of organizational life remain largely unexamined. There is a great variety of such institutional supports, including trust, personal networks, norms of reciprocity, reputational effects, and tacit collusion, to name but a few. More recently, however, researchers have found that dense patterns of association between organizations and their environments are common in high-technology industries (Rogers and Larsen 1984), defense contracting (Stinchcombe 1983), cultural industries (Coser, Kadushin, and Powell 1982; Faulkner 1983), small businesses (Macaulay 1963), and family firms (Ben-Porath 1980).

What is striking about scholarly publishing is the degree of intimacy between the academic community and scholarly publishers. Personal friendships and extended networks among authors and publishers generate strongly defined standards of behavior. Bonds of allegiance shape the processes of access and discovery. Networks of personal relations are also vital to economic success. And, while competition among firms does influence the success or failure of particular publishing houses, these selection pressures are dampened by the dense associational ties and personal relations that support almost all publishing transactions.

The Organization of Environments

To illustrate the nature and the strength of the association between the social science community and Apple and Plum, it is useful to compare scholarly publishing with a somewhat similar institution: public television. Scholarly publishing is much less commercial than trade publishing, and competition among scholarly houses is frequently prestige-driven. Similarly, public television is widely seen as a less commercial alternative to network television. The stated mission of public television is to offer the viewing public higher-quality and more diverse programming. Indeed, John Ryden, director of Yale University Press, has remarked that "university press publishing is rather analogous to public television. We have somewhat the same mission."[3]

Nevertheless, a comparison of the relationships between scholarly publishers and their external constituents with the connections between the employees of a public television station and their external stakeholders reveals a sharp contrast. Exchanges between a scholarly publishing house and its clients are characterized by continuity and a commonality of interests. In public television, the demands of external constituents are typically in conflict not only with one another but with the interests of the television station. Transactions lack continuity—so much so that one public TV executive lamented "the sad fact that nothing that is successful on public TV endures" (Powell and Friedkin 1983:434).

The similarities in the mission and goals of public television and scholarly publishing mask significant differences in the nature of organization-environment relations. These differences require some description and elaboration. It is critical that we recognize that, although organization-environment relations may be a crucial factor in shaping the internal workings of a firm, environments differ greatly in the way they are organized. The consequences, as we shall see, can be significant.

A scholarly publishing house such as Apple or Plum receives its potential "products" from academic authors in search of a publisher. Authors' outputs are publishers' inputs. We know that these "suppliers" have varying rates of success, depending on the strength of their previous affiliation with Apple or Plum. The raw materials go through an editorial winnowing process, and a small percentage are selected for further review. For assistance in evaluating these manuscripts, editors call on academics, particularly those who have been published by the firm. If a manuscript is approved, it is put into production, and, upon publication, Apple and Plum again call on key members of the scholarly community for help in promoting the product. Academics provide blurbs and quotes for use in advertising copy and on the book's jacket. In fact, most authors actually begin the marketing of their book while they are in the process of writing it. Typically, academics ask their colleagues, members of their invisible colleges, to comment on their work in progress, thus helping to promote the book even before it is finished.

A great majority of the books published by scholarly houses are purchased either by members of the academic community or by university libraries. The latter are generally overwhelmed by the flood of new titles released every month. They are guided in their purchasing decisions by the advice of professors at their own universities and by book reviews in scholarly and library journals, the majority of which are written by academics. In sum, it is a community of shared interests: the suppliers, the consumers, and the gatekeepers of scholarly publishing are all members of the academic community. Moreover, inside the publishing houses, the decisions about what to accept are made by a very small number of people, each of whom is closely allied with certain key members of the academic community.

Economic exchange between members of the academy and scholarly publishers takes place within a normative context in which reciprocity, prestige, and career advancement are crucial considerations. Transactions are seldom isolated or atomistic; they commonly fit into ongoing patterns of obligation. The mutuality of interests between authors and publishers can be seen in both the sale of individual titles and in academic promotion decisions. The opinions that academics have with regard to particular books are important to university librarians, as well as to local booksellers. Both service the university community by distributing the products of scholarly publishers. Similarly, reputation and opinion also matter a great deal in academic promotion decisions; such evaluations are based on a candidate's publication record, and if the candidate's publishers are prestigious, that fact can figure prominently in any review.

Public television is also interpenetrated by external constituents, and, as in scholarly publishing, the activities and products of a public television station are a vehicle for the expression of the interests of key outsiders.[4] But we do not find shared understandings or a congruence between the interests of outside stakeholders and the goals of the organization. Instead, we find plural sovereignty, a situation rife with conflict, in which interests diverge and multiple incompatible demands go unresolved. In public television we observe little that is comparable to the close fit between the organizational goals of scholarly publishers and the professional goals of the academy. To demonstrate this point, I treat public television programs as the outputs of a large public television station and discuss the various inputs that are needed to produce a program and the way these resources are transformed by the station into a prime-time show that is disseminated to a national viewing audience.[5]

Public television is a peculiar hybrid, operating under both economic constraints and political control. A large public television station, such as WNET-TV in New York City, is a public agency, because nearly one-third of its operating budget comes from federal, state, and municipal governments, but it also receives as much as 25 percent of its financial support from its members. As in many voluntary nonprofit organizations, there is an ongoing tension between the need for promotional events, such as membership drives and auctions, and the possibility of so irritating supporters that they become disaffected. The remainder of a station's operating expenses, and the *majority* of the funding for nationally distributed programming, comes from corporate underwriters, private foundations, other public TV stations (who purchase the shows produced by the large stations), and the National Endowment for the Arts and the Humanities.

Programs come from a variety of sources, both within and outside the boundaries of a television station. The programming department generates ideas for programs. At the same time, it actively searches for suitable projects created by independent filmmakers, foreign broadcasters, and other public television stations. These outside sources also frequently contact public TV stations, seeking either to sell broadcast rights to their work or to negotiate a joint venture or cooperative financing for a project they are working on or have in mind.

The sources of program ideas may be diverse, but none will ever reach the television screen without financial backing. Public television stations have very limited capital of their own, and even a successful long-term show, such as *Great Performances*, requires new funding each year. Not only is money scarce, but external funding relationships can be unpredictable. A great deal of time and energy is spent by station executives in developing, maintaining, and smoothing relationships with key funding sources. The process of obtaining program-specific financing is labor-intensive and lengthy, sometimes taking several years. Proposals for federal grants usually require review by a panel of experts, and a consensus must be arrived at before final approval is received.

The interests of various funding sources are often at odds with one another. Although the federal government has been the most important continuous source of revenue for public TV, the history of federal support has been marked by political interference and budgetary uncertainty. State governments, through both overt and implied means, place strong constraints on local public-affairs programming.[6] Private foundations were once the largest source of funding for public television, but that support has declined sharply over the past decade. Today, foundation money goes to specific programs; this support has played a crucial role in bringing innovative, "risky" programming to public TV. As foundation support waned and federal money became entangled in political debates and budgetary battles, public broadcasting turned to large corporations for program-underwriting. Although a mere handful of large firms provides most of the corporate donations, which together constitute less than 15 percent of the total budget for public television, corporate underwriting is vital: approximately half of the nationally distributed programs are underwritten in part or in full by corporate sponsors. Corporations naturally prefer highly visible, splendidly produced, noncontroversial shows that reflect favorably on the sponsor.

In sum, both the sources of programming ideas and the financial support needed to translate ideas into viable projects are highly dispersed. The process by which ideas and financial backing are linked is ambiguous and politicized. A former president of the Public Broadcasting System has stated, "Every source of money is tainted. With federal funds we worry about becoming a governmental broadcasting arm. Corporate money makes you steer away from controversy. Membership money means you cater to upper-middle-class viewers. The saving grace is that we have diversified sources."[7]

Once funding for a program has been obtained, the station staff builds a temporary "organization" to produce it. This production team includes actors and actresses, the writing and filming crew, and the supporting staff. Because funding is always meager, considerable opportunity exists for differences of opinion to emerge among the members of this heterogeneous group. Program distribution is a further complication. The 300-odd PBS stations bid on programs offered by large public TV stations and independent producers. The selection process is slow and conservative, and new shows face formidable barriers. Eventually a program is ready for national broadcast. For a major series, this entire sequence of events can take a number of years. Just prior to the scheduled broadcast, the program is made available to television critics, whose reviews then appear in a large number of newspapers around the country. The reviewers seldom concern themselves with the problems of financing, production, and distribution. Like the national viewing audience, the critics are concerned with the merits of the final product. This cycle of production is constant. While not every program involves so complicated a process, the great majority of programs that are aired nationally between 8:00 and 11:00 P.M. do.

A public television station represents an assortment of mini-organizations, each made up of staff members who have their own priorities and varying amounts of allegiance to public TV. Each internal group has a different set of tasks and develops links to different parts of the environment. The environment of a public television station includes a number of large and powerful actors—major corporations, federal and state governments—as well as smaller but also influential constituents—private foundations, the station's members, the viewing audience, critics, and filmmakers. Collectively, these external groups are very loosely coupled and have few interests in common. The process of creating a television program is administratively complex and requires great skill at maneuvering through a minefield of obstacles.

Scholarly publishing and public television thus illustrate the varying ways in which the relational context of organizational environments may be organized. The environments of organizations differ in both the extent of their formal organization and the amount of consensus that is shared among external constituencies. This argument builds on the primary insight of industrial organization economics: the behavior of a firm can depend crucially on the organization of the industry of which it is a party. A key task for organization theory is, first, to extend the observation that many, if not most, organizations are embedded in a larger system of relations and then to begin comparative analyses of the collective properties of environments. We need to move beyond general characterizations of environments as either scarce or munificent and, instead, develop ways of specifying how environments are organized.[8]

A focus on variation in the collective organization of environments may enable us to better explain differences in internal organizational structures, processes, and performance. For example, editors at Apple and Plum had very high rates of success in getting projects approved, while the staff at WNET had low rates of internal approval. Obviously, the difference is explained in part by factors of risk and cost. That is, a scholarly book is neither expensive nor risky, while a public TV program is costly and may be controversial as well. Differential rates of approval also reflect the availability of resources. Less obvious, however, is the importance of patterns of exchange. The acquisition of resources at Apple and Plum takes place in the context of ongoing social relationships marked by loyalty and reciprocity. Both parties gain from the transaction. In public television, the acquisition of some key resources is mandated by federal budgetary allocations. Other resource exchanges are seldom reciprocal. One party (usually the public television station, except in the case of relations with independent filmmakers) is in a strongly dependent position. Transactions are politicized and often coercive; there is little loyalty or continuity. Hence, decision-makers have few commonly held premises to guide their decisions. Every decision seems unique, and it hinges on a particular and idiosyncratic mix of participants, resources, and constraints.

A comparison of Plum Press and WNET in terms of their formal organization is also illuminating. Both employ between 400 and 500 persons. Plum's annual sales in 1982 exceeded $60 million, and WNET's 1982–83 operating budget was of comparable size. Yet Plum has but three departments and one policy-making committee. In contrast, WNET has four divisions, each with six to eight departments, and it has several major policy-making committees. One might try to explain this difference by pointing to the more varied tasks that WNET must perform. But that explanation would not be sufficient. Organizations are constantly in search of external support and legitimacy. When financial support and much-needed credibility are provided by a dispersed and fragmented environment, organizations respond with a varied mix of procedures and policies. Each response may in itself be formally rational, but collectively the responses will exhibit little internal coherence. Organizations located in environments in which conflicting demands are made upon them will be especially likely to generate complex organizational structures with disproportionately large administrative components and multiple boundary-spanning units (see Scott and Meyer 1983, especially pp. 140–49).

Organizations respond to the inconsistent claims generated by pluralistic environments by incorporating structures and policies designed to please and report to a variety of organized constituencies. As a result, structural complexity increases, and the criteria for determining success become less clear. Thus it is not surprising that WNET is structurally more complex than Plum Press and that its control sytems are more cumbersome. Nevertheless, we should not ignore the tradeoffs inherent in these arrangements. The centers of authority and power in WNET's environment are fragmented. Control is primarily financial as opposed to control over the content of programs (although, clearly, the two are somewhat related [see Powell and Friedkin 1983]; in general, when the funding source is highly centralized, a greater degree of control can be exercised over programs). Not surprisingly, individual corporations speak with a more unified voice than federal agencies do. Yet we find nothing comparable to the readers' reports, discussed in chapter 4, in which Apple and Plum authors suggested that manuscripts under review did not correspond to the style of previously published books. This is direct substantive control.

There is yet another and even more consequential tradeoff. Incongruent demands may generate complex reporting and accounting systems, but they also encourage strategic behavior. Elsewhere I have documented how a public TV station is able to satisfy funding sources on a partial, ad

hoc basis by playing one funding source off against another
(see Powell and Friedkin 1983:431–34). In scholarly publishing such opportunism is very difficult. Social ties among
houses and authors are clustered and relatively exclusive, as
opposed to the dispersed and politicized relationships common in public television. As a result, scholarly editors know
that substitution is not easy; not only is it both difficult and
unethical to play one group off against another, but news of
any malfeasance travels quickly through academic networks.
This is even more important when one considers the quasi-
moral character of editor-author relationships, many of
which are close and enduring. The distinction between work
and social life is hard for many editors to draw. This makes it
all the more difficult to act strategically and treat authors as
impersonal providers of supplies that vary with respect to
both quality and marketability.

Access and Networks

What are the consequences of the close alignment between
scholarly publishers and certain influential academics? What
effect do these relationships have on the long-term health of
scholarly publishing houses?

It is my impression, based on hundreds of conversations,
that most academic authors regard the publishing process as
an open market. Academics submit their manuscripts and
assume that publishers will evaluate the merits of their work
as capably and equitably as possible. The process departs
somewhat from the submission of an article to a professional
journal—the author is not anonymous, nor are the initial
reviews done by an author's peers—but the evaluation is not
thought to be fundamentally dissimilar. In contrast, editors
conceive of the process in a completely different light. The
editorial task is like combing a beach that is covered with
rocks and shells of different shapes and colors in search of a
small quota of gems that nicely complement one's existing
collection. It is impossible to search widely or thoroughly;
instead, the skilled collector will learn, over time, to look

along the high-tide line near a certain jetty after a heavy storm.

There are a number of good organizational reasons for editors to restrict access to potential exchange partners. Searching for all the alternatives is a costly process. A system of priorities, such as a work queue, is an efficient means for dealing with overload. There are lower risks involved in dealing with known partners because the transaction is grounded in personal relationships. Recurrent exchanges reaffirm friendships. Trust and reliability are marvelously efficient lubricants to economic transactions. There are, however, drawbacks associated with this course of action. While the major burden is borne by the authors who lack access, the publishing house may suffer as well. Strong, established social networks can create a kind of social inertia, a rigidity that is analogous to a type of brand loyalty that precludes consideration of other, perhaps better, products. This social inertia has two related costs, and these accrue over time. Exclusive, repeat trading can result in parochialism, that is, an intellectual or ideological homogenization of a publisher's list. Authors with different theoretical viewpoints may either lack access to the house or choose not to contact it because its list has become so strongly identified with a particular type of scholarship. An editor's networks can also age or ossify. As an editor grows older, so does his or her network of authors and advisers. If this network has been tightly bounded and entry to it has been severely restricted, the editor may find it very difficult to learn about, or to acquire, work that is new and on disciplinary frontiers. Research in industrial organization has shown that it usually takes some kind of exogenous shock to jolt organizations out of a pattern of repeat purchasing (see Granovetter 1983a:34–37); change is seldom sought by the organization itself. Moreover, given the important resources provided by trading networks, changes that might create disaffection or withdrawal of legitimacy may be very difficult for the organization to pursue (see Hannan and Freeman 1984).

A variety of mechanisms limit an author's opportunity for

first- or even secondhand contact with an editor at a publishing house. There is also considerable variation within the academic community with regard to the willingness of prominent scholars to serve as brokers or patrons for their younger colleagues and thereby provide them with contact with a major publisher. Different degress of access also result from the differential location of individuals within a network of relations. Other things being equal, academics at geographically peripheral universities will have less access, as will scholars located at less prestigious universities. An important exception to this rule is that academics at less prestigious universities in the New York metropolitan area will profit from their geographic proximity to Apple and Plum. Another exception is that even at the most well-connected or prestigious universities the formal structure of academic organization may provide some individuals with more opportunities for access than it provides to others.

What are the implications of restricted access in scholarly publishing? Peter Marsden (1983:704) argues that, when the range of choice for some actors is restricted, they can be forced to exchange resources at a price less than market value because of their lack of alternatives. He then goes on to note that networks distort market value and give a higher exchange value to resources controlled by well-connected actors than these actors would receive under conditions of unrestricted access. Such a process could lead to the creation of a binary opportunity structure, with the rich getting richer and the poor getting poorer. In contrast to Apple and Plum, the leading journals in the social sciences are more pluralistic; they publish articles by authors from a wider variety of academic institutions.[9] This suggests that well-connected academics can easily publish their books, including books that may fall below the normal standards upheld by Apple or Plum, but that academics who unfortunately lack access may be forced to stake their careers and promotion prospects on the publication of journal articles.

Is the pattern of restricted access to Apple and Plum a less than optimal situation for many social scientists? Or, as Morton (1982:863) has argued, am I conflating concern over how manuscripts are evaluated at two publishing houses with concern over the control of the flow of ideas in the social sciences? Many editors contend that, since they determine only what their own house will publish, they are not the arbiters of a manuscript's ultimate fate. In part, this is correct. The number of publication outlets in the social sciences is not shrinking; indeed, the number of specialized scholarly publishers has burgeoned.[10] And the growth in the number of journals and of annual reviews, which bridge journal articles and monograph-length studies, has even outpaced the growth in the number of books published each year. These new publications seem to spawn like mushrooms after a good rain. Such developments in scholarly publishing are in part isomorphic with trends in the social sciences. Research is increasingly sophisticated. Written work now includes charts, tables, graphs, and mathematical notations. There has been a rapid expansion of subfields in the social sciences, and the rise of applied social research has grown apace. The primary danger is certainly not shrinkage of publication outlets. Instead, overproduction appears to be a greater cause for concern. Indeed, it often seems that the many new social science publications are not so much being read as received.

Despite the proliferation of scholarly publishing houses, it is my strong impression that the reputation and influence of the most prestigious ones have grown. This process operates as a contrast effect: in the midst of a large number of houses that are somewhat difficult to distinguish from one another, firms such as Apple and Plum stand out. The power of reputation depends in part on whether a good reputation is hard to obtain and in part on whether many people seek to acquire it (see Kreps and Wilson 1982). My evidence for this argument is fragmentary but strongly suggestive. For example, despite the number of new entrants, annual sales at Apple and Plum have outpaced both inflation and the overall growth rate for scientific and professional books. Interviews with a number of university librarians and booksellers have provided ample illustration of the power of reputational effects. One librarian responsible for her library's acquisitions said, "There are too many new publications to keep track of . . . basically I order the great majority of new titles from five or six of the best houses and wait for reviews or requests from the faculty before ordering other books." (Apple was included in her list of the "best" houses.) As a result, more options can actually lead to less-informed choices. Conversations with the book-review editors at a number of academic journals and journals of opinion also suggest that prestige is a valuable currency. A publisher's logo is particularly important to the fortunes of books by little-known authors. The books of highly visible scholars are typically sent out for review regardless of who their publisher is. But when the book-review editor does not know an author's work, the prestige of the publisher can be a major factor in whether or not the book receives a review. Thus, although acquisition editors do not actually determine a manuscript's ultimate fate, the fact that a prestigious house has selected a manuscript for publication can make an important difference. A book is more likely to be reviewed and to be purchased when it is published by an Apple or Plum press.

Journal articles are, to a certain extent, a barometer of an author's skill in a competition for scarce space. Books are different from journal articles: they are different in part because, while what one has to say is obviously important, whom one knows may determine one's success in getting into print. Books are also different in that we expect a good deal more of a book than of a journal article. A book should have a clear purpose—a detailed, systematic, coherent argument. A journal article need only report on a piece of research or a new idea. For most authors it is much harder to get a book published by Apple or Plum than it is to have an article accepted by a leading disciplinary journal. The publication system is a type of control system. A number of factors— prestige, tradition, and networks of affiliation—limit access and restrict diversity. Both Apple and Plum must, of course, maintain reputations that are reasonable proxies for reality. Otherwise the prestige system collapses.

The principal threat to such houses as Apple and Plum is

the possibility that their networks may either ossify or become too specialized. Many scientific fields are constantly fragmenting and splintering. Sometimes subgroups link up with subgroups in other disciplines; more commonly, subgroups become more and more specialized. This makes it all the more difficult to find books that appeal to broad audiences. The other danger is that, as the networks of authors and advisers age, the house finds that it increasingly lags behind new developments in research and theory. The house may experience a kind of downward mobility as its list becomes associated with the received wisdom of an old guard. The tighter and more homogeneous the circle of authors and advisers becomes, the more likely it is that this will happen. As Edward Shils (1981:213) has observed, "The existence of tradition is at least as much a consequence of limited power to escape from it as it is a consequence of a desire to continue and to maintain it."

I will not attempt to try to forecast the future direction of either Apple or Plum. It is my strong conviction, however, that both houses should be able to ride out periods of austerity. After all, both have prospered in the 1970s and early 1980s—hardly a prosperous era for higher education or for scientific research. Both have pursued strategies designed to lessen their dependence on external resources. Plum has healthy international sales and uses its serial publications as a means of convincing librarians to spend their shrinking budgets by filling out their many serial collections of Plum volumes. Apple continues to enjoy a strong identity, and its diverse list of scholarly, trade, and textbook titles allows it to keep a foot in several camps. The key issues for long-term viability are really perennial ones: how much autonomy will editors be afforded in the course of their duties, and how widely will the houses cast their nets in search of new authors? The answers to these questions will determine the future trajectory of both houses. Whatever that may be, the internal processes of decision-making and control are not likely to change in the immediate future.

APPENDIX

MANUSCRIPT ACQUISITION CODE
DEVELOPED FOR APPLE PRESS

Category 1.   Author initiated contact with the publishing house
   a. Over the transom—cold
   b. Over the transom with supporting materials (letters of reference, use of someone's name, etc.)
   c. Author approached editor/house at a convention, meeting, etc.
   d. Author contacted house cold—makes specific reference to backlist
   e. Author contacted house, but several houses are bidding for manuscript
   f. Other

Category 2.   Author had previous ties to the house or was referred by someone who had a connection with the house
   a. Referral from parent company
   b. Ongoing relationship between the house and an institution (e.g., a research institute or a private foundation)
   c. Serial arrangement (e.g., an annual publication or a referral by a series editor)
   d. Old contract—signed by a previous editor
   e. Paperback or new edition
   f. Referred by another publisher who recommends material

 g. Referred by informal adviser or previous house author

 h. Submitted by an agent known by the editor

 i. Institution/foundation contacted house about manuscript by author affiliated with them, and they suggested a subvention to defray costs of publication

 j. Author had previously been published by the house

 k. Author had previously reviewed manuscripts for the house

 l. Other

Category 3. Manuscript was acquired due to editor's initiative or contacts

 a. Author is a personal friend of editor

 b. The editor solicited the material either on the telephone, on a trip, or at a convention

 c. The editor commissioned the book

 d. An import purchased by the editor-in-chief or an editor on a trip abroad, or paperback rights to a book purchased from another American publisher

 e. Editor signed the book at a previous house and brought it along to his or her new house

 f. Author and editor had discussed manuscript, and the author sent material to the editor when it was completed

 g. A friend told the editor about someone's work in progress, and the editor contacted the author

 h. Serendipity—editor "stumbled upon" author

 i. Other

Category 4. Insufficient information to categorize

NOTES

Notes to Introduction

1. In contrast to the dearth of research on book publishing, there are many studies of the policies and decision-making procedures used by the editors of scientific journals (see Crane 1967 and 1972; Zuckerman and Merton 1971; Schwartz 1975:63–87; Schwartz and Dubin 1978; and Lindsey 1978). The intellectual press is also a frequent target of scrutiny (see Lekachman 1965; Wrong 1970; Kadushin 1974; and Nobile 1974). The key difference between scholarly journals and scholarly books is that books are usually published with the aim of earning a profit. The decision to publish a book is never "pure"; it always rests on a guess about the market for a book as well as on an appraisal of the book's merits. Decisions about journal articles are more formalized and are subject to standards of scholarship, not market potential; as a result, the decision process is easier to study.

2. The weaknesses that characterize most company histories plague the majority of publishing-house histories as well. Many of them are commemorative works, produced to mark a festive occasion. Not surprisingly, the picture they present is rather bland and colorless. At worst, they are exercises in public relations. The best examples of this genre that I have encountered are Exman's (1967) account of Harper and Row, Ballou's (1970) history of the early years of Houghton Mifflin, and Sutcliffe's (1978) history of Oxford University Press.

3. The major histories of the publishing industry include Tebbel's (1972, 1975, 1978, 1981) extremely detailed volumes, Sheehan's (1952) account of publishing in the "Gilded Age," and Lehmann-Haupt's (1951) history of the making and selling of books in the United States from 1630 to 1950. Also valuable are Hart 1950, Madison 1966 and 1974, and Mott 1947.

4. It is not surprising that many of the people associated with the book trade tend to be self-conscious and self-reflexive. As a consequence, few of the memoirs and biographies of editors and publishers provide us with naive accounts. They are designed and intended as partisan documents. For sociologists, the real drawback of this kind of book, and of the company

history as well, is the scarcity of hard data; at best these books give figures on the extreme cases—the highest advance, the largest first printing, and so on. To my mind, Haydn's (1974) autobiography is in a class by itself. Also of interest are Canfield 1971, Cerf 1977, Commins 1978, and Gilmer 1970.

5. I have found Ross 1977, Braudy 1978, and Whiteside 1981 to be particularly useful.

6. Among the various books that deal with the business and financial aspects of book publishing, the following are among the most helpful: Miller 1949, Grannis 1967, Bailey 1970, Dessauer 1974, Balkin 1977, and Shatzkin 1982.

7. For a detailed discussion of the growth of various reading publics, see, in particular, Altick's (1957) entertaining study of reading habits in Victorian England and Watt's (1957) lovely account of the emergence of the novel in eighteenth-century England. Also see Bramstead 1964, James 1963, Q. D. Leavis 1965, and Ward 1974. On the social context in which literature is produced, see Bradbury 1971, Darnton 1971, Gedin 1977, Graña 1964, Sutherland 1976, and Williams 1961.

8. Among the few are Caplette 1981, Coser, Kadushin, and Powell 1982, Lane 1970 and 1975, Powell 1978b and 1982b, and Machlup and Leeson 1978.

9. Kurt Lewin (1951) coined the term "gatekeepers." He noted that information travels through particular communication channels and that specific areas within these channels function as gates, governed either by impartial rules or by individuals empowered to make the decision whether information should be let "in" or remain "out." Lewin's interest in the concept of gatekeeper did not spawn a great deal of subsequent research; however, one important line of inquiry has focused on newspaper editors. White (1950) discussed how a newspaper editor selects what news to print. His analysis of the reasons given for rejecting various types of news stories indicated how highly subjective and reliant on value judgments, based on the gatekeeper's own set of experiences, attitudes, and expectations, the selection of "news" actually is. Geiber (1964), in a review of his research on gatekeepers and civil-liberties news, on telegraph editors, and on editors of small Wisconsin dailies, argued that news is what newspapermen make it to be. Warren Breed's (1955) well-known contribution illustrated the ways in which newspapermen's reporting of the news is guided by the opinions and attitudes of their cohort of superiors and colleagues rather than by anticipation of their audience's reaction. Robert Darnton's beautiful article "Writing News and Telling Stories" (1975) is one of the best recent treatments of the subject. Also see Tuchman 1972, 1973, and 1978 and Roshco 1975.

10. Some attention is also given to the historical trends and large-scale changes that have marked both the past and more recent development of the book industry, but that is not the principal concern of this book. For a more thorough coverage of these issues, see Powell 1978a and Coser, Kadushin, and Powell 1982.

11. Unfortunately, we lack the data necessary to assess the accuracy of Sifton's claim. One of my more frustrating experiences was as a participant in the planning group for an issue of *Daedalus* (Winter, 1983) on the American reading public. While there was no shortage of opinions among

the planning group, there was an almost total absence of hard information on which to ground opinion. The small amount of empirical research that is available suggests that readership is not so much declining as shifting. Caplow et al. (1982:24–25), in their follow-up study of Middletown (Muncie, Indiana), find that the number of library cardholders declined from 48 percent of the population in 1925 to 31 percent in 1975. Yet the average number of books drawn annually by each cardholder increased from fifteen to twenty-two. In 1925, the public library was the principal supplier of books; in the 1970s, numerous bookstores and paperback racks offered the community additional access to books. Most important, library reading habits had shifted markedly: only one out of every six books checked out in the 1930s was nonfiction, but in the 1970s half of the books that circulated were nonfiction.

The Middletown data confirm my own opinion that fiction-reading has declined but that overall reading levels may possibly have increased as specialized reading tastes have burgeoned and popular nonfiction has become the major kind of recreational reading. Data that report the growth in the number of titles by subject area back up this view. For example, in the period 1955–75, there was a 212.7 percent increase in the number of books released annually. Yet, in this same period, the number of fiction titles increased by only 83.6 percent, while books on sports and recreation increased by 512.5 percent and titles in sociology and economics jumped by 1,167.3 percent. The subject categories are based on the Dewey system and are rather broad; still, there is a clear increase in nonfiction as compared to fiction. The information comes from *Social Indicators, 1976*, U.S. Dept. of Commerce, p. 516.

12. See Coser, Kadushin, and Powell 1982:chapter 4.

13. See ibid.: 112–17, 194–97.

Notes to Chapter One

1. Quoted from page 1 of the conference report, edited by Jean V. Naggar, *The Money Side of Publishing: Fundamentals for Non-Financial People* (New York: Association of American Publishers, 1976).

2. William Jovanovich, "The Structure of Publishing," a speech given in 1956 at the Center for Graphic Arts and Publishing of New York University; quoted in Tebbel 1981:722.

3. Quoted in Tony Schwartz, "A Publisher Who Sells Books," *New York Times Book Review*, December 9, 1979.

4. The 1959 and 1966 figures are from *Publishers Weekly*; the 1981 data are from the *U.S. Industrial Outlook*, (Washington, D.C.: U.S. Department of Commerce, 1983), pp. 7–6.

5. The data are from the final 1981 figures published in the Commerce Department's quarterly industry report, *Printing and Publishing*, vol. 22, no. 4, p. 7, edited by William S. Lofquist. The *U.S. Census of Manufactures* defines "company" as "a business organization consisting of one or more establishments under common ownership or control"; a "book-publishing establishment" is defined as "a place where books are published." There were 815 establishments in 1954; in 1977 there were 1,750.

6. The Authors Guild (1977a and b), a trade union representing American writers, has been a vociferous critic of these changes in the industry. It contends that:

> We have seen mergers in every imaginable permutation—hardcover houses merging with each other; hardcover houses merging with paperback houses; the combination thus formed being taken over, in turn, by huge entertainment complexes, involving radio-television networks and motion picture companies. And in some cases, perhaps most distressing of all, we have seen the business of choosing and purveying books, traditionally the province of more or less dedicated book men with one eye on profit and the other on literary and social values, falling under the control of businessmen with no prior interest in books—men, it has sometimes seemed to us, cursed like the Cyclops with having only a single eye, and that eye not trained on literary or social value but steadfastly on the bottom line of a company's financial statement. [Authors Guild 1977a]

In contrast, the industry's trade association, the Association of American Publishers (AAP), has argued that mergers and consolidations have made available the resources without which the remarkable growth of recent years could not have been sustained.

7. Quoted from a speech by Heather Kirkwood to the Pubmart Workshop on Concentration of Ownership in Book Publishing, New York, April 11, 1979.

8. Reported in *BP Report on the Business of Book Publishing*, September 14, 1981 (Knowledge Industry Publications, Inc.). One leading mass-market paperback line, Fawcett, was incorporated into the Ballantine line in 1982. Two smaller lines, Playboy and Ace, were sold to Putnam. And most of Popular Library's titles were sold to Warner. These acquisitions sharply increased concentration, but it should be noted that the rapidly declining number of firms reflects the severe illness of this industry sector; it does not indicate the market power of dominant firms.

9. Reported in *BP Report*, August 13, 1981.

10. U.S. Bureau of the Census report, quoted in *Publisher Weekly*, April 30, 1982, p. 22.

11. Recent developments in book retailing parallel the shifts in marketing strategy inside publishing houses. Some critics go further and charge that the rationalization of book selling is responsible for recent changes in book publishing. It is obviously hard to establish a causal priority, and, at any rate, the developments are mutually reinforcing. That there has been an effort to rationalize book selling is not surprising. Book distribution has always been a vexing problem because of the large number of books issued each year and the policy of publishers to allow booksellers to return unsold copies. ("Gone today, here tomorrow," was Alfred Knopf's sarcastic comentary on the returns policy.) Yet few in the industry anticipated the phenomenal rise of chain bookstores. The chains have spread throughout the country, attracting new buyers to their stores, which are stocked with such high-turnover items as bestsellers and books on the latest fads. For a good reading on how book selling has been transformed, compare Bliven's 1975 account of a traditional book traveler with Powell's 1983 analysis of the chain bookstores and specialty shops.

12. It is possible that this bifurcation of the market may even affect the manner in which authors convey their ideas. The literary critic Leslie Fiedler suggests that novels presently fall into the categories "art or show biz," and not just after they are written and have been sorted out by self-conscious critics and/or the blind mechanism of the marketplace, but in their very conception. Writers tend to write for the academy or for Hollywood, "which is to say as if to be taught, analyzed, and explicated—or to be packaged, hyped, and sold at the box office" (Fiedler 1981:143–44).

13. Richard Snyder, president of Simon and Schuster, did not exaggerate very much when he said, "In a certain sense, we are the software of the television and movie media" (quoted in Whiteside 1981:70).

14. For example, Dessauer (1983:107) reports that adult trade hardcover publishers are particularly dependent on subsidiary-rights income. This category of publishers had a net income of only 5.6 percent in 1980 but had earned-rights income of 15.5 percent, making their loss on their regular operations nearly 10 percent.

15. See Edwin McDowell, "The Loyalty of Authors to Publishers Has New Name: It's Spelled M–O–N–E–Y," *New York Times*, January 22, 1981, p. C12.

16. For data on salaries in publishing, see Stella Dong, "Publishing's Revolving Door," *Publishers Weekly*, December 19, 1980, pp. 20–23; see also Coser, Kadushin, and Powell 1982: chap. 4.

17. As industry analyst John Dessauer notes (1983:95–96), data on the book industry are notoriously scarce and incomplete. The most inclusive and widely used surveys, conducted by the U.S. Bureau of the Census, fall considerably short of capturing the full population of publishing houses. The 1977 *Census of Manufactures for Book Publishing* (SIC 2731) reports on 1,750 publishing establishments, but the R. R. Bowker Company's records suggest that "at least 8,000 bona fide book publishers were actually operating at the time." Late in 1982 Bowker listed 13,000 publishers who had contributed to *The Publishers' Trade List Annual* and *Books in Print*. In addition to excluding very small firms, the *Census* figures are most likely to fail to include publishing subsidiaries of educational, professional, and religious organizations.

18. John Brooks, speaking for the Authors Guild, in his remarks made at the Federal Trade Commission Symposium on Media Concentration, session on Cencentration and Conglomeration in Book Publishing, Washington, D.C., December 14 and 15, 1978.

19. Carroll (1984) notes strong similarities among specialist firms across industries. For example, specialist newspapers are less likely to have their own production facilities or distribution networks, and specialized music-recording labels are less likely than the large record companies to own production studios, to distribute their records, to manufacture them, or to promote their artists as widely.

20. As Freeman and Hannan (1983:1119) put it, "specialist organizations will appear to be leaner than generalists, to have less organizational fat."

21. Similarly, Peterson and Berger (1975) show that, unlike earlier periods in the record industry, when industry concentration was associated

with a narrowing of musical tastes, the renewed market concentration of the 1970s did not lesson musical diversity. A wide range of musical tastes was satisfied because of the institutionalization of the multidivisional form and the aggressive interdivisional competition within record companies.

22. Noble (1982:112) provides figures on book sales by distribution channel. The shares of the market in 1979 were as follows:

General retail stores	23.0%
College stores	14.3
Libraries/institutions	8.2
Schools	18.4
Direct to consumer	27.4
Other	0.9
Export	7.6

23. On the term "invisible colleges," see chapter 2, note 12.

24. In 1979, the eleven leading text houses accounted for 67 percent of college text sales (Noble, 1982:134).

25. For more details on the life-styles of editors, see chapter 4 of Coser, Kadushin, and Powell 1982.

26. Commercial houses tend to avoid these areas because few scholars who are active in them have research grants with which to purchase expensive monographs. Nor do many libraries allocate a large portion of their budgets for the humanities. University presses do, however, publish a considerable number of works in this area. Because trade publishers concentrate on the mass market and monograph publishers focus on the sciences, works of poetry, short stories, and translations are more frequently published by university presses. There is a clear parallel with television, where serious programming is also relegated to subsidized public television stations.

27. For a comparative analysis of the social circles in which scholarly, text, and trade editors are enmeshed, see chapter 3 of Coser, Kadushin, and Powell 1982.

28. Trade paperbacks, the "aristocrats" of paperback publishing, have a somewhat different life-span. Although the distinction between trade and mass-market paperbacks is sometimes blurry, the former are generally produced with better-quality materials and are sold chiefly in bookstores. Mass-market paperbacks are lower in price and smaller in size; intended for popular consumption, they are sold in newsstands, drugstores, supermarkets, bookstores, and anywhere else a paperback display rack can be located. Some trade paperbacks are serious works, of fiction or nonfiction, intended for a well-educated audience. A number of quality trade-paperback lines have been started in the past few years, and books of great merit are now available for the first time in paperback. To my mind, the success of these books has been one of the most exciting developments in recent publishing history. Nevertheless, not all trade paperbacks are books of distinction; much popular and trivial entertainment, such as *The Preppy Handbook*, is also published in trade-paperback format.

29. Harold T. Miller, president of Houghton Mifflin, quoted in *Business Week*, July 4, 1977, p. 50.

Notes to Chapter Two

1. One of the most pronounced changes in recent publishing history has been the shift from individual or family control to corporate ownership. Until the late 1950s most publishing houses were identified with one family or a single individual. In some cases the family's role could be traced back to the nineteenth century. Although there are a few exceptions, such as Harcourt Brace Jovanovich and McGraw-Hill, most large publishing companies today are run by group management. This change is directly tied to the period of expansion, diversification, and mergers in the 1960s and 1970s. With new product lines and specialization, the pursuit of worldwide markets, and the trend toward multimedia ownership, most large previously independent publishing houses became one of many companies operating under the same roof or the same corporate umbrella.

2. The advantages of a series may also extend to the editorial review process. Robert Darnton (1983), in a humorous reflection on the many hurdles that authors must surmount—a situation he observed at first hand during a stint on the editorial board of Princeton University Press—half-facetiously suggests that authors "submit a series." He notes that "we at Princeton turn down books by the hundreds, but as far as I know we have never turned down a series, and we took on half a dozen during my four years on the board."

3. J. David Sapir, an anthropologist who edits a series for a university press, suggests that the term "power" hardly captures his motivation for serving as a series editor. He notes, "If it is power, it is a rinky-dink sort of power." He correctly points out that the task of editing a series is arduous. It is not pleasant to turn people down, nor is it easy to help transform a dissertation into a book in which "several simultaneous levels—the facts of the matter, commentary on the facts, and the theoretical implications of the commentary—are operating together and are constantly at play" (Sapir 1983, personal communication). There is no question but that a well-edited series is difficult work. And certainly the hard work and the infrequent rewards, when a book gets some attention, may outweigh, in an editor's mind, his or her perceived influence. But if one compares the structural position of a series editor to that of an author looking for a publisher, the editor is seen to be in a powerful intermediary position, since his or her sponsorship dramatically increases the author's chances of getting published.

4. Perrow (1985), writing from the perspective of an "established author," argues that annual reviews, conference proceedings, and the like are ideal publication outlets for well-known scholars. These nonrefereed publishing options afford "the opportunity to work one's ideas out in print." They are more willing to accept new lines of inquiry and unconventional and reflective work. Of course, such volumes contain a certain amount of dross, but that is the price to be paid for escaping the orthodoxy of the mainstream journals.

5. For a more extensive discussion of the role of patrons and brokers in scholarly publishing, see Coser, Kadushin and Powell 1982:302–7.

6. We must be careful not to confuse either trust or a norm of reciproc-

ity with some notion of a generalized social morality. Trust is closely tied to self-interest; one trusts best the information generated in the course of one's own experiences. Granovetter (1983b:30) warns that "the widespread preference to transact with partners of known reputation implies that few of us are content to rely on general moral dispositions or on institutional arrangements if more specific information is available." It is evident that in cases of repeated reciprocal exchange, malfeasance is inhibited by the potential for damage to one's reputation.

7. For a discussion of how this myriad of individual transactions can overwhelm publishing houses, see Powell 1983.

8. Such small printings are still common and have changed little since the time of my fieldwork. In a 1983 study of 165 academic authors in economics departments and business schools, Shubik, Heim, and Baumol (1983:369) found that "most scholarly books are destined to have relatively modest sales in the range not exceeding 2,000."

9. Publishers commonly complain that because they produce hundreds of unique, individual products, consumers do not develop "brand-name loyalty." While this may be true for the general reading public, it is not true for librarians and booksellers. Our interviews revealed many instances of such loyalty; librarians and booksellers often base their decisions about which new books to order on a publisher's editorial and marketing reputation.

10. More recent data suggest that advances have not kept pace with inflation. Indeed, advances for scholarly or professional books appear to be the exception rather than the rule. In the study conducted by Shubik, Heim, and Baumol (1983:378), three out of four authors received no advance at all for their books, and the sample included authors of textbooks and trade books as well as professional books. This is unfortunate, though not necessarily because it means less money in authors' pockets. An advance reflects a commitment on the part of the publisher; it shifts part of the risk of publication from the author to the publisher. For example, if royalties never add up to the amount of the advance, the difference is usually borne by the publisher. In addition, it is not altogether uncommon for a house to be acquired by, or merged with, another firm while an author's book is in process. If an author has received an advance, the new owners have a stake in seeing that the book is published.

11. While I was involved in fieldwork at Apple Press, each of the senior editors received several job offers from other houses. The psychology editor left shortly after my observations ended. A year and a half later, unhappy at the house he had joined, he returned to Apple Press. At the time of his departure, the editor-in-chief noted that this editor "was irreplaceable." It was over six months before a suitable replacement was found. At the outset of my fieldwork, two editors had recently left Apple Press for better positions in other companies. Midway through my fieldwork, the marketing director resigned. The editors handled the promotion of their own books for a while, then a free-lance person assisted with the marketing for several months. Eventually a new marketing director was hired.

Only one editor left Plum Press during the course of my fieldwork there, but since then at least three editors have left for positions at other houses. The top administration of Plum Press has also changed significantly: the president has retired, and several top executives have been promoted to positions within the parent company.

12. For a detailed review of the concept of invisible colleges, see Crane 1972.

13. Since the primary focus of this study is on the way that editors select and acquire manuscripts, I have not provided a thorough discussion of the operations of the production, manufacturing, and marketing departments at either house. For an excellent discussion of these functions, see the accounts in the relevant sections of Bailey 1970 and Balkin 1977.

14. For details on interdepartmental conflicts in trade and textbook publishing, see Coser, Kadushin, and Powell 1982:185–99. The reactions of authors to the services provided by the different departments in commercial scholarly houses and university presses are summarized in Powell 1982a.

15. Epstein (1977:435) provides several humorous and incisive comments on this aspect of publishing. He recalls that, when he was an editor, he was visited by an editor from a distinguished English publishing firm:

> In a crisp Oxbridge accent he announced that he was here on a selling trip, attempting to sell the American rights to a number of his firm's titles. From his briefcase he extracted page after page, each one listing a title for sale, a brief description of its contents, a biographical note on the author, and a suggested price. I needed to concentrate, at various points, to recall that we were talking about books and not something else: costume jewelry, say, or cutlery. By the time he had arrived at my office, his better items had already been sold off, and the remaining ones—treatises on land reform in Wales, social scientific studies even more dismally specialized than those produced in the United States—were of no possible interest. We chatted pleasantly until, undefeated and indefatigable, he departed to make his next call. After he left, I thought of the old joke about the man in the circus whose job is to clean up after the elephants. When asked by a friend why he doesn't quit so undignified a job, the man replies, "What! And leave show business!"

16. Goodenough (1963:94) has discussed the social value of "established routines," pointing out that:

> Schedules provide for gratification of otherwise mutually incompatible wants. They acquire value also . . . by making it possible to have fairly reliable expectations . . . Finally, schedules help to space activities in such a way as to give the practice of each a fairly high net efficacy . . . Because they resolve so many different problems, schedules often represent a delicate balance that allows for little alteration without serious dislocation effects.

The disruption of one item in a tight publishing schedule frequently disrupts the entire schedule and throws the whole timetable off.

17. Openness is, of course, a two-way street. I believe, for example, that multiple submissions are reasonable, given the inevitable delays that authors face when they send their manuscripts to one publisher at a time. But it is incumbent upon an author to disclose to the publisher that he has submitted his manuscript to several houses simultaneously. On the other hand, as a book nears its publication date, its author is sometimes kept in

the dark about a number of key decisions. Publishers should provide authors with information about price, how royalties are calculated, the size of the print run, promotion plans, and where review copies have been sent. Such openness helps cement the relationship, and authors may even provide helpful suggestions when they are kept apprised of publication plans.

Notes to Chapter Three

1. A recent profile of editors working in the areas of science, medicine, technology, and the social and behavioral sciences is reported in Summers 1982. The survey presents salary data for editors in the United States, the United Kingdom, the Netherlands, and West Germany. Summers (1982:2109) begins his report by stating:

> Editors are . . . the most expensive and valuable human assets we employ . . . they are the most difficult staff to appoint. Good editors are also among the hardest of all staff to replace—every departure causes a loss of editorial momentum, a faltering of publishing rhythm which no house . . . can afford.

2. This chapter is based for the most part on my field observations at Apple Press and Plum Press. At Apple Press there were two senior editors who each signed approximately thirty books a year. The president of the company and an assistant editor annually signed about ten books between them. The editor-in-chief's "quota" varied, depending on how active his editors were. One year, when the press was without a sociology editor, he signed thirty-five books; the following year, after an editor had been hired, he signed sixteen titles. At Plum Press, my observations were concentrated on two senior editors, each of whom signed between thirty-five and forty books a year. I interviewed the editor-in-chief and an editorial vice-president of Plum, as well as editors who worked for the subsidiary company; however, I did not observe these people in the course of their daily affairs. I also spoke with Plum Press editors who worked in the physical and biological sciences.

In addition, I draw on interviews I had with the director of a leading university press and with his editor-in-chief, two senior editors, and one former editor. I also interviewed four editors at other commercial scholarly houses as well as three editors at three different university presses. I have also made use of interviews and field notes collected by Laurie Michael Roth in her participant-observation study of a large university press and by Annabelle Sreberny in her study of a small university press. Finally, I have utilized information from interviews with editors that were conducted by my research associates as part of a general study of book publishing (see the Appendix in Coser, Kadushin, and Powell 1982).

When I use the term "editor" without any other classification, I am referring to editors whose principal concern is acquisitions.

3. The reputation of a publishing house attracts many submissions. The younger authors whom I interviewed were aware that their chances for publication were somewhat better at Plum Press than at Apple Press. During the years 1975–78, Apple published, at most, three revised dissertations a year. Plum Press has a much larger list than Apple; even so,

dissertations constitute a higher percentage of their total output. From an editor's perspective, most dissertations devote inordinate attention to methodological issues and a review of the existing literature. Editors are more favorably disposed toward manuscripts that are intellectually more speculative and include policy recommendations. The prospects for young writers are not helped by the two- or three-year time lag between a book's publication and the appearance of a review in a professional journal. More prompt reviews could generate interest in what a young writer has to say. Thus it is more feasible for editors to publish established authors, for whom there are ready academic and library sales. Current cutbacks in library budgets, federal research grants, and operating subsidies for university presses now make it even more difficult for young scholars to publish their dissertations.

4. Economists have argued that transaction costs are lowered when there are "lubricants" to the exchange process. Such "lubricants" include personal relationships between actors, which facilitate understanding and reduce opportunism; precedents set by others; and reputational networks, which establish actors' credibility. In author-editor relations, however, the publishing house may suffer from too much familiarity between exchange participants. Not only are editors torn by twin loyalties, but authors may feel a greater allegiance to their editors than to the publishing house. For both authors and editors, the relationship to the publishing house is a formal, contractual quid pro quo, while the relationship between authors and editors may be intrinsically rewarding: the friendship itself is the source of value to the participants. Editors may, on occasion, find themselves in the unpleasant position of being accused by an author of betrayal and accused by their employer of cooptation.

5. Editors in university presses must go through a different and more formal decision-making process. In contrast to commercial scholarly houses, the review process at university presses typically requires two outside readings of a manuscript. If these reviews are contradictory, the editor may solicit a third opinion. In a few cases, particularly for very distinguished authors, outside reviews are not required. As a rule, outside readings are much more crucial in the decision-making process at university presses than at commercial houses. If the outside reviews are favorable, the editor recommends publication to the press's board of advisers, which consists of members of the senior faculty. Some boards are small, such as Princeton's four-member committee. Others are much larger; Chicago has a twelve-member board, California a seventeen-member board. The board's decision is usually based solely on considerations of merit; financial information is seldom provided. If the outside reviews are positive, board approval is typically granted.

The review process at university presses takes considerably more time than at commercial houses. Editorial boards commonly meet only once a month, ten months out of the year. To keep from losing manuscripts to commercial houses, where the pace is speedier and less deliberate, university presses have turned to offering letters of intent and advance contracts (see note 9). Nevertheless, the process at university presses is commonly quite time-consuming. Moreover, while commercial houses may sign a book on a promising topic even if the manuscript needs a good bit of revising, a university press would do so less frequently, because board approval would be hard to obtain.

There is currently much discussion of the need for faster publishing decisions by university presses. At the 1982 annual meetings of the Association of American University Presses, John Gallman, director of Indiana University Press, urged his colleagues to "cut down most in-house committees; they are too time-consuming. Get your faculty committees to allow you to accept a book without all that rigmarole" (Reuter el al. 1982).

6. The process of obtaining approval from the parent corporation of Apple Press has changed somewhat in recent years. A new top executive in the parent company now carefully reviews many of the proposals-to-publish from Apple Press. Proposals are sometimes returned with questions attached. This particular executive seems to enjoy a good argument. Final approval is still routinely granted, but the process now takes more time.

7. Would-be authors are strongly advised to speak with people who have had books published by the particular house to which they intend to send a manuscript. In addition, it is a good idea to examine any volumes that the publisher has released that are comparable to the manuscript that is being submitted. Nor does it hurt to review some of the publisher's relevant promotional materials or catalogues.

8. Twenty-five to thirty-five titles is a rough average of the annual work load for the senior editors at Apple and Plum. In general, scholarly editors handle more books each year than trade or college textbook editors do. Seventy percent of the scholarly editors my colleagues and I interviewed in our general study of book publishing signed more than twenty-five books a year (Coser, Kadushin, and Powell 1982:125). The "average" expectation of the sixty-three publishers from four Western countries, reported in Summers (1982:2111), was that editors would acquire at least twenty new books a year, although some houses expected as many as fifty. Given that a scholarly book earns less than a trade title or textbook, the heavier work load is to be expected.

9. Because of increased competition between university presses and commercial houses, more university presses are now willing to offer an advance contract, or a letter of intent to publish, for an incomplete manuscript. At university presses it is understood that the final manuscript will not be published without favorable outside reviews and board approval. Such quasi-official contracts may provide some security to the author; however, they are not legally binding on the publisher.

10. Editors in scholarly publishing maintain more extensive travel schedules than their counterparts in trade and textbook publishing; however, they are less likely than trade or text editors to initiate an idea and to commission an author to write a book on it.

Notes to Chapter Four

1. The study of the professions is the subject of much debate, as scholars are now questioning the attribute approach (Greenwood 1957; Goode 1960) and are suggesting that much of the research on professionals is

ahistorical and serves the ideological interests of powerful professions. Roth's (1974) vigorous critique of research on the professions points out that much of the literature does not focus on the process of professionalization but on its product, "and typically even this focus is contaminated with the ideology and hopes of professional groups rather than [being] an independent assessment of what they achieve." He claims that professional attributes are largely an ideology designed to protect professionals from threats to their power and demands that they become more accountable. Furthermore, most occupational cultures are composed of common values, folklore, symbols, and argot. What distinguishes the professions from other occupations is power, their ability to obtain a set of rights and privileges from society. Friedson (1970, 1976) has maintained that the constellation of characteristics that are accepted as denoting a profession should realistically be seen either as traits that are derived from the power that professions exercise or as a set of traits that the professions do not actually possess but have been able to convince significant others that they have.

2. Halpenny (1973) observes that students preparing for careers in library work must take advanced courses, become familiar with standard reference works, comprehend principles of classification, and acquire some experience with library research methods. There are even specializations that can be pursued: rare books, legal librarianship, business literature, audiovisuals, and data processing. She goes on to show the contrast between publishers and librarians:

> Librarians are major users of publishers' products, carefully trained to acquire, catalogue, and dispense them and to assist readers to gain access to and take fullest advantage of what has been set down in print or gathered onto film or in a data base. Yet the people in publishing who create these products receive virtually no training for their careers before they embark upon them, have to learn quickly what their responsibilities are and how to meet them, and must catch a general training from the remarks of their seniors, what they can read in a not extensive literature, and what they can acquire in this or that conference or work session to which they may be sent if funds and time permit. [Halpenny, 1973:166]

Johnstone and his colleagues argue that:

> There seems little doubt that, at least in the abstract formal sense, journalism can be considered a profession: it is clearly a full-time occupation; there are established training facilities for its practitioners; several professional associations for working news people are in existence; there is legal sanction, of a kind, for its work territory; and formal codes of ethics have been developed. [Johnstone et al. 1976:102]

On the other hand, neither journalism nor librarianship can be regarded as a powerful profession. Johnstone and his colleagues (1976:102) note that "the extent to which practicing newsmen identify as professionals is quite another question." Furthermore, what fledgling journalists should be taught is a controversy as old as journalism itself. Nevertheless, editors in book publishing have none of the formal professional characteristics of either journalists or librarians.

3. With but a few exceptions there is currently little in the way of formal educational training for careers in publishing. One goal of the AAP Committee for Education in Publishing was to identify existing educational

programs and to suggest how others could be started. Its report stated that publishing is

> A vocation "in which most people find themselves by accident, or at least by indirection, chance, family, or other quirky connections." It has long seemed (erroneously) a perfect refuge for those who "love to read" and/or wanted to write, or who didn't know what to do. Not more than a few publishers ever prepared themselves consciously for a life in publishing. [AAP 1977:11]

The Committee's report illustrates very well how occupational groups' attempts to expand their occupational license are inextricably tied to external forces over which they have limited control. The Committee stated that the industry should be concerned:

> (1) with education *for* publishing, which means the educating of those who might or who plan to enter publishing;
> (2) with the further educating *in* publishing, that is, the training and development of those already employed; and
> (3) with education *about* publishing, for those who do not work in publishing but whose good opinion and access to reliable information about publishing is of considerable importance.

With the latter point, the Committee recognized that there are special constituencies—among them, booksellers, librarians, authors, agents, the educational community, reviewers and critics, the financial community, printers, legislators, and the reading public—whose opinions affect the prestige and rewards of publishers.

4. For a detailed discussion of editorial careers, see chapter 4, "Climbing the Editorial Ladder," in Coser, Kadushin, and Powell 1982.

5. In the course of my fieldwork I saw many instances of manuscript referral. The editor-in-chief at a house that was one of Apple Press's prime competitors referred a manuscript to Apple because he felt that the manuscript was "a bit too academic for my tastes." The book subsequently became one of Apple Press's leading titles, selling well both in hardcover and in a later paperback edition. Both the editor-in-chief and the sociology editor at Apple Press frequently referred manuscripts they felt were "too specialized" to editors they knew in monograph houses. They remarked on several occasions that friends of theirs had started small publishing firms and that they were glad to send manuscripts their way. While I was at Apple Press, a manuscript came in from a monograph publisher (which in this case was Plum Press). It had been favorably reviewed by a Plum series editor; however, the acquisitions editor at Plum Press felt that it was too popular a treatment of the subject matter for Plum and suggested to the author that he send the manuscript to Apple Press.

6. The old cliché that variety is the spice of life obviously has some merit. Medoff and Abraham (1980:732) suggest that the "passage of time can come to have a negative effect on productivity, mediated by what might be called 'on-the-job sensory deprivation'" (also see Pfeffer 1983:320–26). For detailed reviews of the literature on turnover, see Price 1977 and Bluedorn 1982.

7. The comments the editor-in-chief at a competing scholarly house

made to me bear directly on the issue of editorial autonomy and the tolerance of mistakes:

> In general, every proposal is accepted as long as in a fundamental way it doesn't disgrace us or isn't a commercial disaster. I believe in a lot of discussion to bring the assumptions about a book out into the open. But it's very rare for a project which is proposed by an editor—one which he really wants—to be vetoed. It's very difficult to second-guess an editor. But if they make too many mistakes, I'll fire them. I believe in editorial freedom as long as they don't blow it.

8. The impact of several years of inflation may require these figures on editors to be adjusted upward. Summers' (1982) survey, drawing on 1981 data, reports a salary range of $23,000 to $43,000 for editors at monograph houses in the United States, with an average salary of $30,750. For salary information of the various branches of book publishing in the United States, see Coser, Kadushin, and Powell 1982:111–12. Our data were reported by editors in 1977 and 1978. Inflation does not, however, seem to have affected starting salaries. An August 15, 1982, *New York Times Book Review* column states that the average entry-level pay is about $9,000 a year.

9. The empirical support for contingency-theory or resource-dependence arguments has been modest. Critics of contingency theory argue that it exaggerates the constraints under which organizations operate (Child 1972). There have been weak empirical tests of contingency theory, in part because of inadequate conceptualization of technology, environment, and organizational effectiveness (Mohr 1971). Pfeffer and Salancik's (1978) resource-dependency theory avoids some of the problems that contingency theory has encountered in trying to explain the "fit" between an organization's structure and its environment. Their concern is to discover how the internal distribution of organizational power is determined by the differential ability of subgroups to solve problems related to critical environmental uncertainty. Critics such as Williamson (1981), however, contend that the power argument is both tautological and imprecise. Williamson's (1975, 1981) transaction cost approach would suggest that editorial discretion is the outcome of an efficient assignment of information and resources to the parts of the enterprise that are the most critical for competitive viability. The debate over whether aspects of organizational structure reflect power or efficiency maximization holds much promise as a research topic.

10. Perrow (1979:50–52) points out that this is an idea about which Max Weber was rather explicit, although few have properly recognized it. To Weber, a person has a set of skills, expertise, or experience and a sense of career with a firm. These skills, expertise, and experience can be developed, and he expects to utilize them; indeed, he wants to. It is therefore wise to allow him the freedom to exercise these skills and to use his discretion, for that is why experts are employed. He should, however, exercise his skills in the service of organizational goals that are set for him. He is not expected, or encouraged, to inquire into the legitimacy of those goals.

11. Warren Breed (1955:328) presents an excellent account of how reporters learn to please their editors. It is a process devoid of any formal instruction.

> When the new reporter starts work, he is not told what policy is. Nor is he ever told. This may appear strange, but interview after interview confirmed the condition. The standard remark was "Never in my —— years on this paper, have I ever been told how to slant a story." No paper in the survey had a "training" program for its new men; some issue a "style" book, but this deals with literary style, not policy. Further, newsmen are busy and have little time for recruit training. Yet all but the newest staffers know what policy is. On being asked, they say they learn it "by osmosis." Basically, the learning of policy is a process by which the recruit discovers and internalizes the rights and obligations of his status and its norms and values. He learns to anticipate what is expected of him so as to win rewards and avoid punishments. The staffer reads his own paper every day; some papers require this. It is simple to diagnose the paper's characteristics. Unless the staffer is naive or unusually independent, he tends to fashion his own stories after others he sees in the paper. This is particularly true of the newcomer. The news columns and editorials are a guide to the local norms. Thus a southern reporter notes that Republicans are treated in a "different" way in his paper's news columns than Democrats. The news about whites and Negroes is also a distinct sort. Should he then write about one of these groups, his story will tend to reflect what he has come to define as standard procedure. Certain editorial actions taken by editors and older staffers also serve as controlling guides. "If things are blue-pencilled consistently," one reporter said, "you learn he [editor] has a prejudice in that regard."

12. I was, at one point, offered a position as an associate editor by a leading scholarly publishing house. I met with their editorial director, and we discussed what my duties would be. I asked about my first assignment. He commented, "We have about four or five manuscripts in the house that desperately need an editor. You would inherit these. They need editing, and this would give you an idea of what we do around here. If you are interested, you can take one or two of them with you."

13. Perrow (1979) suggests that the consequences of effective premise-setting should lead organization theorists to reconsider traditional notions about the span of control. It has long been held that authority must be delegated if a manager has ten or fifteen people to supervise, because a manager cannot watch each employee; if a manager has four or five employees, then direct supervision and control are feasible. Perrow argues that a sensible alternative view is that a narrow span of control allows one to shape premises more effectively and thus avoid the costs of close supervision. A broad span of control is likely to be associated with little delegation, repetitive work, and little control over premises but much control over behavior. Perrow's hypothesis helps explain Blau's (1968) findings that a narrow span of control was associated with more decentralization of decisions than a broad span of control.

14. In houses where sales from the backlist are minimal, the influence of the house's tradition plays a minor part in the decision-making process. Generally this is the case in newly formed companies and in trade houses that do not publish "serious" fiction or nonfiction but produce, instead,

mass-market, trendy materials. At both houses I studied, the backlist accounted for more than 60 percent of total annual sales; hence the types of books previously done by the house were of major consequence in all publishing decisions.

15. One editor suggested that I overstated Apple's lack of interest in highly theoretical work. He said, "Sure, we have our own tastes, but we are also professionals." The difference lies in how various manuscripts are processed. The editor gave the following illustration:

> A book that is interesting and accessible in substance or style is likely to get signed faster, and perhaps without outside review. If we have reason to believe a very theoretical work is important, we certainly would do it. However, it is much more likely to be sent out for one or two reviews. And I'll have to have my facts together when I make a case for the manuscript.

16. Schudson (1978:16) makes a similar point with regard to print journalism, where there are important traditions that urge reporters to move beyond organizational routines. He suggests that "in journalism, as in medicine, one will get nowhere without mastery of the standard procedures, but one will not get somewhere unless one has also acquired and demonstrated the ability to exercise judgment in ways one's colleagues admire."

Notes to Chapter Five

1. As a member of a panel at the American Sociological Association meetings in Chicago, Illinois, in September, 1977, I presented the Columbia Press figures to illustrate the volume of materials with which publishers must cope. The editor-in-chief of Columbia University Press, also a member of the panel, was distressed by my presentation of this data, for he felt that I was implying that manuscripts do not receive sufficient attention. He responded, "Every manuscript gets looked at for at least ten minutes." I was tempted to interject, "I rest my case." Another panelist, Erwin Glikes, then president of Basic Books and an editorial director at Harper and Row, commented that if Basic "were to give every manuscript equal attention, they would each get a three-minute glance."

2. See Brett 1913 and Bessie 1958.

3. A notable exception to this rule occurs when a regular author submits an inferior manuscript; the editor is not impressed with it but does not personally want to say no. These are the "political" problems that can cause editors to lose sleep at night.

4. At Apple Press I initially used a network questionnaire, an instrument that my colleagues and I hoped to use at a number of publishing houses in order to keep track of manuscripts under review. We also anticipated that the responses to the questions would enable us to map both the informal organizational structure and the patterns of external ties—who works with whom, who consults with whom on what projects, and so on. The responses of the various editors to the questionnaire made us realize how extremely difficult such a mapping process would be. Regretfully, we abandoned our quest for network data. In particular, the senior

editors and the editor-in-chief replied that the question that asked for the names of the manuscripts or books on which they were currently working was not answerable. One senior editor wrote the following reply on the questionnaire:

> Not possible to answer. I'm always working on books and thinking about possibilities for new ones. I have twenty-three books scheduled for 1977; about half are in production, and the others are being worked on by me or by the authors. As of this writing, I have the same number scheduled for 1978, six of which are in and being worked on by me. About seven have been signed for 1979, but none is in the house. Also, of course, I have about forty books under active consideration, and consideration plus the red tape of doing a proposal equals "work." Zat what you mean?

The editor-in-chief could not interpret what "working on" was intended to mean. He responded, "Do you mean trying to sign, developing, on the spring list, the fall list, just out, or what? I am probably 'working on' over one hundred books at this time. I couldn't possibly recall the names of all the people I've spoken with in the course of my efforts."

5. The research strategy adopted at Plum differed from the approach I used at Apple for several reasons. My fieldwork could not be as detailed or intensive, because Plum had fifteen times the number of employees that Apple had. Second, at the outset we agreed that my fieldwork would last for a period of less than six months. And, third, individual editors operated much more on their own, working on their own lists and paying little attention to the overall Plum list. At Apple each editor felt that he or she was contributing to the overall list and was willing to talk about the character of the general Apple list. At Plum the editors were willing to talk only about their books, and, given the large number of books that each of them signed, it often happened that, unless they kept good records of correspondence, there were a number of books for which information on the method of acquisition was missing. In addition, the press had a west-coast office, staffed by several editors who also acquired books. The extensive use of series editors further confounded data collection; for Plum editors who received unsolicited manuscripts in a series editor's field of competence would often immediately forward the materials to the series editor, who would give the manuscript its initial scanning. Finally, many authors submitted their manuscripts to a series editor rather than directly to Plum.

6. This is not to say that speed is never a concern. Presented with an opportunity to publish a new book by Lester Thurow or Fernand Braudel (both of whom are published by trade publishers), scholarly publishers would surely move with dispatch. But this would be an exception to the general pattern. For an excellent case study of the "leisurely" decision-making process at scholarly presses, see Erwin and Sapir 1977 for a description of a project that involved six presses and more than three years of waiting time.

7. In category 3, editorial initiative, there are important differences between trade editors—who often hit on an idea for a book and then secure an author to execute it—and scholarly editors. The latter seldom initiate a project. After all, most scholars spend several years doing research before

they begin writing. More commonly, a scholarly editor learns about a research grant or a fellowship award or hears that someone is working on a project; the editor then visits the persons involved on their home campus or writes them and expresses interest. The key to category three for scholarly editors is to learn about a project in its early stages, actively follow up on this information, and eventually persuade an author to submit a manuscript for review.

8. Would-be authors should note that a five-minute conversation with an editor at a convention booth does not constitute "personal contact." In coding category 3 for personal contact, I asked each editor whether he or she expected the arrival of a manuscript. If the answer was yes, I asked several questions to assess the extent of the editor's personal knowledge of the author. A "no" to any of these questions meant that the manuscript was classified in category 1.

9. Authors with no prior contact with a publishing house should be aware that they face several disadvantages. Not only will the review process be perfunctory, but editors will also frown on the fact that an unsolicited manuscript has been simultaneously submitted to several other houses. In cases of extreme work overload, this fact alone may be grounds for rejection. For obvious reasons, publishers dislike multiple submissions. Granting a publisher the exclusive right to review a manuscript, however, puts an author at a considerable disadvantage (see Coser, Kadushin, and Powell 1982: chap. 9). I always recommend that authors be upfront and tell publishers about their intention to send a project to several houses, for to reveal this after a review has been completed can provoke considerable anger on an editor's part. It is, of course, reasonable for authors to stipulate that, if they have not heard from a publisher within a certain amount of time, they will submit their manuscripts elsewhere. But unpublished authors must recognize that, if they choose to send their manuscripts to many houses at once, they are probably hurting their chances of publication at each individual house.

10. There are occasional exceptions to this axiom. Some very prominent academics prefer not to be hounded by editors until they have completed their book. Once finished, they will contact the publisher of their choice. If an individual's reputation is widely known, he or she will receive more expeditious treatment than others who send in unsolicited manuscripts.

11. Barron's rating of the competitiveness of universities, measured on the basis of the SAT scores of the entering class, was used as a general rating of university prestige. Though not as accurate a measure as the various rankings of specific departments, the Barron's ratings are much easier to use.

12. The importance of networks is by no means unique to the contemporary publishing scene. In their study of the British house of Macmillan, Tuchman and Fortin (1980) found that previous contact with the house greatly enhanced an author's chances of publication. They argue that differential access to appropriate social networks and unequal educational opportunities account for the higher rate of rejection for women novelists at Macmillan during the period from the late 1860s to the late 1880s.

13. Although university-press publishing is probably still more "comfortable" than commercial publishing, the nature of this business has changed somewhat since this 1978 interview. Rising costs, the declining purchasing power of libraries, and, in some cases, cuts in support from parent universities have forced some belt-tightening on the part of university presses. The chief casualty of this economic regime appears to be the specialized monograph, particularly the revised dissertation. Nevertheless, university presses still receive support in a wide variety of ways, such as authors' waivers of royalties and submission of camera-ready copy, free rent, endowment income, and annual operating subsidies from parent universities.

14. Quoted in Wendroff 1980:25.

15. An advance is not, properly speaking, a production cost, for, if the book succeeds, the advance will be recovered by deductions from the author's royalties. However, it does represent an initial cost.

16. Subventions have become a controversial issue in scholarly publishing. At the 1982 annual meetings of the Association of American University Presses, a panel on subventions attracted the most controversy. John Gallman of Indiana University Press asserted that "books that require subsidy are not worth publishing." He went on to note that "subsidies mean loss of integrity; there is a subtle loss of control, since agencies giving money do expect special attention." He noted several exceptions, however, particularly in regard to translations and mammoth projects. Nor was Indiana averse to large block grants or endowments. Another panelist, Sheldon Meyer, of Oxford University Press, remarked that Oxford has several centuries-old subsidies, most notably various editions of the Bible and the *Oxford English Dictionary*. John Goellner, of Johns Hopkins University Press, argued that "the paramount reason for university publishing is to publish scholarly monographs, and such publishing is impossible without title subsidies." Moreover, he asserted that trade books (popular titles on health and diets, for example) could never support scholarly books and that, in fact, trade books are peripheral to a university press's purpose. Johns Hopkins has several operating rules for handling subsidies: "Never accept a subsidy from the author's own pocket; don't make publishing conditional on getting the subsidy; and don't ask the author to be solely responsible for obtaining the subsidy." (I was in the audience at this panel; however, the direct quotes are from Reuter et al. 1982). An article in the *New York Times* (September 30, 1983, p. C20) reports that, according to a study by the Association of American University Presses, 68.6 percent of the books published in 1982 by university presses were subsidized in some measure by endowments, foundations, or private organizations.

At both Apple and Plum, acquiring editors very rarely searched for title subsidies. On occasion, however, manuscripts arrived with support in hand. For example, a manuscript might report the results of a three-year research project, and the sponsoring foundation or agency would subsidize publication costs; or the manuscript might be a revised version of a United Nations or foundation-sponsored inquiry into a particular political or social problem, and the original sponsor wanted the report to reach a broader audience. Unlike some university presses, few commercial scholarly houses are engaging in widespread searches for title subventions.

Notes to Chapter Six

1. An important exception is Richardson 1972.

2. There are, of course, a variety of ways of carving up the terrain of organization theory. Astley and Van de Ven 1983, Barney and Ulrich 1982, and Pfeffer 1982 are among the more interesting recent efforts at synthesis. My reference in the text to the dominant perspectives in organization theory includes three schools of thought. (1) The *rational adaptation* perspective, of which there are numerous variants (the best known are structural contingency theory and resource dependence theory), argues that the key to organizational survival is adaptation to the threats and opportunities posed by the environment (see Thompson 1967; Pfeffer and Salancik 1978). (2) *Transaction cost analysis* argues that organizations are driven to engage in exchanges in a manner that minimizes overhead and enforcement costs. This effort is complicated by problems of uncertainty, asset specificity, and small numbers; thus various governance forms arise to mediate difficult kinds of transactions (see Williamson 1975 and 1981, and also Williamson 1985). (3) *Population ecology* focuses on the distribution of organizational forms across environmental conditions. It argues that organizational change is a consequence of an environmental selection process that operates via the replacement of organizations that are dominant at one period of time by a new set of dominant organizations (see Aldrich 1979; Hannan and Freeman 1977, 1984).

3. John Ryden, quoted in a news article by Edwin McDowell, "Publishing: What University Presses Are Doing," *New York Times*, April 20, 1984, p. C22.

4. For a more detailed comparative analysis of scholarly publishing and public television, see Powell 1984.

5. The discussion draws on interviews and fieldwork conducted between 1980 and 1982 at WNET-TV (New York, N.Y., and Newark, N.J.) and several smaller public TV stations. WNET is the largest public TV station in the United States and is commonly referred to as the public broadcasting system's "flagship" station. It produces a significant portion of the programs that are nationally broadcast by public TV stations.

6. As one former WNET executive noted, "Most stations simply can't do public affairs shows that look critically at their own state government . . . There is a terrible baggage that comes with state money" (Powell and Friedkin 1983:417–18).

7. Lawrence Grossman, quoted in *Newsweek*, November 20, 1978, p. 139.

8. For a promising approach of this type that deals with specific relations among the component parts of an organizational field, see DiMaggio 1984.

9. Compare the review process at Apple or Plum with a recent study by Cole, Cole, and Simon (1981) of the evaluation process used by the National Science Foundation for grant proposals in the fields of chemical dynamics, economics, and solid-state physics. They argue that the peer-review system at NSF is essentially free of systematic bias because grant proposals from eminent scientists do not have substantially higher probabilities of receiving favorable ratings than proposals from scientists who are

not eminent. Contrary to the view that science is characterized by general agreement about what constitutes good work, these researchers found real and legitimate differences of opinion among experts about what good science is or should be. They conclude (p. 885) that "the fate of a particular grant application is roughly half determined by the characteristics of the proposal and the principal investigator, and about half by apparently random elements which might be characterized as luck of the reviewer draw."

The disagreement found among reviewers of NSF grant proposals partially reflects the fact that the pool of reviewers is heterogeneous. The selection of reviewers is part of an effort to draw on a broad cross-section of scientists. In contrast, Apple and Plum, when they do call on academic reviewers (remember that this does not always occur), draw on a fairly small stable of authors they have published. The consensus is high. At NSF, unlike at Apple and Plum, there is no profit consideration that encourages prompt decision-making. NSF can afford to be pluralistic and to take its time; Apple and Plum cannot.

10. It is worth noting that the recent expansion of publication outlets has occurred in the context of a number of widely perceived and much ballyhooed threats to the health of scholarly publication. Library budgets have shrunk, federal support to higher education has failed to keep pace with inflation, soaring journal prices have cut into the already reduced acquisition budgets of libraries, and the demographics of higher education are not propitious. Scholarly books have become more expensive; hence there are fewer buyers, shorter print runs, and, as a result, higher price tags. So the vicious cycle goes. Nevertheless, the number of scholarly publishing houses has grown. The explanations are many and varied. In chapter 1 I noted that scholarly presses have moved into the niches vacated by large trade publishers, who have gone off in pursuit of "blockbuster" books. This newly opened terrain has afforded many houses important opportunities. Although widely available high-quality photocopying equipment enables some potential buyers to avoid purchasing new books, computer technology has greatly aided scholarly publishers in developing pinpoint mailing lists with which to target likely buyers. And, of course, the pressure to publish continues to increase within the academy. The demand for good books is fairly elastic, for scholars need to stay abreast of developments in their field in order to advance their own careers.

REFERENCES

Akerlof, George A.
  1984   "Gift Exchange and Efficiency-Wage Theory: Four Views."
          American Economic Review 74, no. 2 (May):79–83.
Aldrich, Howard E.
  1979   *Organizations and Environments.* Englewood Cliffs, N.J.:
          Prentice-Hall.
Aldrich, Howard E., and Donna Fish
  1982   "Origins of Organizational Forms." Paper presented at the
          American Sociological Association annual meetings, Septem-
          ber, San Francisco.
Altick, Richard D.
  1957   *The English Common Reader: A Social History of the Mass
          Reading Public, 1800–1900.* Chicago: University of Chicago
          Press.
Arrow, Kenneth
  1974   *The Limits of Organization.* New York: Norton.
Association of American Publishers
  1977   "The Accidental Profession: Education, Training, and the
          People of Publishing." Report of the AAP Education for
          Publishing Committee. New York: Association of American
          Publishers.
  1976   *The Money Side of Publishing: Fundamentals for Non-
          Financial People.* Report of a conference sponsored by the
          Association of American Publishers, General Publishing Divi-
          sion, prepared by Jean V. Naggar. New York: Association of
          American Publishers.
Astley, W. Graham, and Andrew Van de Ven
  1983   "Central Perspectives and Debates in Organization Theory."
          Administrative Science Quarterly 28:245–73.

Authors Guild
1977a   Statement on the Continuing Trend to Concentration of Power in the Publishing Industry. Issued June 6, New York, N.Y.
1977b   Supplemental Memorandum on Concentration in the Book Club Market and Mass Paperback Market. Issued August 2, New York, N.Y.

Bachrach, Peter, and Morton S. Baratz
1963   "Decisions and Nondecisions: An Analytical Framework." *American Political Science Review* 57:632–42.
1962   "Two Faces of Power." *American Political Science Review* 56:947–52.

Bailey, Herbert S.
1970   *The Art and Science of Book Publishing*. New York: Harper & Row.

Balkin, Richard
1977   *A Writer's Guide to Book Publishing*. New York: Hawthorn Books.

Ballou, Ellen B.
1970   *The Building of the House: Houghton Mifflin's Formative Years*. Boston: Houghton Mifflin.

Bandura, Albert
1977   *Social Learning Theory*. Englewood Cliffs, N.J.: Prentice-Hall.

Barnard, Chester
1938   *The Functions of the Executive*. Cambridge, Mass.: Harvard University Press.

Barney, Jay, and Dave Ulrich
1982   "Perspectives in Organization Theory: Resource Dependence, Efficiency, and Ecology." Unpublished manuscript, School of Management, University of California at Los Angeles.

Becker, Howard S.
1978   "Arts and Crafts." *American Journal of Sociology* 83:862–89.
1974   "Arts as Collective Action." *American Sociological Review* 39:767–76.

Ben-Porath, Yoram
1980   "The F-Connection: Families, Friends, and Firms in the Organization of Exchange." *Population and Development Review* 6:1–30.

Bessie, Simon Michael
1958   "American Writing Today." *Virginia Quarterly Review* 34: 253–63.

Blau, Peter M.
1968   "The Hierarchy of Authority in Organizations." *American Journal of Sociology* 73:453–67.
1964   *Exchange and Power in Social Life*. New York: Wiley.

Bliven, Bruce, Jr.
1975   *Book Traveller*. New York: Dodd, Mead.

Bluedorn, Allen
1982   "The Theories of Turnover: Causes, Effects and Meaning." In
        S. Bacharach, ed., *Research in the Sociology of Organizations*,
        vol. 1. Greenwich, Conn.: JAI Press.

Bourdieu, Pierre
1977   *Outline of a Theory of Practice*. Translated by Richard Nise.
        New York: Cambridge University Press.

Bradbury, Malcolm
1971   *The Social Context of Modern English Literature*. New York:
        Schocken Books.

Bramstead, Ernest K.
1964   *Aristocracy and the Middle Classes in Germany: Social Types
        in German Literature, 1830–1900*. Rev. ed. Chicago: Univer-
        sity of Chicago Press.

Braudy, Susan
1978   "Paperback Auction: What Price 'Hot' Book?" *New York
        Times Magazine*, May 21, pp. 18–19, 91–95, 106–9.

Breed, Warren
1955   "Social Control in the Newsroom: A Functional Analysis."
        Social Forces 33:326–35.

Brett, George P.
1913   "Book Publishing and Its Present Tendencies." *Atlantic
        Monthly* 111 (April): 454–62.

Burns, Tom, and G. M. Stalker
1961   *The Management of Innovation*. London: Tavistock.

Canfield, Cass
1971   *Up and Down and Around: A Publisher Recollects the Time of
        His Life*. New York: Harper & Row.

Caplette, Michele
1981   "Women in Publishing: A Study of Careers in Organizations."
        Ph. D. dissertation, Department of Sociology, SUNY at Stony
        Brook.

Caplovitz, David
1963   *The Poor Pay More*. New York: Free Press.

Caplow, Theodore
1964   *Principles of Organization*. New York: Harcourt, Brace &
        World.
1954   *The Sociology of Work*. Minneapolis: University of Minnesota
        Press.

Caplow, Theodore; Howard M. Bahr; Bruce Chadwick; Reuben Hill; and
Margaret Holmes Williamson
1982   *Middletown Families: Fifty Years of Change and Continuity*.
        Minneapolis: University of Minnesota Press.

Carroll, Glenn
   Forth-   "Concentration and Specialization: Dynamics of Niche Width
   coming.   in Populations of Organizations. *American Journal of Sociolo-
               gy,* in press.
   1984   "The Specialist Strategy." *California Management Review* 26,
               no. 3 (Spring): 126–37.
Cerf, Bennett
   1977   *At Random.* New York: Random House.
Chandler, Alfred D.
   1977   *The Visible Hand: The Managerial Revolution in American
               Business.* Cambridge, Mass.: Harvard University Press.
Child, John
   1972   "Organization of Structure, Environment and Performance:
               The Role of Strategic Choice." *Sociology* 6:1–22.
Child, John, and Janet Fulk
   1982   "Maintenance of Occupational Control: The Case of Profes-
               sionals." *Work and Occupations* 9:155–92.
Cicourel, Aaron
   1970   "The Acquisition of Social Structure: Toward a Developmen-
               tal Sociology of Language." Pp. 136–68 in Jack D. Douglas,
               ed., *Understanding Everyday Life.* Chicago: Aldine.
Cohen, Michael D., and James G. March
   1974   *Leadership and Ambiguity.* New York: McGraw-Hill.
Cohen, Michael D.; James G. March; and Johan P. Olsen
   1972   "A Garbage Can Model of Organizational Choice." *Adminis-
               trative Science Quarterly* 17:1–25.
Cole, Jonathan, and Stephen Cole
   1973   *Social Stratification in Science.* Chicago: University of Chicago
               Press.
Cole, Stephen
   1978   "Scientific Reward Systems: A Comparative Analysis." *Re-
               search in Sociology of Knowledge, Sciences and Art* 1:167–90.
Cole, Stephen; Jonathan R. Cole; and Gary A. Simon
   1981   "Chance and Consensus in Peer Review." *Science* 214
               (November 20): 881–86.
Collins, Randall
   1979   *The Credential Society.* New York: Academic Press.
Commins, Dorothy
   1978   *What Is An Editor? Saxe Commins at Work.* Chicago: Uni-
               versity of Chicago Press.
Cook, Karen S.
   1977   "Exchange and Power in Networks of Interorganizational Re-
               lations." *Sociological Quarterly* 18:62–82.
Cooley, Charles Horton
   1929   "Case Study of Small Institutions as a Method of Research."

In Ernest W. Burgess, ed., *Personality and the Social Group.* Chicago: University of Chicago Press.

Coser, Lewis A.
1979   "Asymmetries in Author-Publisher Relations." *Society* 17: 34–37.

Coser, Lewis A.; Charles Kadushin; and Walter W. Powell
1982   *Books: The Culture and Commerce of Publishing.* New York: Basic Books.

Coser, Rose Laub
1984   "The Greedy Nature of *Gemeinschaft.*" Pp. 221–39 in Walter W. Powell and Richard Robbins, eds., *Conflict and Consensus: Essays in Honor of Lewis A. Coser.* New York: Free Press.
1961   "Insulation from Observability and Types of Conformity." *American Sociological Review* 26:28–39.

Crane, Diana
1972   *Invisible Colleges: Diffusion of Knowledge in Scientific Communities.* Chicago: University of Chicago Press.
1967   "The Gatekeepers of Science: Some Factors Affecting the Selection of Articles for Scientific Journals." *American Sociologist* 2:195–201.

Croce, Benedetto
1968   *Aesthetic.* Translated by Douglas Ainslie. New York: Noonday Press.

Crozier, Michel
1981   "Comparing Structures and Comparing Games." Pp. 97–110 in C. C. Lemert, ed., *French Sociology: Rupture and Renewal since 1968.* New York: Columbia University Press.
1964   *The Bureaucratic Phenomenon.* Chicago: University of Chicago Press.

Cyert, Richard M., and James G. March
1963   *A Behavioral Theory of the Firm.* Englewood Cliffs, N.J.: Prentice-Hall.

Darnton, Robert
1983   "A Survival Strategy for Academic Authors." *American Scholar* 52:533–37.
1975   "Writing News and Telling Stories." *Daedalus* 104:175–94.
1971   "Reading, Writing, and Publishing in Eighteenth-Century France: A Case Study in the Sociology of Literature." *Daedalus.* 100:214–56.

Dearborn, DeWitt C., and Herbert A. Simon
1958   "Selective Perception: A Note on the Departmental Identifications of Executives." *Sociometry* 21:140–44.

Dessauer, John P.
1983   "Book Industry Economics in 1982." Pp. 95–110 in *Publishers Weekly Yearbook, 1983.* New York: R. R. Bowker.

1974   *Book Publishing: What It Is, What It Does.* New York: R. R. Bowker.

DiMaggio, Paul J.
1984   "Structural Analysis of Organizational Fields." Unpublished manuscript, Department of Sociology, Yale University.

DiMaggio, Paul J., and Walter W. Powell
1983   "The Iron Cage Revisited: Institutional Isomorphism and Collective Rationality in Organizational Fields." *American Sociological Review* 48:147–60.

Doebler, Paul
1976   "Editors and Other Creative People Are Introduced to the Financial Side of Book Publishing." *Publishers Weekly*, March 15, pp. 33–35.

Driscoll, James
1980   "Myths about Work." Paper presented at the Academy of Management Meetings, August, Detroit.

Duncan, Robert B.
1972   "Characteristics of Organizational Environments and Perceived Environmental Uncertainty." *Administrative Science Quarterly* 17:313–27.

Eccles, Robert, and Harrison C. White
1984   "Firm and Market Interfaces of Profit Center Control." Working paper, Harvard Business School.

Edwards, Richard
1979   *The Contested Terrain: The Transformation of the Workplace in the Twentieth Century.* New York: Basic Books.

Emerson, Richard M.
1962   "Power-Dependence Relations." *American Sociological Review* 27:31–41.

Epstein, Joseph
1977   "Life and Letters: Marboro Country." *American Scholar* 46:432–40.

Erwin, Robert, and J. David Sapir
1977   "The Writer vs. the University Press." *Book Forum* 3:508–17.

Exman, Eugene
1967   *The House of Harper: One Hundred and Fifty Years of Publishing.* New York: Harper & Row.

Faulkner, Robert
1983   *Music on Demand: Composers and Careers in the Hollywood Film Industry.* New Brunswick, N.J.: Transaction.

Feldman, Martha S., and James G. March
1981   "Information in Organizations as Signal and Symbol." *Administrative Science Quarterly* 26:171–86.

Fiedler, Leslie
1981   "The Death and Rebirths of the Novel." *Salmagundi* 15:143–52.

Freeman, John, and Michael T. Hannan
  1983   "Niche Width and the Dynamics of Organizational Popula-
          tions." *American Journal of Sociology* 88:1116–45.
Friedson, Eliot
  1976   *Doctoring Together.* New York: Elsevier.
  1970   *The Profession of Medicine.* New York: Dodd, Mead.
Frugé, August
  1976   "The Ambiguous University Press." *Scholarly Publishing* 8:
          1–10.
Fulton, Oliver, and Martin Trow
  1974   "Research Activity in American Higher Education." *Sociol-
          ogy of Education* 47:29–73.

Gedin, Per
  1977   *Literature in the Marketplace.* Translated by George Bissett.
          Woodstock, N.Y.: Overlook Press.
Geertz, Clifford
  1978   "The Bazaar Economy: Information and Search in Peasant
          Marketing." *American Economic Review* 68, no. 2 (May):
          28–32.
Geiber, Walter
  1964   "News Is What Newspapermen Make It." Pp. 172–82 in
          L. Dexter and D. White, eds., *People, Society, and Mass
          Communications.* Glencoe, Ill.; Free Press.
Gilmer, Walker
  1970   *Horace Liveright: Publisher of the Twenties.* New York: David
          Lewis.
Gilroy, Angele A.
  1980   *An Economic Analysis of U.S. Domestic Book Publishing:
          1972–Present.* Congressional Research Service Report No.
          80-79E. Washington, D.C.: U.S. Government Printing Office.
Goode, William J.
  1960   "Encroachment, Charlatanism, and the Emerging Profession:
          Psychology, Sociology, and Medicine." *American Sociological
          Review* 25:902–14.
Goodenough, Ward H.
  1963   *Cooperation in Change.* New York: Russell Sage Foundation.
Graña, Caesar
  1964   *Bohemian versus Bourgeois.* New York: Basic Books.
Grannis, Chandler B.
  1967   *What Happens in Book Publishing.* 2d ed. New York: Co-
          lumbia University Press.
Granovetter, Mark
  1983a   "Economic Action and Social Structure: A Theory of Embed-
          dedness." Unpublished manuscript, Department of Sociolo-
          gy, SUNY at Stony Brook.

1983b   "Labor Mobility, Internal Markets and Job-Matching: A Comparison of the Sociological and Economic Approaches." Unpublished manuscript, Department of Sociology, SUNY at Stony Brook.

1974   *Getting a Job: A Study of Contacts and Careers.* Cambridge, Mass.: Harvard University Press.

Greenwood, Ernest

1957   "Attributes of a Profession." *Social Work* 2 (July): 45–55.

Hackman, J. Richard, and Greg R. Oldham

1980   *Work Redesign.* Reading, Mass.: Addison-Wesley.

Hage, Jerald, and Michael Aiken

1967   "Relationship of Centralization to Other Structural Properties." *Administrative Science Quarterly* 12:72–92.

Hagstrom, Warren

1976   "The Production of Culture in Science." *American Behavioral Scientist* 19:753–68.

Hall, Richard H.

1975   *Occupations and the Social Structure.* 2d ed. Englewood Cliffs, N.J.: Prentice-Hall.

Halpenny, Frances

1973   "Education and Training for Scholarly Publishing." *Scholarly Publishing* 4:165–74.

Hannan, Michael T., and John Freeman

1984   "Structural Inertia and Organizational Change." *American Sociological Review* 49:149–64.

1977   "The Population Ecology of Organizations." *American Journal of Sociology* 82:929–64.

Hargens, Lowell, and Warren Hagstrom

1967   "Sponsored and Contest Mobility of American Academic Scientists." *Sociology of Education* 40:24–30.

Harman, Eleanor, and R. M. Schoeffel

1975   "Our Readers Report . . ." *Scholarly Publishing* 6:333–40.

Hart, James D.

1950   *The Popular Book: A History of America's Literary Taste.* New York: Oxford University Press.

Haug, M. R.

1977   "Computer Technology and the Obsolescence of the Concept of Profession." In M. R. Haug and J. Dofny, eds., *Work and Technology.* Beverly Hills: Sage.

Haydn, Hiram

1974   *Words and Faces.* New York: Harcourt Brace Jovanovich.

Hickson, D. J.; C. R. Hinings; C. A. Lee; R. E. Schneck; and J. M. Pennings

1971   "A Strategic Contingencies' Theory of Intraorganizational Power." *Administrative Science Quarterly* 16:216–29.

Hirsch, Paul M., and Thomas Whisler
    1982   "The View from the Boardroom." Paper presented at the Academy of Management Meetings, August, New York, N.Y.

Inkeles, Alex
    1969   "Social Structure and Socialization." Pp. 615–32 in D. A. Goslin, ed., *Handbook of Socialization Theory and Research.* Chicago: Rand-McNally.

Jacobs, David
    1981   "Toward a Theory of Mobility and Behavior in Organizations: An Inquiry into the Consequences of Some Relationships between Individual Performance and Organizational Success." *American Journal of Sociology* 87:684–707.

James, Louis
    1963   *Fiction for the Working Man, 1830–1850.* London: Oxford University Press.

Jamous, H., and B. Peloille
    1970   "Work and Power." In G. Esland and G. Salomon eds., *The Politics of Work and Occupations.* Milton-Keynes, Eng.: Open University Press.

Johnstone, John W. C.; E. J. Slawski; and W. W. Bowman
    1976   *The News People: A Sociological Portrait of American Journalists and Their Work.* Urbana: University of Illinois Press.

Kadushin, Charles
    1974   *The American Intellectual Elite.* Boston: Little, Brown.

Kanter, Rosabeth Moss
    1983   *The Change Masters.* New York: Simon & Schuster.
    1977   *Men and Women of the Corporation.* New York: Basic Books.
    1968   "Commitment and Social Organization: A Study of Commitment Mechanisms in Utopian Communities." *American Sociological Review* 33:499–517.

Kelsell, R. K.
    1955   *Higher Civil Servants in Britain.* London: Routledge & Kegan Paul.

Kerr, Chester
    1974   "What to Publish at Yale." *Scholarly Publishing* 5:211–18.

Knight, Frank
    1921   *Risk, Uncertainty and Profit.* New York: Harper & Row.

Knoke, David, and Ron S. Burt
    1982   "Prominence." In R. S. Burt and M. J. Minor, eds., *Applied Network Analysis: Structural Methodology for Empirical Social Research.* Beverly Hills: Sage.

Kreps, David M., and Robert Wilson
    1982   "Reputation and Imperfect Information." *Journal of Economic Theory* 27:253–79.

Lane, Michael
  1980   *Books and Publishers.* Lexington, Mass.: D. C. Heath.
  1975   "Shapers of Culture: The Editor in Book Publishing." *Annals of the American Academy of Political and Social Science* 421:34–42.
  1970   "Publishing Managers, Publishing House Organization and Role Conflict." *Sociology* 4:367–83.
Larson, Magali Sarfatti
  1977   *The Rise of Professionalism.* Berkeley: University of California Press.
Lawrence, Paul R., and Jay W. Lorsch
  1967   *Organization and Environment.* Cambridge, Mass.: Harvard University Press.
Leavis, Q. D.
  1965   *Fiction and the Reading Public.* New York: Russell & Russell.
Lehmann-Haupt, Helmutt, in collaboration with L. C. Roth and R. G. Silver
  1951   *The Book in America: A History of the Making and Selling of Books in the United States.* 2d ed. New York: R. R. Bowker.
Lekachman, Robert
  1965   "The Literary Intellectuals of New York." *Social Research* 32:127–40.
Lewin, Kurt
  1951   "Psychological Ecology." In D. Cartwright, ed., *Field Theory in Social Science.* New York: Harper & Bros.
Lieberson, Stanley, and James F. O'Connor
  1972   "Leadership and Organizational Performance: A Study of Large Corporations." *American Sociological Review* 37:117–30.
Lin, Nan; Walter M. Ensel; and John C. Vaughn
  1981   "Social Resources and Strength of Ties." *American Sociological Review* 46:393–405.
Lindblom, Charles
  1959   "The Science of Muddling Through." *Public Administration Review* 19:79–99.
Linder, Staffan B.
  1970   *The Harried Leisure Class.* New York: Columbia University Press.
Lindsey, Duncan
  1978   *The Scientific Publication System.* San Francisco: Jossey-Bass.
Lorsch, J. W., and J. J. Morse
  1974   *Organizations and Their Members: A Contingency Approach.* New York: Harper & Row.
Luce, Robert Duncan, and Howard Raiffa
  1957   *Games and Decisions.* New York: John Wiley.

Macaulay, Stewart
  1963   "Non-Contractual Relations in Business: A Preliminary
          Study." *American Sociological Review* 28:55–67.
Machlup, Fritz, and Kenneth Leeson
  1978   *Information through the Printed Word.* Vol. 1: *Book Pub-
          lishing.* New York: Praeger.
Madison, Charles A.
  1974   *Irving to Irving: Author-Publisher Relations, 1800–1974.* New
          York: R. R. Bowker.
  1966   *Book Publishing in America.* New York: McGraw-Hill.
March, James C., and James G. March
  1977   "Almost Random Careers: The Wisconsin School Superin-
          tendency, 1940–1972." *Administrative Science Quarterly*
          22:377–409.
March, James G.
  1978   "Bounded Rationality, Ambiguity, and the Engineering of
          Choice." *Bell Journal of Economics* 9:587–608.
March, James G., and Johan P. Olsen
  1983   "Organizing Political Life: What Administrative Reorganiza-
          tion Tells Us about Government." *American Political Science
          Review* 77:281–96.
  1976   *Ambiguity and Choice in Organizations.* Bergen, Norway:
          Universitetsforlaget.
  1975   "The Uncertainty of the Past." *European Journal of Political
          Research* 3:147–71.
March, James G., and Herbert Simon
  1958   *Organizations.* New York: Wiley.
Marsden, Peter V.
  1983   "Restricted Access in Networks and Models of Power." *Amer-
          ican Journal of Sociology* 88:686–717.
Mechanic, David
  1962   "Sources of Power of Lower Participants in Complex Orga-
          nizations." *Administrative Science Quarterly* 7:349–64.
Medoff, James, and Katharine Abraham
  1980   "Experience, Performance, and Earnings." *Quarterly Journal
          of Economics* 95:703–36.
Menaker, Daniel
  1981   "Unsolicited, Unloved MSS." *New York Times Book Review,*
          March 1, pp. 3, 22.
Merton, Robert K.
  1968   "The Matthew Effect in Science." *Science* 159:56–63.
  1957   "Some Preliminaries to a Sociology of Medical Education."
          Pp. 3–79 in *The Student Physician,* edited by R. K. Merton et
          al. Cambridge, Mass.: Harvard University Press.

Meyer, John W., and Brian Rowan
1977   "Institutionalized Organizations: Formal Structure as Myth and Ceremony." *American Journal of Sociology* 83:340–63.
Miller, William
1949   *The Book Industry.* New York: Columbia University Press.
Mills, C. Wright
1963   "Language, Logic, and Culture." In I. L. Horowitz, ed., *Power, Politics, and People: The Collected Essays of C. W. Mills.* New York: Oxford University Press.
Mintzberg, Henry
1973   *The Nature of Managerial Work.* New York: Harper & Row.
Mischel, Walter
1973   "Toward a Cognitive Reconceptualization of Personality." *Psychological Review* 80:252–83.
Mohr, Lawrence B.
1971   "Organizational Technology and Organizational Structure." *Administrative Science Quarterly* 16:444–59.
Morton, Herbert C.
1982   "The Book Industry: A Review of Books: The Culture and Commerce of Publishing." *Science* 216 (May 21): 862–63.
Most, Harry R.
1977   "Today's Best Book Profits Are in Professional Publishing." *Publishers Weekly,* March 21, p. 39.
Mott, Frank Luther
1947   *Golden Multitudes: The Story of Best Sellers in the United States.* New York: R. R. Bowker.
Nobile, Phillip
1974   *Intellectual Skywriting: Literary Politics and the "New York Review of Books."* New York: Charterhouse.
Noble, J. Kendrick
1982   "Book Publishing." Pp. 95–141 in B. M. Compaine, ed., *Who Owns the Media?* 2d ed. White Plains, N.Y.: Knowledge Industry Publications.
Oppenheimer, M.
1973   "The Proletarianization of the Professional." Sociological Review Monographs no. 20, pp. 213–27.
Ouchi, William G.
1980   "Markets, Bureaucracies, and Clans." *Administrative Science Quarterly* 25:129–44.
Perrow, Charles B.
1985   "Journaling Careers." In L. L. Cummings and P. J. Frost, eds., *Publishing in the Organizational Sciences.* Homewood, Ill.: Irwin.
1979   *Complex Organizations: A Critical Essay.* 2d ed. Glenview, Ill.: Scott, Foresman.

1977   "The Bureaucratic Paradox: The Efficient Organization Centralizes in Order to Decentralize." *Organizational Dynamics* 5 (Spring): 2–14.

1976   "Control in Organizations: The Centralized-Decentralized Bureaucracy." Paper presented at the Annual Meetings of the American Sociological Association, August, New York.

1974   "Is Business Really Changing?" *Organizational Dynamics* 2 (Spring): 31–44.

1967   "A Framework for the Comparative Analysis of Organizations." *American Sociological Review* 32:194–208.

1961   "The Analysis of Goals in Complex Organizations." *American Sociological Review* 26:854–66.

Peters, Thomas J.
1978   "Symbols, Patterns, and Settings: An Optimistic Case for Getting Things Done." *Organizational Dynamics* 6 (Autumn):3–23.

Peterson, Richard A., and David G. Berger
1975   "Cycles in Symbol Production: The Case of Popular Music." *American Sociological Review* 40:158–73.

1971   "Entrepreneurship in Organizations: Evidence from the Popular Music Industry." *Administrative Science Quarterly* 16:97–106.

Pfeffer, Jeffrey
1983   "Organizational Demography." Pp. 299–357 in L. L. Cummings and B. Staw, eds., *Research in Organizational Behavior*, vol. 5. Greenwich, Conn.: JAI Press.

1982   *Organizations and Organization Theory*. Marshfield, Mass.: Pitman.

1981   "Management as Symbolic Action: The Creation and Maintenance of Organizational Paradigms." Pp. 1–52 in L. L. Cummings and B. Staw, eds., *Research in Organizational Behavior*, vol. 3. Greenwich, Conn.: JAI Press.

1977   "Toward an Examination of Stratification in Organizations." *Administrative Science Quarterly* 22:553–67.

Pfeffer, Jeffrey, and Gerald Salancik
1978   *The External Control of Organizations*. New York: Harper & Row.

Porter, Michael
1980   *Competitive Strategy*. New York: Free Press.

Powell, Walter W.
1984   "Institutional Sources of Organizational Structure: A Comparative Analysis of Scholarly Publishing and Public Television." Paper presented at the American Sociological Association annual meetings, August, San Antonio, Texas.

1983   "Whither the Local Bookstore?" *Daedalus* 112:51–64.

1982a   "Adapting to Tight Money and New Opportunities." *Scholarly Publishing* 14:9–20.

1982b   "From Craft to Corporation: The Impact of Outside Ownership on Book Publishing." Pp. 33–52 in J. S. Ettema and D. C. Whitney, eds., *Individuals in Mass Media Organizations: Creativity and Constraint.* Beverly Hills: Sage.

1978a   "Getting into Print." Ph.D. dissertation, Department of Sociology, SUNY at Stony Brook.

1978b   "Publishers' Decision Making: What Criteria Do They Use in Deciding Which Books to Publish?" *Social Research* 45: 227–52.

Powell, Walter W., and Rebecca Friedkin
1983   "Political and Organizational Influences on Public Television Programming." Pp. 413–38 in E. Wartella and D. C. Whitney, eds., *Mass Communication Review Yearbook,* vol. 4. Beverly Hills: Sage.

Pressman, J. L., and Aaron B. Wildavsky
1973   *Implementation.* Berkeley: University of California Press.

Price, James
1977   *The Study of Turnover.* Ames: Iowa State University Press.

Pugh, D. S.; D. J. Hickson; C. R. Hinings; and C. Turner
1968   "Dimensions of Organization Structure." *Administrative Science Quarterly* 13:65–105.

Quant, Mary
1965   *Quant by Quant.* London: Cassell.

Quirk, Dantia
1977   *KIP Studies: The College Publishing Market, 1977–1982.* White Plains, N.Y.: Knowledge Industry Publications.

Reuter, Madalynne; John F. Baker; and Chandler B. Grannis
1982   "Scholarly Publishers Meet in a Can-Fix-It Mood." *Publishers Weekly,* July 30, pp. 30–42.

Richardson, G. B.
1972   "The Organisation of Industry." *Economic Journal* 82: 883–96.

Rogers, Everett M., and Judith K. Larsen
1984   *Silicon Valley Fever: Growth of High-Tech Culture.* New York: Basic Books.

Roshco, Bernard
1975   *Newsmaking.* Chicago: University of Chicago Press.

Ross, Irwin
1977   "The New Golconda in Book Publishing." *Fortune* 96 (December): 110–20.

Roth, Julius A.
1974   "Professionalism—The Sociologist's Decoy." *Sociology of Work and Occupations* 1:6–23.

Salancik, Gerald R., and Jeffrey Pfeffer
    1977   "Constraints on Administrator Discretion: The Limited Influence of Mayors on City Budgets." *Urban Affairs Quarterly* 12:475–98.
    1974   "The Bases and Use of Power in Organizational Decision Making: The Case of a University." *Administrative Science Quarterly* 19:453–73.

Schapiro, Meyer
    1964   "On the Relation of Patron and Artist: Comments on a Proposed Model for the Scientist." *American Journal of Sociology* 70:363–69.

Schudson, Michael
    1978   "A Critique of the 'Production of Culture' Perspective in the Study of Mass Media." Paper presented at the annual meeting of the American Sociological Association, September, San Francisco.

Schwartz, Barry
    1978a   "The Social Ecology of Time Barriers." *Social Forces* 56: 1203–20.
    1978b   "Queues, Priorities, and Social Process." *Social Psychology* 41:3–12.
    1975   *Queuing and Waiting: Studies in the Social Organization of Access and Delay.* Chicago: University of Chicago Press.

Schwartz, Barry, and Steven C. Dubin
    1978   "Manuscript Queues and Editorial Organization." *Scholarly Publishing* 9:253–59.

Scott, W. Richard
    1965   "Reactions to Supervision in a Heteronomous Professional Organization." *Administrative Science Quarterly* 10:65–81.

Scott, W. Richard, and John W. Meyer
    1983   "The Organization of Societal Sectors." Pp. 129–53 in J. Meyer and W. R. Scott, eds., *Organizational Environments: Ritual and Rationality.* Beverly Hills: Sage.

Shatzkin, Leonard
    1982   *In Cold Type: Overcoming the Book Crisis.* Boston: Houghton Mifflin.

Sheehan, Donald
    1952   *This Was Publishing: A Chronicle of the Book Trade in the Gilded Age.* Bloomington: Indiana University Press.

Shils, Edward
    1981   *Tradition.* Chicago: University of Chicago Press.

Shubik, Martin; Peggy Heim; and William J. Baumol
    1983   "On Contracting with Publishers: Author's Information Updated." *American Economic Review* 73, no. 2 (May): 365–81.

Sifton, Elisabeth
    1982   "What Reading Public?" *Nation* 234:627–32.

Simmel, Georg
1950   *The Sociology of Georg Simmel.* Translated and edited by Kurt H. Wolff. Glencoe, Ill.: Free Press.

Simon, Herbert
1957   *Administrative Behavior.* New York: Free Press.

Stinchcombe, Arthur L.
1984   "Contracts as Hierarchical Documents." Institute of Industrial Economics Reports, no. 65. Bergen, Norway.
1980   "Three Origins of Red Tape." Unpublished manuscript, Department of Sociology, Northwestern University, Evanston, Ill.
1959   "Bureaucratic and Craft Administration of Production: A Comparative Study." *Administrative Science Quarterly* 4: 168–87.

Summers, David
1982   "STM Editors in Profile." *Bookseller,* June 5:2109–11.

Sutcliffe, Peter
1978   *The Oxford University Press: An Informal History.* London: Oxford University Press.

Sutherland, J. A.
1976   *Victorian Novelists and Publishers.* Chicago: University of Chicago Press.

Tebbel, John
1972,   *A History of Book Publishing in the United States.* 4 vols. Vol.
1975,   1: *The Creation of an Industry, 1630–1865.* Vol. 2: *The Expan-*
1978,   *sion of an Industry, 1865–1919.* Vol. 3: *The Golden Age be-*
1981   *tween Two Wars, 1920–1940.* Vol. 4: *The Great Change, 1940–1980.* New York: R. R. Bowker.
1974   *The Media in America.* New York: New American Library.

Thompson, James
1967   *Organizations in Action.* New York: McGraw-Hill.

Thompson, James, and A. Tuden
1959   "Strategies, Structures, and Process of Organizational Decision." Reprinted in W. Rushing and M. Zald, eds., *Organizations and Beyond.* Lexington, Mass.: D. C. Heath, 1976.

Thornton, Russell, and Peter M. Nardi
1975   "The Dynamics of Role Acquisition." *American Journal of Sociology* 80:870–85.

Tuchman, Gaye
1984   "When the Prevalent Don't Prevail: Male Hegemony and the Victorian Novel." Pp. 139–58 in Walter W. Powell and Richard Robbins, eds., *Conflict and Consensus: Essays in Honor of Lewis A. Coser.* New York: Free Press.
1982   "Culture as Resource: Actions Defining the Victorian Novel." *Media, Culture, and Society* 4:3–18.

1978   *Making News.* New York: Free Press.
1973   "Making News by Doing Work: Routinizing the Unexpected." *American Journal of Sociology* 79:110–31.
1972   "Objectivity as Strategic Ritual: An Examination of Newsmen's Notions of Objectivity." *American Journal of Sociology* 77:660–79.

Tuchman, Gaye, and Nina Fortin
1980   "Edging Women Out: Some Suggestions about the Structure of Opportunities and the Victorian Novel." *Signs* 6:308–25.

Van Maanen, John
1978   "People Processing: Strategies of Organizational Socialization." *Organizational Dynamics* 7, no. 1:19–36.

Ward, Albert
1974   *Book Production: Fiction and the German Reading Public, 1740–1800.* London: Oxford University Press.

Watson, Tony J.
1980   *Sociology, Work and Industry.* London: Routledge & Kegan Paul.

Watt, Ian
1957   *The Rise of the Novel.* Berkeley: University of California Press.

Weick, Karl E.
1976   "Educational Organizations as Loosely Coupled Systems." *Administrative Science Quarterly* 21:1–19.
1969   *The Social Psychology of Organizing.* Reading, Mass.: Addison-Wesley.

Wendroff, Michael
1980   "Should We Do the Book? A Study of How Publishers Handle Acquisition Decisions." *Publishers Weekly* August 15, pp. 25–28.

Wheelock, John Hall
1950   *Editor to Author: The Letters of Maxwell Perkins.* New York: Scribner's.

White, David
1950   "The Gatekeeper: A Case Study in the Selection of the News." *Journalism Quarterly* 27:383–90.

White, Harrison
1983   "Agency as Control." Working paper, Harvard Business School.
1981   "Interfaces." Paper presented at the Social Science Research Council Conference on Organizational Indicators, December.

Whiteside, Thomas
1981   *The Blockbuster Complex.* Middletown, Conn.: Wesleyan University Press.

Williams, Raymond
1961   *Culture and Society, 1780–1950.* London: Penguin.

Williamson, Oliver E.

1985   *The Economic Institutions of Capitalism.* New York: Free Press.

1981   "The Economics of Organization: The Transaction Cost Approach." *American Journal of Sociology* 87:548–77.

1980   "The Organization of Work: A Comparative Institutional Assessment." *Journal of Economic Behavior and Organization* 1:5–38.

1975   *Markets and Hierarchies.* New York: Free Press.

Wrong, Dennis

1970   "The Case of the *New York Review.*" *Commentary* 50, no. 5 (November): 49–63.

Zerubavel, Eviatar

1979   *Patterns of Time in Hospital Life.* Chicago: University of Chicago Press.

Zucker, Lynne

1983   "Organizations as Institutions." Pp. 1–47 in S. Bacharach, ed., *Research in the Sociology of Organizations,* vol. 2. Greenwich, Conn.: JAI Press.

Zuckerman, Harriet

1970   "Stratification in American Science." *Sociological Inquiry* 40, no. 2 (Spring): 235–57.

Zuckerman, Harriet, and R. K. Merton

1971   "Patterns of Evaluation in Science." *Minerva* 9:66–100.

INDEX

Marsden, Peter, 204
Mass-market paperback pub-
  lishing: of Apple Press, 52; as
  category, 23; industry concen-
  tration in, 6, 15; major features
  of, 33, 34, 216; profitability of,
  13–14, 24–25
Matthew Effect, 178
MCA, 6
Mechanic, David, 147
Medicine, occupational control in,
  137–38
Medoff, James, 224
Menaker, Daniel, 170–72
Merger(s), 5–6, 16–18, 39, 214,
  217; and Apple Press, 39; Plum
  Press, 43, 44
Merton, Robert K., 126, 178, 211
Meyer, John W., 80, 201
Meyer, Sheldon, 230
Middletown study, 213
Miller, Harold T., 216
Miller, William, 3, 212
Mills, C. Wright, 152
Mintzberg, Henry, 55, 126, 146
Mischel, Walter, 150
Mobility: of authors, 12; of edi-
  tors, 12, 126, 141–42. See also
  Turnover, editorial
Mohr, Lawrence B., 225
"Money Side of Publishing, The"
  (seminar), 1
Monograph houses, 23, 30–32.
  See also Scholarly publishing
Monograph series, development
  of, 115–16
Morley, John, 157
Morse, J. J., 136
Morton, Herbert C., 204–5
Most, Harry R., 24
Mott, Frank Luther, 211
Muddling through, science of, 93
Multiauthored books, 48, 123–25
Multitiered lists, 177–78

Naggar, Jean V., 213
Name of the Rose, The (Eco), 17
Nardi, Peter M., 159

National Endowment for the Arts
  and the Humanities, 197
National Science Foundation,
  231–32
Networks, 24; and academic status, 181–83; consequences of
  reliance on, 76, 202–7; functions of, 74–76, 195–96; implications of, for organization
  theory, 190–94; methods of using, in editorial search, 90–93;
  and promotion, 59–60. See also
  Author-publisher relationship
New Republic, 60, 123
Newspaper industry, resource par-
  titioning in, 18
New Yorker, 29–30
New York metropolitan area, access to publishers in, 182–83,
  204
New York Review of Books, 29–
  30, 52–53, 60
New York Times, 12, 82
New York Times Book Review,
  69, 225
Nobile, Philip, 211
Noble, J. Kendrick, 4, 12–14, 17,
  216
Nondecision, power of, 81
Northanger Abbey (Austen), 22
Norton, W. W., Company, 31
Novels, 22; acceptance rate for,
  162, 170–72

Occupations: control of, 137–44;
  craft versus bureaucratic, 7–10
O'Connor, James F., 61
Oldham, Greg R., 145
Olsen, Johan P., 96, 97, 99, 164
Oppenheimer, M., 138
Organization(s): of Apple Press,
  54–62, 68–69; and conflict, 63–
  64; decision-making in, 93–102;
  domain of, 45; and environment, relationship between,
  189–202; heteronomous, 138–
  39; informal controls in, 145–
  46; management of tensions in,